ANSWERS *for* EACH DAY

Bayless Conley

P.O. Box 417
Los Alamitos, CA 90720
answersbc.org

Published by DUNHAM BOOKS

Published 2007

ISBN: 978-0-9787116-5-8

Printed in the United States of America

For more information:
DUNHAM BOOKS
15455 Dallas Parkway, Sixth Floor
Addison, Texas 75001

Foreword

I want to personally welcome you to the 365 day *Answers for Each Day* devotional. I don't believe it is an accident that you have a copy of this book in your hands. I believe God can use it in a powerful way to help you grow in your relationship with Him.

The reason I wrote this devotional is very simple: To help you—on a daily basis—plant the seeds of God's Truth in your heart.

As you take the time to read and think about the truth that each daily devotional uncovers, I believe that the Holy Spirit will show you how to apply that truth to your life.

Consider either starting or ending each day with the *Answers* devotional. Or perhaps take some time during your daily schedule to stop and meditate on God's Word by using this tool.

If you will spend the time, on a consistent basis, to feed on the truths presented in the following pages, I believe it will help your daily walk with God to flourish.

Bon appétit!

Bayless Conley

Day 1

Aiming at God's Pleasure

In John, chapter 8, Jesus made a statement that I wish I could make. He said, "*I always do those things that please the Father.*" Wouldn't it be great if we could all say that?

Paul points us in that direction in 2 Corinthians 5:6-9,

> *So we are always confident, knowing that while we are at home in the body we are absent from the Lord. For we walk by faith, not by sight. We are confident, yes, well pleased rather to be absent from the body and to be present with the Lord. Therefore we make it our aim, whether present or absent, to be well pleasing to Him.*

Whether we are still in this earthly body or we are standing before the Lord in heaven, he says, "We make it our aim to be well pleasing to Him."

But you know what? You cannot aim at a target that you can't see. You can't make it your aim to be well pleasing to Him if you don't know what pleases Him. And it is to your advantage to find out, as Paul points out in verse 10,

> *For we must all appear before the judgment seat of Christ, that each one may receive the things done in the body, according to what he has done, whether good or bad.*

So let me ask you, what is your aim today? Are you aiming at what pleases God? My prayer is that you will come to truly know and understand what pleases God as you spend time each day with me in this devotional...and that you will make that your aim!

Day 2

Making a Priority of Faith

When we talk about what pleases God, I think we must put faith at the top of the list. Very simply, faith pleases God.

Hebrews 11—often called the faith chapter—makes it very clear how vital faith is to pleasing God. In fact, Hebrews 11:6 tells us,

> *But without faith it is impossible to please Him, for he who comes to God must believe that He is, and that He is a rewarder of those who diligently seek Him.*

Notice it doesn't say, "Without faith it is very difficult to please Him." No, it is impossible to please God without faith. You and I must learn to trust God if we are to bring a smile to the face of God.

Some people say, "Well, there is just too much teaching on faith." I disagree. Why? Because it takes faith to please God. Without it, we have no chance at all of pleasing Him. In fact, Hebrews 10:38 states,

> *Now the just shall live by faith; but if anyone draws back, My soul has no pleasure in him.*

That is pretty black and white, isn't it? If you desire to please God, it starts with faith, trusting God completely.

I challenge you today to ask yourself, "Do I really trust God with every part of my life? Do I place my faith in Him moment by moment? Or do I refuse to trust Him as I should?"

If this is an area of struggle for you, determine today to spend time in the Word of God. For the Bible tells us that faith comes by hearing the Word of God. Ask God to speak to you through His Word. Your faith and trust in Him will grow. Our great God is worthy of your trust.

Day 3

The Nature of Faith

In our last devotional, we talked about how important faith is to pleasing God. It is not just important, it's essential, because without it, you and I cannot please God.

The natural question is, "What is faith?"

In Hebrews 11:1, the writer gives us the technical definition of biblical faith,

> *Now faith is the substance of things hoped for, the evidence of things not seen.*

Faith deals with unseen reality. In fact, Weymouth's translation says, *"Faith is a conviction of the reality of things we do not see."*

You might think, "That's a nice definition, but what does that really mean?" That is a good question. And it is answered by the examples given in Hebrews 11, which show different ways people expressed their faith in God, because there is not just one way to demonstrate faith in God:

- Abel shows us that faith is giving our best to God. He deserves our first and our best.
- Enoch shows us that faith is walking with God. It is living a life in constant connection with God, even when you can't sense or feel Him.
- Noah shows us that faith is making preparations as though Christ is coming back today, even when there is seemingly no evidence.
- Abraham shows us that faith is obeying God, even though you may not know where He is leading you.
- Sarah shows us that faith is receiving God's promise, even when public opinion says, "No way!"
- Moses shows us that faith is living life in light of eternity, and allowing that focus to affect all of life's decisions.

Commit today to live this life of faith. If you do, you will truly please God!

Day 4

Standing in the Gap

Justice is turned back, and righteousness stands afar off; for truth is fallen in the street, and equity cannot enter. So truth fails, and he who departs from evil makes himself a prey. Then the LORD saw it, and it displeased Him that there was no justice. He saw that there was no man, and wondered that there was no intercessor; therefore His own arm brought salvation for Him; and His own righteousness, it sustained Him (Isaiah 59:14-16).

God is not pleased at injustice nor when truth and righteousness do not prevail. When He sees those who turn from evil becoming a prey, He is not happy.

I remember a young man who had lived a particularly sordid life. He heard the gospel and had an amazing conversion experience. Within a month or so of accepting Christ, he was diagnosed with testicular cancer.

What happened? He departed from evil and became a prey! God was not responsible for his situation, nor was He pleased.

Why did it happen? At least part of the answer is found in verse 16. There was no man serving as an intercessor. No one was keeping a hedge of protection around that young man through prayer.

Before and after people turn from evil we need to intercede to God on their behalf.

I challenge you today to be one of those who stands in the gap and makes up the hedge for new babes in Christ. May God find pleasure in you and me as we take our position as intercessors.

Day 5

God's Pleasure…Your Blessing

In Psalm 35:27 we are told,

> *Let them shout for joy and be glad, who favor my righteous cause; and let them say continually, "Let the LORD be magnified, Who has pleasure in the prosperity of His servant."*

This psalm says it clearly—God is pleased when you are blessed. The Revised Standard Version translates this verse this way, *God delights in the welfare of His servant.*

In Luke 12, when talking about God meeting our practical, physical, and material needs, Jesus says, *"Do not fear, little flock, for it is your Father's good pleasure to give you the kingdom."*

You do not need to somehow convince God to meet your needs. In fact, God desires to bless you.

It is like the son who felt his father had not provided for him when his dad passed away. His father left one sibling some property, another one some valuable stock, and all the son got was a box of what looked to him like junk.

One day, because of financial trouble, the son had to move out of his apartment. As he cleaned things out, he found the box of junk he had thrown in the back of a closet. Noticing there were some stamps and trading cards in the box, he decided to see if they were worth anything.

It turned out the trading card collection was filled with rare baseball cards in mint condition. And every one of the stamps was very rare—very valuable. The combined appraisal of the two collections was over $450,000!

His father had provided for him, but the son had lived far below those privileges because he didn't believe his father had blessed him!

Our heavenly Father delights in, He takes pleasure in, the prosperity of His servant. And that means you!

Day 6

A Prosperous Attitude

In our previous devotional, we learned that God is pleased to bless us. But that prosperity must be accompanied by a special attitude... an attitude that is captured in 1 Kings 3.

This passage records God's appearance to Solomon in a dream at Gibeon. In the dream God said to Solomon, "Ask! What shall I give you?"

What an incredible statement, and question! Equally incredible is Solomon's response, which revealed the attitude of his heart, the attitude which must accompany our prosperity. That response is captured in verses 7-10,

> *"Now, O LORD my God, You have made Your servant king instead of my father David, but I am a little child; I do not know how to go out or come in. And Your servant is in the midst of Your people whom You have chosen, a great people, too numerous to be numbered or counted. Therefore give to Your servant an understanding heart to judge Your people, that I may discern between good and evil. For who is able to judge this great people of Yours?" The speech pleased the LORD, that Solomon had asked this thing.*

God is pleased when, in our hearts, we put others before ourselves. God delights in prospering us when prosperity is not our chief aim. When we get it right, and in our hearts we do place others before ourselves, God can bless us beyond our wildest dreams.

God will give you everything you need to fulfill His plan for your life. He will give you richly all things to enjoy, as long as you have a prosperous attitude that puts His plans and His people first.

Day 7

Fitting into God's "Foolishness"

In 1 Corinthians 1:21, Paul gives us an interesting insight into how you and I please God.

> *For since, in the wisdom of God, the world through wisdom did not know God, it pleased God through the foolishness of the message preached to save those who believe.*

God's methods are astounding. To bring men and women into His family through the foolishness of preaching! When people hear the gospel preached and believe it, God is pleased.

Now how is the gospel preached? Through your life and mine. Every one of us has been entrusted by God with some gift to communicate the gospel. Perhaps you have been entrusted by God with unusual wealth. Or maybe a marvelous singing voice, or the ability to communicate, or perhaps the skill to assimilate facts.

Whatever it is, God has put something in each of us that somehow fits into His great master plan of winning this lost world to Jesus Christ.

God has chosen to use these weak, fallible vessels to share the simple gospel message that the world is separated from Him because of sin. In His mercy, God reached down to the human race when He sent His own Son, Who willingly gave up His life on the cross and died for our sins. The price was paid. God's eternal justice was satisfied. And the Holy Spirit raised Jesus Christ from the dead.

That is the message our world so desperately needs to hear today! God is pleased when you share that "foolishness." So however God has gifted you, use that gift today to present a living Jesus to our dying world!

Day 8

Pleasing God...Even in Your Sorrow

In Psalm 69, David shares his innermost thoughts as he cries out to God, afflicted, sorrowful, beaten down, and distressed. David felt like he was sinking in floodwaters, caught in the quicksand of difficulties.

If you are like me, I am sure you have been there too. In fact, you may feel like you are there right now. Floodwaters of trouble have come into your life. You are treading water, and it seems like you are about to go down for the third time.

For most of us, our response is to get down and depressed, to feel sorry for ourselves. And to hope we will receive comfort and encouragement from those around us.

David's reaction was different. And a model for how we should respond to those times of sorrow and trouble in a way that pleases God. In verses 30 and 31 of Psalm 69 he states,

> *I will praise the name of God with a song, and will magnify Him with thanksgiving. This also shall please the LORD better than an ox or bull.*

You know, anyone can sing when the sun is shining. It is easy to praise God and shout the victory when things are going your way. But to praise God when the chips are down...that brings pleasure to God.

To worship God, to magnify Him and to thank Him even when it looks like you are not going to make it, that pleases the heart of God. It shows Him something about you. It demonstrates that you have faith in Him, and it opens a way for Him to work in your life.

If your life feels full of sorrow and trouble, begin to praise God, and watch God work!

Day 9

Fearing God

In Psalm 147:10-11, David gives us insight into two things that please God—two things that may seem disconnected from each other.

> *He does not delight in the strength of the horse; He takes no pleasure in the legs of a man. The LORD takes pleasure in those who fear Him, in those who hope in His mercy.*

First, God delights in those who fear Him, those who have a reverential respect and awe for Him. Second, God is pleased with those who hope in His mercy.

In today's devotional, I want to focus on what it means to truly fear God. And, in tomorrow's devotional, we will look at what it means to hope in mercy, and how these two are connected.

Scripture constantly admonishes us to fear God. But how do you do that? I believe the Bible gives us at least four ways:

1. Through a hatred of evil. Proverbs 8:13 says, *The fear of the Lord is to hate evil.*
2. Through radical obedience. To fear the Lord means to radically obey Him, as Abraham did in Genesis 22 when he was willing to sacrifice his son.
3. With an awareness that God is always watching you. Scripture makes it clear there is nowhere you can go that God does not see.
4. With the knowledge that one day you will have to stand before God as your Judge. Jesus even tells us that one day, when we stand before Him, we will have to give an account of every idle word we have spoken.

Pray today that God will help you live your life by these four principles. Because God delights in those who fear Him.

Day 10

Hoping in God's Mercy

In our last devotional, Psalm 147:10-11 showed us how important fearing God is to pleasing Him.

> *He does not delight in the strength of the horse; He takes no pleasure in the legs of a man. The LORD takes pleasure in those who fear Him, in those who hope in His mercy.*

In today's devotional, I want to look at the second thing that pleases God, according to this psalm, those who hope in God's mercy.

You have to wonder why the Lord put those two things together, the fear of Him and hoping in His mercy. At first blush, they do not seem to go together, but they do.

They show how God truly understands our nature. That even those who reverence Him, and truly fear Him, and try to live for Him, sometimes fall short. And in those moments of failure, they need the mercy of God.

In fact, we are told in the Book of Proverbs that the righteous man falls seven times, but gets up again.

You know, I love God, and I do my best to serve Him and walk with Him. But I'm super grateful for His mercy! Thank God He is a merciful God! Because there are times when I so desperately need it. And I am sure you do, too!

My friend, if you have stumbled and today feel like you are a million miles away from God, do not despair. God finds pleasure in those who hope in His mercy. He is delighted when you ask for His mercy. He will not be angry.

Remember, only the guilty need mercy. And God finds pleasure when in your guilt you call out to Him, and hope in His mercy.

Day 11

Rejoicing in God's Mercy

We all are familiar with the story of the Prodigal Son. After he had wasted his inheritance, he came to his senses and returned home, hoping he could just be a servant to his father.

His father wouldn't even consider it. He put the best robe on him, put a ring on his finger, sandals on his feet, and then had the fatted calf killed for a party. The father delighted in showing mercy to his son!

But what about the older brother? He stood outside the party and wouldn't come in to celebrate. He was so angry! He had never messed up and yet his father had never thrown him a party!

Sometimes, if we are not careful, we can have the attitude of that older son. We can look at the lives of others and think, "That is not fair. I know he's been messing up, and God is blessing him. What's up with that? I haven't been as bad as him!"

We need to remember that God delights in showing mercy to the guilty when, from a sincere heart, they seek that mercy. He delights when you and I ask for His mercy when we have blown it.

Micah 6:7-8 says,

> *Will the LORD be pleased with thousands of rams, ten thousand rivers of oil? Shall I give my firstborn for my transgression, the fruit of my body for the sin of my soul? He has shown you, O man, what is good; and what does the LORD require of you but to do justly, to love mercy, and to walk humbly with your God?*

God delights in showing mercy. So be a person of mercy, and rejoice when God shows mercy to someone who needs it.

Day 12

Becoming a Person of Mercy

Luke 6:38 tells us,

"Give, and it will be given to you: good measure, pressed down, shaken together, and running over will be put into your bosom. For with the same measure that you use, it will be measured back to you."

It is not unusual to hear this verse used in connection with giving money to the Lord's work. And while there is a principle concerning money embedded in this verse, Jesus was not talking about giving an offering when He made this statement. That was not the subject under discussion.

In order to understand what He was really talking about, you need to read verses 35-37,

"But love your enemies, do good, and lend, hoping for nothing in return; and your reward will be great, and you will be sons of the Most High. For He is kind to the unthankful and evil. Therefore be merciful, just as your Father also is merciful. Judge not, and you shall not be judged. Condemn not, and you shall not be condemned. Forgive, and you will be forgiven."

Jesus wanted to impress on us this truth: If you give forgiveness, and you give love, and you give mercy, they come back to you in good measure, pressed down, shaken together.

He wanted us to understand that by the same measure you and I give these things, it will come back to us. But if you and I measure out judgment and condemnation, guess what gets measured back to us?

Make a commitment today to become a person of mercy, not seeking anything in return. Become known as someone who reflects our God of mercy to a broken and needy world.

Day 13

Obedience and Respect

I am sure most Christian parents, at one time or another, have pointed their children to Colossians 3:20,

> *Children, obey your parents in all things, for this is well pleasing to the Lord.*

Or to Ephesians 6:1-3,

> *Children, obey your parents in the Lord, for this is right. "Honor your father and mother," which is the first commandment with promise: "that it may be well with you and you may live long on the earth."*

These two character qualities of obeying and honoring parents are vital to pleasing God. But it is important to understand that obedience has to do with an outward act, while honoring has to do with an inward attitude of the heart.

As parents, we all can remember those times when our children may have been outwardly obedient but were being inwardly disrespectful. You may have gotten them to sit down in the corner, but while they sat there, they were thinking, "I may be sitting down on the outside, but I'm standing up on the inside!"

If you are a parent, it is critical for you to deal just as swiftly with a disrespectful attitude as it is with a disobedient act. It is part of your God-given role of teaching your children obedience and respect for authority.

As your children learn how to obey and respect, you will not only bring them peace, they will experience God's blessing in their lives.

So as you work to raise your children to be the people God desires them to be, make a priority of teaching your children the qualities of respect for authority and obedience. Someday they will bless you for it!

Day 14

Embracing the Blessings of God

Ephesians 1:3 is a verse that is often misunderstood. It tells us,

> *Blessed be the God and Father of our Lord Jesus Christ, who has blessed us with every spiritual blessing in the heavenly places in Christ.*

I used to read that and wonder what in the world a spiritual blessing in a heavenly place in Christ really was! I truly believed that I had been blessed with it, but I didn't have a clue what it meant.

Then one day as I studied, I found out that the word *spiritual* literally means Holy Spirit-conferred. The Amplified Bible helps clarify the meaning when it says, *He has blessed us with every Holy Spirit-given blessing.*

What it means, literally, is that the blessings you and I enjoy as believers in Jesus Christ come from heaven's vast resources. And they have already been conferred on us. Isn't that awesome?!

But there is something more. These Holy Spirit-conferred blessings include any blessing and benefit we get from God, be it material, physical, emotional, or spiritual.

So, when God heals you, it is a blessing being conferred through the agency of His Spirit. When God brings peace to your troubled heart, that is a blessing from the Holy Spirit. And when God supernaturally supplies material needs, that is the Holy Spirit at work blessing you from the vast resources of heaven!

But here is what I really want you to grasp. Based on this verse, all those blessings have already been given. They have been issued. On God's side of the ledger, they are a done deal. He has already signed them and sent them.

So praise God for...and embrace...His blessings in your life!

Day 15

Enjoying the Fullness of Your Inheritance

In Galatians 4:1-5, the apostle Paul helps us understand what it means to be part of God's family,

> *Now I say that the heir, as long as he is a child, does not differ at all from a slave, though he is master of all, but is under guardians and stewards until the time appointed by the father. Even so we, when we were children, were in bondage under the elements of the world. But when the fullness of the time had come, God sent forth His Son, born of a woman, born under the law, to redeem those who were under the law, that we might receive the adoption as sons.*

Adoption in Roman society was very different from adoption today. When a flesh and blood son reached the age of maturity, he was "adopted" into his own family. Until that time, he was considered a child, and he was under the tutelage of a household slave.

We are heirs because of adoption. What does this mean? It means that God is well pleased when we assume our place as mature sons of God, exercising our authority and enjoying the fullness of our inheritance. But most Christians don't do this.

Not long ago, I learned about a particular website that can tell you if you have any money anywhere that you don't know about. There are literally hundreds of millions of dollars sitting unused in trust funds or accounts that people don't know about.

A lot of Christians operate this way. They have this incredible inheritance that belongs to them, this incredible authority that has been given to them, and they are unaware of it. And, friend, that does not bring pleasure to God.

Day 16

Delivered!

Do you realize that the devil has absolutely no authority over you?

In Colossians 1:12-13, the apostle Paul tells us,

> *Giving thanks to the Father who has qualified us to be partakers of the inheritance of the saints in the light. He has delivered us from the power of darkness and conveyed us into the kingdom of the Son of His love.*

You and I have been delivered from the power of darkness. We are out from under the authority of the devil.

That was a happy day for me when I realized this truth. After I was saved, I was afraid of the devil because I had been so deeply involved in the occult. I literally had a fear that hung upon me and followed me everywhere I went. So I just prayed over and over, "God, please make me so I'm not afraid of the devil."

I started to constantly read the New Testament. As I did, I realized what Christ had done for me, and I was set free.

As I thought about this truth, I was reminded of being in elementary school. We had this kid who terrorized a lot of other kids. I was so afraid of him. One day, he just pushed one of my buttons. All of a sudden I was on top of him holding his arms down, and I was thinking, "Why in the world was I ever afraid of this kid?" He was absolutely helpless!

Just like that bully, the devil is a defeated foe. And part of your inheritance is authority over all the power of the enemy. It is a happy day when you realize it.

Day 17

Blessed to Be a Blessing

Our capitalistic society is geared toward one purpose...people accumulating wealth. While there is nothing wrong with material abundance, many Christians today have lost sight of why God has blessed them with prosperity.

They believe it is for their own good and benefit, but God's perspective is quite different. For example, here is what the writer of Hebrews tells us in Hebrews 13:16,

> *But do not forget to do good and to share, for with such sacrifices God is well pleased.*

Now the phrase "to share" means to share with others. One translation says, *Share what you have.* Another version translates this, *Be generous.* Another says, *Contribute to the needy.*

You see, God blesses us to make us a blessing! That ought to be the main motivation for desiring and praying for God's blessing in our lives. God told Abraham, "I'm going to bless you, and you will be a blessing." God says the fringe benefit is that, "I will give you richly all things to enjoy." But the main flow of God's purpose in blessing us is so we can help other people.

It is also the reason we should desire the inheritance that Christ has given to us, all of those Holy Spirit-conferred blessings, which we discussed on day 14. Why? Because we can't give what we don't have. You can't bless someone if you don't have anything to bless them with!

God is well pleased to see us walk in our inheritance as sons, but He is also well pleased to see us share what He has blessed us with.

Day 18

You Can't Out-Give God

Tucked away in the pages of the New Testament is a very powerful promise to those who are generous givers. It is found in Philippians 4:18-19,

> *Indeed I have all and abound. I am full, having received from Epaphroditus the things sent from you, a sweet-smelling aroma, an acceptable sacrifice, well pleasing to God. And my God shall supply all your need according to His riches in glory by Christ Jesus.*

The Philippian church had made the financial support of the apostle Paul a priority. In these verses Paul acknowledges their generosity and also states a vital principle for every believer to grasp... you can't out-give God!

Not too long ago I came across a letter from a lady who had sacrificially given to the work of God. Here is what she said in her letter:

> "My husband and I were in dire straits. He is a Vietnam War veteran who was exposed to Agent Orange. Due to his benefit claims being denied and his being unemployed for three years, we lost nearly everything. We had to put our home up for sale, but nothing was happening. During this time, I gave every penny I could get my hands on and always prayed. So one miracle after another began to take place. First, we were able to move into my husband's deceased mother's home. Then we signed papers for the sale of our former home. Next, my husband's claim for benefits was approved and awarded, and the award was backdated three years. Then he found a job! Our income has tripled, and God continues to do miraculous things for us."

My friend, become a generous giver today. Because you can't out-give God!

Day 19

The Priority of Purity

We live in a highly sexualized society. It is amazing the number of people, even pastors, who fall to sexual temptation.

In 1 Thessalonians 4:3-5 we are told straight out,

For this is the will of God, your sanctification: that you should abstain from sexual immorality; that each of you should know how to possess his own vessel in sanctification and honor, not in passion of lust, like the Gentiles who do not know God.

God expects for you and me to live in sexual purity. You need to know how to possess your body in sanctification and honor; otherwise your body will possess you.

God has created a strong sexual drive that is an awesome blessing in marriage! But, you know, it is so strong that sometimes it just wants to flow out of the banks and go somewhere it shouldn't go.

We must learn how to possess our bodies in sanctification and honor, and live morally pure lives that bring pleasure to God. Here are three practical ways:

1. <u>Avoid temptation</u>. 2 Timothy 2:22 says, *Flee youthful lusts.* Avoid the very scenes of temptation. Stay away when you know you might get in trouble.
2. <u>Feed your spirit, not your flesh</u>. In Romans, we are told of the great war every Christian experiences, the war between our spirit and our flesh. Whatever you feed is going to be stronger, so make sure to feed your spirit.
3. <u>Rely on the Holy Spirit and His power</u>. If you will acknowledge Him and look to Him for strength, you will find He is a very present help in your time of need.

Make a commitment today to practice these three principles for purity. If you do, you will live in the sexual purity God desires.

Day 20

Perfect and Complete

Your faith in God has incredible potential to make your life complete. To take you from the place of deficiency, to the place of being perfect and complete, lacking nothing.

James puts it this way in James 1:2-4,

> *My brethren, count it all joy when you fall into various trials, knowing that the testing of your faith produces patience. But let patience have its perfect work, that you may be perfect and complete, lacking nothing.*

Faith in God can make you complete, but your faith will be contested. It will be opposed, even as we read here. Your faith will go through the fire of trial.

If you lack spiritually in your life, you can get to the place of holiness. If you are lacking materially, you can get to a place where your needs are met. Whatever your lack, your faith in God has the potential to take you from where you are, and where you are lacking, to this place that the Bible speaks of...being perfect and complete, lacking nothing.

But, the path to that completeness is one of trial. Your faith will not get you there until it first goes through testing. You do have an adversary. You will be opposed. The Bible says, *Your adversary, the devil, walks about as a roaring lion seeking whom he may devour.*

The devil knows what is at stake, and he will do all he can to keep you from trusting God. So as your faith encounters the turbulence of trials, do what James says, and count it all joy. You are on your way to becoming perfect and complete in Christ.

Day 21

Passing the Test of Your Faith

In yesterday's devotional, we saw how God desires for us to be perfect and complete, lacking in nothing; but the road to that is the testing of our faith.

The natural question is, "What does it take to succeed when the test comes?" There are two cooperating forces which must be at work. James 1:4-5 shows us what those two forces are,

> *But let patience have its perfect work, that you may be perfect and complete, lacking nothing. If any of you lacks wisdom, let him ask of God, who gives to all liberally and without reproach, and it will be given to him.*

The first force is patience. James' point is, "Don't quit before the answer comes. Let patience have full play, that you may be perfect and complete, lacking nothing."

Hebrews 10:36, says it this way,

> *For you have need of endurance, so that after you have done the will of God, you may receive the promise.*

You and I may actually have done the will of God, done what God wants us to do, but if we don't exercise endurance, we won't receive the promise. That is the importance of patience.

The second cooperating force at work to pass the test of your faith is wisdom. If you lack wisdom, if you can't see the forest for the trees in the midst of your trial, you can ask God and He will give it...liberally and without reproach.

God delights when you ask for wisdom. And He won't belittle you or find fault with you for asking.

So if you find your faith on trial, if you are being sorely tested, ask God for wisdom and patiently endure. Without these two forces, you will never know victory!

Day 22

Gaining the Wisdom of God

I think every Christian desires wisdom from God. But they don't get it because they don't understand how to receive it.

In Psalm 51:6, we are told,

...in the hidden part You will make me to know wisdom.

When God communicates His wisdom to us, He does it in that secret part. Whether it's as we read His Word and a Scripture speaks to us, or whether the Holy Spirit just whispers to us. As Proverbs 20:27 tells us, *The spirit of a man is the lamp of the Lord.* In other words, God illuminates us through our spirit.

For example, maybe you are in a difficult financial situation and you just don't know what to do. You are working, you are tithing, you are trusting God, you are doing all you need to do, but it seems like you can't make ends meet.

Maybe what you need is wisdom. If you ask for it, God may speak something as simple to your heart as, "Go talk to this person." Or, "Advertise in this magazine." Or, "Call so-and-so and ask them to forgive you for the way you treated them." Or He may just say, "Hold steady."

Shortly after I was saved, I developed a physical condition I could not get any relief from. So I went to God and I said, "God, give me wisdom." God spoke to me and said, "You need to stop drinking coffee."

Now I did not want to hear that because I was a big coffee drinker. But you know what? After obeying God in that, almost immediately, that condition cleared up, and it has never been back.

God's wisdom. He will speak to you. If you ask, He will make His wisdom known in the hidden part.

Day 23

The Requirement for Receiving God's Wisdom

In yesterday's devotional, we talked about how, when you ask for God's wisdom, He reveals it in your spirit...that hidden place. But there is a critical requirement for God to reveal that wisdom to you. You have to ask for it in faith.

James 1:6-8 tells us,

> *But let him ask in faith, with no doubting, for he who doubts is like a wave of the sea driven and tossed by the wind. For let not that man suppose that he will receive anything from the Lord; he is a double-minded man, unstable in all his ways.*

You can't vacillate between two opinions. If you don't anchor yourself on God's promise that He will give you His wisdom, you will be blown about by the opinions of others, by your feelings, by the way the circumstances look, and you won't receive anything from God.

Not too long ago I went with some friends in a small boat to Catalina (an island 26 miles off the coast of Southern California). Just as we were arriving at about eight in the evening, the engine seized. We paddled in to a depth where we could drop the anchor.

After calling Vessel Assist, a storm came up and the wind began to blow and the rain began to fall. We had to wait a couple of hours before help arrived.

You know what? If we hadn't dropped anchor, the wind would have blown us somewhere out in the middle of the Pacific Ocean.

My friend, you have to drop your anchor. You have to ask in faith. You can't vacillate. You can't be double-minded if you are going to receive the wisdom of God.

Day 24

True Faith

James 2:14-20 tells us the substance of true faith,

> *What does it profit, my brethren, if someone says he has faith but does not have works? Can faith save him? If a brother or sister is naked and destitute of daily food, and one of you says to them, "Depart in peace, be warmed and filled," but you do not give them the things which are needed for the body, what does it profit? Thus also faith by itself, if it does not have works, is dead. But someone will say, "You have faith, and I have works." Show me your faith without your works, and I will show you my faith by my works. You believe that there is one God. You do well. Even the demons believe—and tremble! But do you want to know, O foolish man, that faith without works is dead?*

My favorite translation of this last verse is, "Faith without actions that correspond is dead." Faith must have actions that correspond with it.

You can talk about catching fish, about what lures you are going to use, and how you are going to cook them after you catch them, but if you never throw a line in the water, you are not going to catch a fish.

Or it's like the golfer who comes to a 3-par hole with a lake right in front of the green and says, "No problem, I can hit that green with my six iron." Then he digs out an old ratty golf ball. If he truly believes he can hit the green, he will hit his brand new $3 golf ball!

For faith to be genuine, it has to have corresponding actions.

Day 25

The Motive of Faith

When speaking of faith, it is critical to talk about the motive of our faith. James 4:2-3 tells us what a wrong motive is,

> *You lust and do not have. You murder and covet and cannot obtain. You fight and war. Yet you do not have because you do not ask. You ask and do not receive, because you ask amiss, that you may spend it on your pleasures.*

God is very concerned about the "why" behind our prayers of faith. He is very interested in the state of our hearts. And I think it is good to check our motives from time to time.

Why do we want what we want? Is it ego driven? Am I asking for it because I want to impress someone? Are my motives right?

Now, you don't have to overdo it. You can overanalyze things to the point that you become spiritually frozen and don't do anything. I think if you will get honest and lay your heart out before God, He will very quickly put the spotlight on the things that should not be there.

Our dog always stands at the back door and scratches on the glass like he really loves us and wants to come in and be with us. But the moment you open the door he runs right by you into the kitchen looking for food.

Why do you want the thing you want? What is the purpose behind asking? Is it for the glory of God? Is it to help people? Is there a pure motive there?

When your motive is right, God will not be long in answering. But if your motive is not right, God won't answer until it gets right.

Day 26

Faith Hears the Rain

Over the last few devotionals, we have looked at faith—what true faith looks like, and the motive behind the faith that pleases God.

In James 5:15 we are told,

> *And the prayer of faith will save the sick, and the Lord will raise him up. And if he has committed sins, he will be forgiven.*

Clearly, James wants us to know that when we pray a prayer of faith, God will answer it. In this passage, we are told that through that prayer God will indeed heal those who are sick, and raise them up.

So what is it that makes up the prayer of faith? There are three components, all of which we have touched on in the last few days.

The prayer of faith is a prayer that:

1. <u>Does not waver</u>. It doesn't vacillate, moving back and forth. It is anchored on the promise of God.
2. <u>Is followed by corresponding actions</u>.
3. <u>Is prayed from right motives</u>.

The example James cites of someone who prayed a prayer of faith is Elijah. I encourage you to read his story in 1 Kings 17. There you find that, through the prayer of faith, God shut up the heavens and there was no rain. And then, by another prayer of faith, the heavens were opened and rain came down.

Elijah expressed his faith when he said he *heard the sound of abundance of rain.* He made that statement before there was a cloud in the sky or before a drop of rain ever fell!

When you and I don't waver in our faith, when we show our faith by corresponding action, and when we pray with right motives, God will act. As surely as Elijah heard that rain by faith, you can hear the rain...whatever that represents in your life. That is the prayer of faith.

Day 27

The Importance of Revival

Psalm 85:6 asks a powerful question,

> *Will You not revive us again, that Your people may rejoice in You?*

Notice that the psalmist says, "again." This tells me that the nation of Israel was once in a state of revival, but that had waned, it had declined, and they had come again to the place where they needed to be revived.

Perhaps today you are in a place where you need to be revived.

Revival has been described as the inrush of the Spirit into the body that threatens to become a corpse. That is a good definition. Something needs to be revived when it is dying or when it has lost its strength or momentum.

Revival brings new life. It brings fresh vigor. It brings renewed momentum to that which is in a weakened or dying state.

In 2 Timothy 1:6, Paul writes to Timothy, *Stir up the gift of God which is in you.* The word for *stir up* literally means to rekindle. In other words, a fire was there at one time, but it has begun to burn low. And now it needs to be refueled and tended to.

The Amplified Bible says, *Rekindle the embers, fan the flame and keep burning the gracious gift of God, the inner fire.*

Maybe you have felt spiritually flat lately. Maybe the fire that once burned white hot for God is now just a glowing ember. If so, it is time to rekindle those embers and fan to flame what He has put within you.

As God goes to work in your life, you will find that once again your life will be filled with purpose, and you will once again rejoice in God.

Day 28

The Vital Sign of Joy

In yesterday's devotional, I challenged you to consider whether God needs to do a work in your life to revive you spiritually. Perhaps you feel it, but you just don't know what it is.

Over the next few days, I want to point you to the vital signs that may indicate the need for spiritual revival in your life. The first one we find in Psalm 85. It is lack of joy. Look at the language in verse 6,

> *Will You not revive us again, that Your people may rejoice in You?*

When a person is sullen and depressed spiritually, cheerless and despondent, it is a sure sign that they need revival.

You might say, "Well, you know, if my circumstances would just change, then I would rejoice." No. Joy is not dependent upon your circumstances. In fact, let me give you a great example.

2 Corinthians 8:1-2 states,

> *Moreover, brethren, we make known to you the grace of God bestowed on the churches of Macedonia: that in a great trial of affliction the abundance of their joy and their deep poverty abounded in the riches of their liberality.*

Notice this language. The Macedonians were not in a little trial. They were in a "great trial of affliction." They were experiencing deep poverty, tremendous lack in their life, and yet they had abundant joy.

What was their secret? Living in the grace of God.

More than anything else, joy is dependent upon understanding the grace of God, knowing that God's grace is at work even in your affliction.

If you are joyless today, ask the Spirit of God to fill your heart. If you do, there will be a joy regardless of what you are facing.

Day 29

The Vital Sign of Prayer

One of the truest indicators of whether an individual's spiritual life is progressing or declining is prayer. And if your prayer life is declining, it is a sure sign your spiritual life is in need of reviving.

Psalm 80:18 puts it this way,

Then we will not turn back from You; revive us, and we will call upon Your name.

Prayer is to the spiritual life what breathing is to the physical life. If your breathing is shallow and intermittent, something is wrong. It is a sign that there is a lack of health. If your breathing is deep and regular, it is a sign of health.

I once read a story about a World War II soldier who was called in before his commanding officer and accused of spying. The officer said, "You have been seen slipping off into a wooded area where we know enemy patrols have been seen, and we think you're passing information to them."

The commanding officer demanded, "Why did you go there?" and the soldier said, "I just slipped away for a quiet hour of prayer." The officer then commanded him to get on his knees and show him how he prayed.

So the soldier hit his knees, thinking he was likely to get executed for treason, and began to cry out to God. Immediately it was evident that he had an intimacy with God. The commanding officer stopped him and said, "That's enough. You can go." He turned to another officer and said, "No one could pray like that without a long apprenticeship."

Where are you when it comes to prayer? Is it deep and regular? Or is it shallow, sporadic, and intermittent? If it is shallow, it is a sign that your heart needs to be revived.

Day 30

The Vital Sign of Hunger for God's Word

It is not unusual for someone who becomes physically sick to lose their appetite. In fact, when a person is deathly ill, the doctor will often pull loved ones aside and say, "Try to get them to eat something. If they're going to recover, they have to eat."

The same is true when someone is sick spiritually. They lose their appetite for spiritual things. They lose their appetite for the Word of God. In fact, when you see a believer who has lost his or her hunger for God's Word, it is a sure sign that person needs to be revived.

At least three times in Psalm 119, the psalmist tells us that one of the ways God will revive you when you are spiritually weak is through His Word.

In verse 25 he says,

> *My soul clings to the dust; revive me according to Your word.*

In verse 107 he says,

> *I am afflicted very much; revive me, O LORD, according to Your word.*

And then in verse 154 he says it again,

> *Plead my cause and redeem me; revive me according to Your word.*

If you are going to be revived, it will be in large part according to or through the Word of God. In fact, what the psalmist is literally saying is, "Give me life. Revive me through Your Word." The more you feed on God's Word, the more you hunger for it.

So a critical vital sign of the spiritual life is a hunger, an appetite, for God's Word. There is a renewed hunger for spiritual truth when you are revived. As you feed upon His Word, it will give you more life, it will give you more strength, and it will give you spiritual vitality.

Day 31

The Vital Sign of Passion to Reach the Lost

One of the major signs that someone needs to be revived is a lack of concern for the lost. In David's psalm of repentance, Psalm 51:10-13, he says,

> *Create in me a clean heart, O God, and renew a steadfast spirit within me. Do not cast me away from Your presence, and do not take Your Holy Spirit from me. Restore to me the joy of Your salvation, and uphold me by Your generous Spirit. Then I will teach transgressors Your ways, and sinners shall be converted to You.*

When David says, *Renew a steadfast spirit in me...Restore to me the joy of Your salvation*, he is saying, "God, revive me, restore me, renew me." One of the fruits we find in a heart that has been revived is a desire to see others converted. *Then I will teach transgressors Your ways, and sinners shall be converted to You.*

When a person's spiritual life wanes, there is very little thought and very little action aimed at reaching the lost. Yet, someone who has been revived and is spiritually healthy will be actively engaged in the evangelization of the lost.

Read carefully these words from Elton Trueblood, a Quaker scholar. He said, "Evangelism occurs when Christians are so ignited by their contact with Christ that they in turn set other fires. It is easy to determine when something is aflame. It ignites other material. Any fire that does not spread will eventually go out."

When you are spiritually revived, you will think about the spiritual state of the people that you rub shoulders with every day. It is inevitable that when your heart is revived and close to God, you will have a concern for the lost.

Day 32

The Vital Sign of Spiritual Insight

In the Old Testament, we find the story of Ezra and a large group of Israelites who returned to Jerusalem to reestablish the temple and the worship of God. In the midst of this incredible effort, Ezra prays a powerful prayer, as recorded in Ezra 9:8,

> *"And now for a little while grace has been shown from the LORD our God, to leave us a remnant to escape, and to give us a peg in His holy place, that our God may enlighten our eyes and give us a measure of revival in our bondage."*

Ezra prays that their eyes would be enlightened spiritually. It is reminiscent of Paul's prayer in Ephesians 1, when he prayed that the eyes of the Ephesians would be enlightened, spiritually opened.

One vital sign of the need for revival is when we are spiritually dull and insensitive to God's promptings, and the Holy Spirit's direction and creativity.

Perhaps you can remember something creative that once operated in your life, but sadly, it has waned. It has declined. It has gone dormant.

It shouldn't be that way! The Holy Spirit wants to prompt you and guide you and give you knowledge and creativity. But when you are living in a spiritual fog, and you have become accustomed to living in that fog, you can be assured you have become spiritually dull.

That is when you need to be revived. And when you are, there is an enlightening of the eyes. There is a renewed sense and an awareness of the prompting, and the wooing, and the guiding of God's Spirit. That is what comes with revival.

When you are spiritually revived, you will be sensitive to God's Spirit, and you will gain from Him supernatural insight and enlightenment.

Day 33

The Vital Sign of Pride

Pride and self-sufficiency are unmistakable signs of a heart that is in desperate need of reviving. Isaiah 57:15 tells us,

> *For thus says the High and Lofty One who inhabits eternity, whose name is Holy: "I dwell in the high and holy place, with him who has a contrite and humble spirit, to revive the spirit of the humble, and to revive the heart of the contrite ones."*

To have a contrite heart literally means you break easily. Even at the thought of grieving God's Spirit you break and repent very quickly. It means you walk softly in your heart before God.

God says He will revive those with a humble spirit and a contrite heart. But one of the great dangers among Christians today—especially for those living in the western world with all of its abundance—is a belief that we don't need anything.

More than ever we need to read the words of Jesus in Revelation 3:17,

> *"Because you say, 'I am rich, have become wealthy, and have need of nothing'—and do not know that you are wretched, miserable, poor, blind, and naked."*

How can you be miserable and naked and not know it? It's obvious that Jesus is speaking of their inward, spiritual condition. Apparently, their outward wealth blinded them to their inward poverty. They fell into the trap of pride, which is one of the inherent dangers that comes with prosperity. As Christians living in a very prosperous western world, we need to heed this word!

At Disneyland there is a ride with cool little cars. I remember once seeing a little boy on the ride with his dad, and his feet didn't even reach the pedals! But Junior thought he was driving, oblivious to the fact that Daddy was actually driving the car and making it go.

We need to remember that our feet don't even reach the pedals, and that Daddy, our God, is the One who makes this thing go. We need to maintain a humble heart.

Day 34

View from the Top

I sometimes think Jesus views the Church much differently than we view the Church. In fact, there is a really alarming verse that points to this. It is Revelation 3:1,

> *"And to the angel of the church in Sardis write, 'These things says He who has the seven Spirits of God and the seven stars: "I know your works, that you have a name that you are alive, but you are dead."'"*

WOW! That was written to a church that on the outside looked like they had it all together!

They had a reputation of being a living, vibrant church! People who saw them went to seminars to find out how they were doing it, and people applauded them for their success. But Jesus says, "You're dead!"

The Knox Bible puts it this way, *How thou dost pass for a living man and all the while art a corpse.* The Living Bible says, *I know your reputation as a live and active church, but you're dead.*

You see, activity is not synonymous with life. Sometimes people and churches that are decaying spiritually cover it up with activity. They are still "going through the motions," but there is really a spiritual decay eating away inside.

People think they are doing great, but Jesus sees right to the heart of the matter, both in our individual lives and in the Church.

May God keep you and me from being so misled. May we look to Him always for our daily bread, recognizing and acknowledging that every blessing we possess, every stride of progress we make, is the result of His goodness and His grace alone.

He is the One whose view really matters!

Day 35

The Slippery Spiritual Slope

The slippery slope to spiritual decline is one that is almost imperceptible. One day you are on fire for God, and then before you know it, you are dull and lethargic.

How does spiritual decline happen? I think there are at least four ways:

1. Through neglect. If you neglect a garden, the weeds grow. If you don't water the garden, it will eventually dry up. Sometimes we get into a state where we need to be revived due to neglect.
2. Through the storms of life. Life can sometimes beat you up. Some people have been so beaten up that they are just worn down; and when you couple that with neglect, it is a recipe for spiritual disaster.
3. Through the influence of wrong company or wrong relationships. 1 Corinthians 15:33 says, *Do not be deceived. Evil company corrupts good habits.*" And the very next word is *awake. Awake to righteousness, and do not sin.* Do not be deceived. Evil company, bad company, corrupts good habits.
4. Through willful disobedience. I don't know anyone who hasn't been guilty at one time or another of willful disobedience. And when that is not repented of, when it is not taken care of, it brings us into a state of spiritual decline that can be very dangerous.

So what do you do if you find yourself in spiritual decline? Let me leave you with this verse, Hosea 6:1,

> *Come, and let us return to the LORD; for He has torn, but He will heal us; He has stricken, but He will bind us up.*

The same Spirit that convicts also comforts. If you are convicted, repent. Repentance is an inward change of heart resulting in an outward change of direction. Return to the Lord and let Him heal you and bind you up.

Day 36

Patience in Repentance

In yesterday's devotional, I mentioned Hosea 6:1 as a challenge to repent if indeed God is convicting you.

> *Come, and let us return to the LORD; for He has torn, but He will heal us; He has stricken, but He will bind us up.*

God is indeed a God of compassion Who wants you to return to Him. That is the nature of His grace!

It's not unusual to truly repent of a sin, to seek to return to God and walk with Him, but not feel anything right away. And perhaps, to get discouraged.

The verse that follows Hosea 6:1 gives us a good word as a clear encouragement. Here is what Hosea 6:2 says,

> *After two days He will revive us; on the third day He will raise us up, that we may live in His sight.*

You need to understand that the evidence of revival may not be perceivable right away. That is why I believe Hosea says, *After two days He will revive us; on the third day He will raise us up.*

You need to be careful not to say, "Well, Lord, you have until lunchtime today to do something. And if it doesn't happen by then, I'm out."

God wants you to stick with your commitment to repent. He wants to know you are serious in your desire to walk with Him.

Remember the words of Zechariah 1:3, "*Return to Me," says the Lord of hosts, and "I will return to you.*" Returning to God is something you can do. But only God can do God's part.

If you will return to Him, He will return to you.

Day 37

In the Pits?

There are times when each of us is in the pits, when life just seems to be upside down and nothing seems to be going right.

As you read the Psalms, you realize King David often felt this way. Take Psalm 88 for example. In verses 2-6 he says,

> *Let my prayer come before You; incline Your ear to my cry. For my soul is full of troubles, and my life draws near to the grave. I am counted with those who go down to the pit; I am like a man who has no strength, adrift among the dead, like the slain who lie in the grave, whom You remember no more, and who are cut off from Your hand. You have laid me in the lowest pit, in darkness, in the depths.*

Pretty descriptive of how you and I can sometimes feel, *when our soul is full of troubles...like one who has no strength...adrift among the dead...whom You* [God] *remember no more.*

When you are in the pits, it can often seem like there is no way out. Your soul is full of trouble, you are despondent, you are overwhelmed by the problems of life, you can almost feel like something has died inside of you, and you might feel totally cut off from God, like He has somehow forgotten you.

What I want you to see in today's Scripture is that you are not alone. Every one of us has gone through these difficult days. Even King David!

God knows your struggles. Like David, take time today to share with God all that is on your heart, and in the next few days, I will show you how you can get out of the pits!

Day 38

Waiting on God

To get out of a pit, it's really not complicated. Psalm 40:1-2 tells us the first step,

> *I waited patiently for the LORD; and He inclined to me, and heard my cry. He also brought me up out of a horrible pit, out of the miry clay, and set my feet upon a rock, and established my steps.*

The first step in getting out of the pit of despair is to cry out to God. He will hear your cry, and He will bring you up and out.

But His answer is not always instant. Notice David said, *I waited patiently for the Lord.* The answer to his cry wasn't apparent for a while. If you've spent a long time getting yourself into a mess, it may take some time for your deliverance.

A number of years back I went hunting with a friend. I was to fly on a little plane into a meadow about 20 miles into the wilderness where he was going to meet me.

For a variety of reasons, I ended up being six hours late to the drop-off point. My friend wasn't there, so for 20 minutes the pilot of that little plane tried to convince me not to stay. He said there were mountain lions, grizzly bears, packs of wolves...I would get eaten alive!

He finally left, and at about two in the morning I heard a noise. It wasn't a grizzly bear; it was my friend with the horses!

I think the devil is like that airplane pilot. He is always trying to talk us into quitting and giving up. But we can miss the greatest blessings in our lives when we are not patient.

Cry out to God, He will answer you. Period! But be prepared to exercise patience.

Day 39

Have You Dug a Pit for Others?

In order to get out of the pits, you need to make sure you haven't dug any pits for others. Psalm 7:14-16 tells us,

> *Behold, the wicked brings forth iniquity; yes, he conceives trouble and brings forth falsehood. He made a pit and dug it out, and has fallen into the ditch which he made. His trouble shall return upon his own head, and his violent dealing shall come down on his own crown.*

Then there is Psalm 9:15-16,

> *The nations have sunk down in the pit which they made; in the net which they hid, their own foot is caught. The LORD is known by the judgment He executes; the wicked is snared in the work of his own hands.*

Finally, Psalm 57:6,

> *They have prepared a net for my steps; my soul is bowed down; they have dug a pit before me; into the midst of it they themselves have fallen.*

When people dig a pit for somebody else, they end up falling into it themselves. In fact, Proverbs 26:27 says it most directly,

> *Whoever digs a pit will fall into it, and he who rolls a stone will have it roll back on him.*

Pretty plain, isn't it? If you are asking God to get you out of a pit, you need to take time to consider if it is a pit of your own construction. If you have done something to get someone else in trouble—even if you think you are justified in doing it because that person has hurt you—you need to repent. Until there is repentance, God will not intervene.

God is not going to get you out of your pit while you have a shovel in your hand.

Day 40

Are You Rebelling Against Authority?

If you are in the pits, you need to make sure you are not in rebellion against God's established authority, or aligned with those who are.

In Numbers 16 there is an instructive story of Korah and his followers. They openly confronted Moses and Aaron, and challenged whether they were really God's ordained leaders.

Moses and Aaron were flawed and fallible just like every one of us, but Korah wanted to usurp authority that did not belong to him.

God had placed Moses and Aaron in their position of authority, but Korah tried to undermine that authority and lead people against them.

Look at the result of Korah's rebellion. Moses is speaking in verses 30 and 31,

> *"But if the LORD creates a new thing, and the earth opens its mouth and swallows them up with all that belongs to them, and they go down alive into the pit, then you will understand that these men have rejected the LORD." Now it came to pass, as he finished speaking all these words, that the ground split apart under them, and the earth opened its mouth and swallowed them up, with their households and all the men with Korah, with all their goods.*

Notice that it was not just Korah who was destroyed. All those who were aligned with him also went into the pit.

I don't think the ground is going to open up under you if you rebel against the authority that God has set up. But you may find yourself in an emotional, physical, or financial pit that you cannot get out of until you get the rebellion out of you.

If you are in a pit today, check your heart and make sure you are not in rebellion against God's ordained authority.

Day 41

Are You Obeying God's Warnings?

The third thing you should check in your life, if indeed you are in the pits, is to make sure you have obeyed God's warnings.

God does warn us, but we must listen to those warnings. As Job 33:14-18 says,

> *For God may speak in one way, or in another, yet man does not perceive it. In a dream, in a vision of the night, when deep sleep falls upon men, while slumbering on their beds, then He opens the ears of men, and seals their instruction. In order to turn man from his deed, and conceal pride from man, He keeps back his soul from the Pit, and his life from perishing by the sword.*

God always tries to warn us to keep us out of the pits and to keep our lives from danger. And He speaks in many different ways. Sometimes, as we read here, God will speak to us even through a dream.

As I look at my own life, I can see that I have fallen into pits at various times because I did not listen to God's warnings. There have been times I have been too busy to perceive the fact that God was talking to me. It wasn't that God wasn't warning me. He was. I just had a bunch of other things going on in my life and was not taking time to listen to Him.

He is always faithful to warn us. It's just that we are not always faithful to listen. So if you find yourself in a pit today because you did not heed God's warning, just say, "God, I'm sorry." Repent. God will forgive you. And you will be in the position to receive His deliverance.

Day 42

The Pit of Immorality

In the last several devotionals, we have discovered a variety of ways to get out of the pits. Today, I want you to focus on something that is an increasing problem in the Church today. Immorality.

Solomon tells us in Proverbs 22:14,

The mouth of an immoral woman is a deep pit; he who is abhorred by the LORD will fall there.

And he says in Proverbs 23:27,

For a harlot is a deep pit, and a seductress is a narrow well.

Immorality is a deep pit. A pit that is difficult to get out of once you have gotten yourself into it. Not only do you get physically involved with another, there is an emotional entanglement that is not that easy to get out of.

Solomon also says immorality is a narrow well. It is binding, restrictive, and it suffocates your spiritual life. If you are seeking God for deliverance while continuing to engage in immoral behavior, your effort is fruitless.

If you are in the pits today because of an immoral relationship, you must cut off that relationship before seeking God's deliverance. If you will ask God for help after you have repented and cut off that relationship, He will help you beyond anything you could imagine.

God is a merciful God. And He has the ability to work something for good even in a situation like this. If you are truly repentant and broken, God can do something good.

God is the only One who can break something and make it more valuable. I break things, and they lose their value. But when God breaks something, it becomes more valuable.

If you are in an immoral relationship, stop it, repent, and He will forgive you, and bring you out of your pit.

Day 43

The Pit of Pride

The fifth and the final reason your life may be in the pits is pride. We always need to check our hearts for pride.

In Isaiah 14:13-15 we read,

> *For you have said in your heart: "I will ascend into heaven, I will exalt my throne above the stars of God; I will also sit on the mount of the congregation on the farthest sides of the north; I will ascend above the heights of the clouds, I will be like the Most High." Yet you shall be brought down to Sheol, to the lowest depths of the Pit.*

This passage records God's rebuke of Satan when he was kicked out of heaven. Satan was talking real big with pride oozing from every word that he said.

But God said, "That's what you think. I'm going to throw you down to the pit." And because of the pride in his heart, Satan will indeed be thrown down to a pit for all eternity (read Revelation 20!).

Pride is a dangerous thing. In fact, so dangerous we are told in 1 Timothy 3:6 to not put a novice into a leadership role in the Church, lest being puffed up with pride, he or she falls into the same condemnation as the devil.

Pride goes before destruction and a haughty spirit before a fall.

Pride is a weird thing. It's like bad breath. Everybody seems to know you have it before you do! But pride will not only get you into a pit, it will destroy you.

I want to challenge you today. If your life is in the pits, check to see if it is because of your pride. If so, humble yourself, otherwise you are not going to get out!

Day 44

Avoiding the Pit

Over the last few days, we have looked at what it takes to get out of the pits—what to do when life seems to be turned upside down.

There is one pit, though, that every person is headed for except for the grace and provision of God. Some of the most marvelous verses of Scripture are found in Psalm 49:6-9. These verses point us to the one and only way to avoid the pit for eternity.

> *Those who trust in their wealth and boast in the multitude of their riches, none of them can by any means redeem his brother, nor give to God a ransom for him—for the redemption of their souls is costly, and it shall cease forever—that he should continue to live eternally, and not see the Pit.*

These are powerful words for our day and age. It is so easy for many to believe that their wealth, their power, and their goodness will someday be enough to save them.

But the only way to have eternal life and not see the pit of eternal destruction is to realize that you can do nothing and pay no amount to redeem your own soul. Why? Because the price of your soul is very costly—more than you could ever pay.

The purchase price was the shed blood of the Son of God upon Calvary's cross. Only through embracing His sacrifice can your soul be ransomed. No good works can do it. No personal sacrifice can do it. The price has been paid.

I trust you have accepted God's gift of eternal life through Jesus Christ. If so, praise Him today for rescuing you from the pit of hell and for paying that high price for you.

Day 45

Falling into Crisis

In 1 Kings, we have the story of the prophet Elijah. In chapter 18, we see a great victory over the priests of Baal, an incredible victory that demonstrated the power of the one true God for all to see.

In the next chapter, we see Elijah on the run (1 Kings 19:1-3),

> *And Ahab told Jezebel all that Elijah had done, also how he had executed all the prophets with the sword. Then Jezebel sent a messenger to Elijah, saying, "So let the gods do to me, and more also, if I do not make your life as the life of one of them by tomorrow about this time." And when he saw that, he arose and ran for his life, and went to Beersheba, which belongs to Judah, and left his servant there.*

How could Elijah, a prophet of God who had been used in such a powerful way, now be on the run? (He eventually even became suicidal.) While there are a number of things we could look at, I want to give you one truth today to consider.

After any great spiritual victory, it is always wise to keep your armor on. Over and over, there are examples of tremendous trials and temptations after great victories.

King David, after God had supernaturally spoken to him, fell morally, and committed adultery with Bathsheba. Or there is Samson who, after God used him to bring great deliverance, got messed up with Delilah. Then there is Jesus who, after being with the Father on the mount of transfiguration, came to the bottom of the mountain and was met by a demon-possessed boy.

Sometimes we are the most vulnerable after the highest and brightest times we have with God. So today, let me encourage you to always keep your armor on (see Ephesians 6:11).

Day 46

The Power of Zero

Perhaps you are in a very stressful time in your life right now, and you feel you can't go on. I want you to know that you are not alone. In fact, some of the greatest men and women of God have gone through what you are going through right now.

One of those individuals is the prophet Elijah whom I mentioned in yesterday's devotional. After a great spiritual victory over the priests of Baal, we find him on the run, wondering whether life is even worth it.

We catch the story in 1 Kings 19:4-6,

> *But he himself went a day's journey into the wilderness, and came and sat down under a broom tree. And he prayed that he might die, and said, "It is enough! Now, LORD, take my life, for I am no better than my fathers!" Then as he lay and slept under a broom tree, suddenly an angel touched him, and said to him, "Arise and eat." Then he looked, and there by his head was a cake baked on coals, and a jar of water. So he ate and drank, and lay down again.*

Elijah had reached that "zero" place in his life. There was nothing left. He had given it all and the tank was empty.

Maybe that describes you right now, you are on the verge of quitting. You figure, "I've had enough. I'm done. Enough pressures, enough hassles, I cannot ride this thing out anymore. My strength is gone!"

Well, did you notice that when Elijah was at the end of his strength, that was when God intervened? Being out of strength, being at zero, is not a bad place to be. If you will look to God, He is prepared to meet you in your moment of need.

Day 47

Your Weakness, God's Power

2 Corinthians 12:9 is a powerful reminder of God's provision for you and me when we reach the end of our strength.

> *"My grace is sufficient for you, for My strength is made perfect in weakness."*

When Paul wrote these words, he was being harassed everywhere he went by an evil spirit that he referred to as "a thorn in the flesh." It was a messenger sent from Satan to buffet him, to constantly harass him.

The constant harassment of this spirit finally got to him, and he begged God three times to take it away. Paul was clearly at the end of his rope.

But, even though Paul prayed for God's intervention three times, the spirit did not depart. And God's response to Paul was the verse we read above. His strength is made perfect in weakness.

What does *perfect* mean? It means that His power comes to full maturity...it blossoms...it is fully expressed in our weakness.

What was Paul's response? He went on to say in verses 9-10 of that same chapter,

> *Therefore most gladly I would rather boast in my infirmities that the power of Christ may rest upon me. Therefore I take pleasure in infirmities, in reproaches, in needs, in persecutions and distresses for Christ's sake. For when I am weak, then I am strong.*

It seems that sometimes we have to get to the end of ourselves before we will look fully to God. But when we do, we find that He is more than enough. If you are there today or close to that point, take hold of God's strength.

Put your trust in Him. He will bring you to the place of your breakthrough, and you will find the strength and direction you need.

Day 48

Lightening the Load

When we get into the storms of life, it is often difficult to know what to do. It can feel like the noise of our troubles drowns out everything else.

In Acts 27 we find the apostle Paul caught in the midst of a horrible storm. The ship was being tossed all over the place, and the situation was becoming quite serious.

Embedded in this story is a spiritual truth that can guide you and me when we get caught in the storms of life. It is found in verses 18-19,

> *And because we were exceedingly tempest-tossed, the next day they lightened the ship. On the third day we threw the ship's tackle overboard with our own hands.*

Notice that when the storm got bad and threatened to capsize the ship, they lightened the load.

Sometimes in a storm you need to throw some things overboard. In fact, it is a great time to evaluate any baggage that you are carrying in your life. There are some things that may not be a sin to you, but they are a weight to you.

One of the things you need to carefully evaluate is your relationships. There are some relationships you need to cut loose because they are hanging you up, holding you back, and they are hindering you from getting to where God wants you to go.

Or maybe it's something as simple as too much TV. Watching TV may not be a sin, but it can sure be a weight! It can sure be a hindrance to you hearing from God, especially when you are in a time of crisis.

If you really want to hear from God and get yourself unstuck, lighten your ship.

Day 49

Rest

In the last several devotionals, we have looked at how we respond to the storms of life. Today and tomorrow we will look at two more principles for handling life when the storms hit.

Today, I want to go back to the story of Elijah in 1 Kings 19. In verses 5-6 we read,

> *Then as he lay and slept under a broom tree, suddenly an angel touched him, and said to him, "Arise and eat." Then he looked, and there by his head was a cake baked on coals, and a jar of water. So he ate and drank, and lay down again.*

Notice that in the midst of his crisis, Elijah rested and ate. He took care of his body.

Some of the crises you experience come because you are sleep deprived and you don't eat right. And you know what? Your body, your soul, and your spirit are all tied together. What you do to one affects the other two. It affects the whole.

We are intricately woven together. And the wisest thing you can do when you get into a crisis is just give your body a rest, because it affects every other part of your life.

When you are exhausted and physically weak, it is easy for everything to be blown out of proportion. When you are tired, it can look like your whole world is falling apart when it really is not. It is like Mark Twain said, "I am an old man and have known a great many troubles, but most of them never happened."

You and I do need to rest. If you are in the midst of a storm today, make sure not to neglect the rest you need.

Day 50

The Still Small Voice

In the last three devotionals, we have looked at principles on how we should respond when our life is in crisis. The last principle is found in 1 Kings 19:11-12,

> *Then He said, "Go out, and stand on the mountain before the LORD." And behold, the LORD passed by, and a great and strong wind tore into the mountains and broke the rocks in pieces before the LORD, but the LORD was not in the wind; and after the wind an earthquake, but the LORD was not in the earthquake; and after the earthquake a fire, but the LORD was not in the fire; and after the fire a still small voice.*

If your life is in crisis today, you need to remind yourself how God leads. Do not look for it in outward, powerful manifestations—the strong wind, an earthquake, or fire.

Rather, listen for that "still small voice."

That is how Jesus speaks to us today. Read carefully the words of John 16:13,

> *"However, when He, the Spirit of truth, has come, He will guide you into all truth; for He will not speak on His own authority, but whatever He hears He will speak; and He will tell you things to come."*

God has given you and me His Holy Spirit to lead and guide us. And, friend, when God leads you, it is going to be through the still small whisper of the Spirit in your heart.

Yet many people want more than that. Some people think, "I'm in a desperate situation. I need something more!" You and I need nothing more, because through the indwelling Holy Spirit, we have God on the inside.

So if God is going to guide you, He is going to do it from within...through that still small voice.

Day 51

PRAISE: The First Step in Effective Prayer

Praying consistently will change your life. In fact, many of the blessings God wants you to enjoy will never be realized unless you pray.

I think all Christians know they are supposed to pray, and all Christians want to pray. But many of God's people, if they are completely frank and transparent about the issue, would have to admit their prayer life is somewhere between mediocre and non-existent.

Over the next few devotionals, I want to share with you four simple points which I have put into an acronym: P-R-A-Y. If you can spell the word *pray*, hopefully you will be able to remember how to make your prayer life more effective, and you will be inspired to pray more consistently.

Psalm 100 helps us understand the first letter, "P", in the word P-R-A-Y, which stands for *praise*. Psalm 100:1-4 states it well,

> *Make a joyful shout to the LORD, all you lands! Serve the LORD with gladness; come before His presence with singing. Know that the LORD, He is God; it is He who has made us, and not we ourselves; we are His people and the sheep of His pasture. Enter into His gates with thanksgiving, and into His courts with praise. Be thankful to Him, and bless His name.*

Verse 2 tells us, *Come before His presence with singing*. And in verse 4 notice the words "enter into." In other words, praise is how you are to enter God's presence. It is the best way to begin your prayer.

When you want to come to God, you start with thanksgiving. You start with singing. You start with praise. Or, as *The Message* says, *Enter with the password: "Thank you!"*

Today, and every day, make praise the starting point of every conversation with God!

Day 52

REPENT: The Second Step in Effective Prayer

Yesterday we began to look at what makes for effective prayer by using the acronym P-R-A-Y. The first step is *praise*. Today, I want to focus on the second letter of our acronym, "R", which stands for *repent*.

By repentance in prayer, I mean taking the time before God to search your heart and repent of anything that has come between you and Him. Psalm 19:12-13 expresses it well,

> *Who can understand his errors? Cleanse me from secret faults. Keep back Your servant also from presumptuous sins; let them not have dominion over me. Then I shall be blameless, and I shall be innocent of great transgression.*

Verse 12 begins with the question, "Who can understand his errors?" The psalmist is telling us, "You will not always know when you do something wrong. You will not always know when you get into an area that is not right."

What David is pointing to are the secret faults and presumptuous sins which can still have dominion over you—even though you may not be aware that what you did was wrong.

For example, sometimes we can allow attitudes to get into our hearts that we don't realize are inconsistent with God's character. Or sometimes we can do and say things that are detrimental, not only to us, but to others, and not really understand the damage we have done.

How do you deal with these sins? You come before God and say, "God, put the spotlight on anything in my life that has raised a barrier between You and me, and I will repent of it."

So when you pray, ask God to reveal any sin in your life you may be overlooking. God will honor your heart of repentance.

Day 53

ASK:
The Third Step in Effective Prayer

So far we have discovered that *praise* and *repentance* are the first two steps to effective prayer. Today I want to show you the very important third step of *asking*.

Yesterday we talked about how repentance is searching your own heart and asking God to put the spotlight on it, and then repenting of anything that He shows you. When your heart is clean, you can have confidence before God when you ask. As 1 John 3:21-22 says,

> *Beloved, if our heart does not condemn us, we have confidence toward God. And whatever we ask we receive from Him, because we keep His commandments and do those things that are pleasing in His sight.*

In Matthew 7:7-11, Jesus tells us,

> *"Ask, and it will be given to you; seek, and you will find; knock, and it will be opened to you. For everyone who asks receives, and he who seeks finds, and to him who knocks it will be opened. Or what man is there among you who, if his son asks for bread, will give him a stone? Or if he asks for a fish, will he give him a serpent? If you then, being evil, know how to give good gifts to your children, how much more will your Father who is in heaven give good things to those who ask Him!"*

Pretty clear, isn't it? God loves you and wants the very best for you. Be careful not to water down the words of Jesus, or somehow try and explain them away or complicate them. He meant just what He said.

But there are some conditions. And tomorrow we will look at those conditions for receiving what you ask God for.

Day 54

The Conditions for Answered Prayer

Yesterday we talked about the "A" in the acronym P-R-A-Y, which is our way of understanding the steps in effective prayer. That "A" stands for *ask*, and I have come to believe that too many Christians don't believe that God wants them to ask.

God wants you to ask. He really does. But there are some conditions He gives in order to answer your requests. In John chapters 14-16 we find a number of these conditions.

We need to remember that these are Jesus' last hours with the disciples; and He wants them to understand how prayer really works. Over and over He emphasizes the need to ask, but His answers will be based on three conditions.

First, in John 14:13, Jesus says your request must glorify God,

> *"And whatever you ask in My name, that I will do, that the Father may be glorified in the Son. If you ask anything in My name, I will do it."*

Second, in John 15:7, He says your request must be consistent and in harmony with His Word,

> *"If you abide in Me, and My words abide in you, you will ask what you desire, and it shall be done for you."*

And finally, in John 16:23-24, Jesus sets the condition that your request bring you joy,

> *"And in that day you will ask Me nothing. Most assuredly, I say to you, whatever you ask the Father in My name He will give you. Until now you have asked nothing in My name. Ask, and you will receive, that your joy may be full."*

Over and over, Jesus commands you to ask. But when you ask, make sure your request will glorify God, that it is consistent with His Word, and that it will bring you joy.

Day 55

YIELD: The Fourth Step in Effective Prayer

Psalm 37:4 provides us the "Y" in the acronym P-R-A-Y, the four elements to effective prayer we have been discussing over the last few devotionals.

Here is what Psalm 37:4 says,

Delight yourself also in the LORD, and He shall give you the desires of your heart.

Now the Hebrew word for *delight* in this verse literally means to become soft or pliable. This means that "delighting" in the Lord is assuming a yielded posture before God.

So the "Y" in P-R-A-Y stands for *yield*. The question is: How do you practice yielding to God when you pray? Yielding is when you stop talking, and you wait, listen, and seek to hear from God.

In my own practice of prayer, I will often bow before God and ask Him, "God, is there anything You want to say to me? Do You have any instructions for me? Is there anything You want me to change?"

Then I silently wait for Him to speak to me.

As you assume this posture of being yielded and waiting quietly before Him, you will be surprised at some of the things that come to your attention: "You need to spend more time with your daughter," "Take your wife out on a date," "Bake your neighbor a pie and build a bridge over which the gospel can travel," "Spend more time praising Me," "Show your gratitude and appreciation for those who have been helping you in your life."

You will indeed hear from God if you ask Him to speak into your heart, and wait silently before Him.

That is the last element of effective prayer: *praise, repent, ask, yield*. Your prayers can indeed be effective if you commit to these four principles. That is how to P-R-A-Y.

Day 56

Pressing On

In Philippians 3:12, Paul says,

> *Not that I have already attained, or am already perfected; but I press on, that I may lay hold of that for which Christ Jesus has also laid hold of me.*

Paul's challenge in this verse is for you and me to press on, to keep growing. I believe one of the greatest assets in life that you and I have is the capacity to grow and change. We have the capacity to press on.

One of the first steps in pressing on is to realize that you have not yet arrived. Even the apostle Paul acknowledged and recognized that he had not yet arrived. He said, *Not that I have already attained, or am already perfected.*

Paul understood that he had a lot of room for growth. And if he did, so do we.

If you have grown stagnant in your spiritual life, you need to ask the question, "Why?" Why is your spiritual life stunted? Why are you not growing? Why are you stymied in your spiritual progress? What are your barriers to growth?

I believe that if we are willing to admit that we need to grow, then identify the barriers that are keeping a lid on our spiritual lives, and finally, by the grace of God, deal with those barriers and remove them, we will begin to press on and grow.

If you were to take a catfish and put it in a small fish tank, that fish would only grow to be 12 inches long and it might weigh a quarter of a pound. But if you took that identical catfish and placed it into a lake, it might grow to be three feet long and weigh 60 pounds.

What was the barrier to its growth? The tank kept it contained. It grew to the limit that the environment allowed.

Remove the barriers to your spiritual growth and press on!

Day 57

Growing Up

The Scripture says in Ephesians 4:15 that we should grow in all things. In today's and tomorrow's devotionals, I want to give you ten areas in which the Bible teaches us we should grow. I hope you will take time to read each passage and answer the question of whether you are growing as you should in each of these areas.

1. In Colossians 1:10 we are told we should increase in the knowledge of God. You ought to know more about God and His Kingdom this week than you did last week.
2. Psalm 71:21 tells us we are to be growing in our influence. I hope I have not reached the pinnacle in my life when it comes to the influence I have for good in the lives of others. If you call yourself a leader and no one is following you, then you are not influencing them, you are just taking a walk. You and I need to grow in influence.
3. In Proverbs 13:11 it says we are to be growing and increasing materially. I don't know of many who couldn't grow in this area!
4. Isaiah 29:19 speaks of increasing in joy. From appearances, some people seem to grow more and more sour as the days go by and have less and less of a sense of humor. Listen, the more you advance in age, the more your capacity to laugh at life's ups and downs should grow.
5. 2 Thessalonians 1:3 teaches us that we should grow in faith. Now faith certainly touches all areas of life; and, hopefully, today you don't freak out like you used to when you are faced with a trial, because your faith has grown and you have tasted and seen that the Lord is good.

In tomorrow's devotion we will complete this list.

Day 58

Growing Up (Part Two)

Yesterday we began a list of ten areas in which Scripture says we should be growing. In today's devotional, I want to complete that list for you.

6. 1 Thessalonians 3:12 and 1 Thessalonians 4:9-10 teach us that we should grow in our love for others. I would hate to think that I have plumbed the depths of love for my wife, for my children, for my friends, or for God.
7. Ephesians 2:21 speaks to us of growing in unity. You and I ought to grow better and better at getting along with other believers, especially those in our church.
8. Luke 2:52 speaks of growing in wisdom. God is so anxious to provide you and me with His wisdom, but it is something we need to seek. Are you growing in wisdom?
9. Luke 2:52 also speaks of growing in favor. Are you obnoxious and hard to get along with? Do you find it difficult to get along with others? I challenge you, if that is true, to consider the model of Jesus for our lives. He grew in favor with both God *and* men.
10. 2 Peter 3:18 says that we can grow in grace. I don't know about you, but I am deeply grateful for God's grace in my life. And for those who extend me grace when I blow it. Is grace a hallmark of your life?

According to Scripture, these ten areas—the five from yesterday and the five today—are vital areas in which you and I are to grow. I challenge you to read each Scripture and take each area before the Lord and ask Him to reveal where you need to grow.

You will be amazed at the change for good that will come about in your life!

Day 59

Focus

In Philippians 3:13, Paul says,

> *Brethren, I do not count myself to have apprehended; but one thing I do, forgetting those things which are behind and reaching forward to those things which are ahead.*

The phrase I want to direct you to today is Paul's statement, *One thing I do.* These are echoes of words King David spoke when he said, "One thing I desire," and Jesus, who said to the rich young ruler, "There is one thing you lack."

Then there is the blind man, who had been blind from birth, whom Jesus healed. When he was questioned, he said, "There is one thing I know: I was blind, now I see." One thing I do; one thing I desire; one thing you lack; one thing I know.

Each of these statements points to a vital thing needed if you are to grow in your spiritual life: FOCUS.

The problem with many people is they are far too scattered. They are trying to do everything and be everything. They try to be a jack-of-all-trades and end up being a master of none.

If that describes you today, let me ask you a question: What is the one main thing that should be the focus of your life?

I have a very gifted friend who drives me crazy. We can spend an hour in the car; and, in that hour, he has shared 21 new ideas with me. He is trying to be so many things and do so many things that he is not as effective as he could be at anything!

My question to you is this: If you died and stood before God today, what is the one thing He is going to ask you about? Paul said, "One thing I do." What is that one thing for you?

Day 60

Forgetting the Past

Yesterday we looked at Philippians 3:13. I want to draw our attention to this verse again today, but for another reason.

> *Brethren, I do not count myself to have apprehended; but one thing I do, forgetting those things which are behind and reaching forward to those things which are ahead.*

The key word I want to have you focus on today is *forgetting*. I want you to understand the importance of forgetting the past so you can move forward.

Some people—perhaps you—cannot reach forward because they are continually looking backwards. Their focus is on their past sins, their past mistakes, their past failures, their past hurts.

God does not want you to live in the past, but rather focus on the future.

A while back I was visiting a friend who had a great impact on my life as a young believer. As I was sitting at a meal with him and his wife, he began to share with me a great personal failure.

About ten years earlier, when he was pioneering a church, he fell into an adulterous relationship. It rocked the foundation of his marriage; but he repented, got out of the relationship, and over time, God healed his marriage. But he has not been in ministry since.

As he told me, tears began to stream down his face. He got up from the table, went to the bathroom, and his wife looked at me and said, "Bayless, if you can help him, please do. My husband has lived a holy life for the last ten years. God has forgiven him, I have forgiven him, but he hasn't forgiven himself."

This man chained himself to this one past failure, and he couldn't get on with what God had called him to do.

Bury your past so you can uncover your future.

Day 61

Running Inside the Lines

In Philippians 3:14, Paul provides a powerful insight into his passion. Here is what he says,

I press toward the goal for the prize of the upward call of God in Christ Jesus.

Paul clearly had a goal in mind, a sense of his destiny. And he was undaunted in seeking to reach it.

In fact, the phrase "I press toward the goal" could literally be translated from the Greek text this way, "I run within the lines." It paints the picture of a runner, running down a track, staying in his lane.

He is not overreaching his bounds, running in someone else's lane. Rather, as he goes for the goal, he is running within the lines with the goal in mind.

In a little mission in Medford, Oregon, many years ago, there was a young man with a terrible drug and alcohol problem. One night God got a hold of his life. It was a truly dramatic conversion.

I was that young man. And for several decades now, I have been seeking to lay hold of the reason for which He laid hold of me. I knew that night that God had a destiny for my life. And that is the goal I strive and press forward to achieve.

God has a destiny for your life, too. God laid hold of your life just like He did mine, for a purpose. If you have not already done so, you must understand and press forward to fulfill the destiny God has for your life.

If you don't know what that might be, then start asking God to reveal that to you. Ask Him to show you the lane you are to run in.

Day 62

Your Lane

Yesterday we discovered that God has given each of us a call...a destiny designed by God for His glory.

In Philippians 3:12, Paul gives us some additional insight into that call,

> *Not that I have already attained, or am already perfected; but I press on, that I may lay hold of that for which Christ Jesus has also laid hold of me.*

Paul—when he was still an unbeliever and on the road to Damascus—had an encounter with Jesus. Our Lord laid hold of him and Paul realized God had not only put a call on his life, but that the call was unique.

He was driven to fulfill that call. He states it this way, "Since that day, I have been trying to lay hold of the reason for which He laid hold of me."

You also have a unique call. And whatever it is, you need to stop comparing yourself to others and competing with others. That is a terrible way to live. Find out what your lane is, what your gifting is, your calling, and run in that lane.

You are unique! God has not called anyone else to do exactly what you do. Find out who you are and forget about what anybody else thinks. God is not comparing you to another person. You do not have to compete with anyone or be compared to anyone. Just do what He has asked you to do.

That is running in your lane. Do not run in somebody else's lane. Now you can certainly learn from others, but you don't want to copy them. You were born an original; you don't want to die a copy.

Determine God's unique design for your life and run in the lane of that design. That is when you will know satisfaction, blessing, and contentment.

Day 63

The Prize

If you have read the last couple of days' devotionals, you know we have been focusing on Philippians 3:12-14. Today I want to give you one final truth from this passage of Scripture.

It is found in verse 14 where Paul says,

> *I press toward the goal for the prize of the upward call of God in Christ Jesus.*

What I want to focus our thoughts on today is the prize. According to this passage, there is a reward for finishing, a reward that will be given openly to all those who are faithful.

In fact, the Greek word translated *prize* literally means a reward that is given publicly. This is not something that is given in private.

In 2 Timothy 4:7-8, Paul says,

> *I have fought the good fight, I have finished the race, I have kept the faith. Finally, there is laid up for me the crown of righteousness, which the Lord, the righteous Judge, will give to me on that Day, and not to me only but also to all who have loved His appearing.*

This crown of righteousness is synonymous with the "prize." Paul said, "It will be given to me on that Day." Not the day Paul died, but rather on a day that has yet to arrive, when we are gathered before God's throne.

On that day, everyone will be there. King David, Samuel the prophet, Elijah, Elisha, Isaiah, Moses, the apostle Paul, Peter…every saint who has lived for God in every generation since the Resurrection.

On that day, we are going to be standing before God giving an account of our lives. We are going to be rewarded publicly if we have fulfilled our job description and run within the lines of our calling while on this earth.

I urge you to prepare for that day!

Day 64

Your Three-Way Calling

In Jude 1:1, we read the following greeting,

> *Jude, a bondservant of Jesus Christ, and brother of James, to those who are called, sanctified by God the Father, and preserved in Jesus Christ.*

The Greek word for *called* here is used in three different ways. As believers in Jesus Christ, this word tells us we are called to three things:

1. It is used for those who are summoned to an office, duty, or a responsibility. Friend, every believer has been called. You have a duty, you have an office, and you have a responsibility. We have all been called to do something for Christ. We are ambassadors for Christ, and we need to represent Him to a lost and dying world.
2. The word *called* is also used in the Greek language to summon someone to a feast or a festival. And you know what? You have been called to the marriage supper of the Lamb, and you will sit down one day to enjoy all the things God has planned for eternity.
3. Finally, the word translated *called* in this passage is used to summon someone into court to give an account for themselves, or to summon them to judgment. One day we will have to give an account of our lives. One day every one of us will stand before the judgment seat of Christ and give an account for the works done in the body.

You have a responsibility to represent Christ to our dying world, to someday celebrate the marriage supper of the Lamb, and to ultimately give an account of your life.

I pray you will embrace and fulfill your calling today!

Day 65

Your Calling to Judgment

One of the three ways in which we are called as believers, which we looked at in yesterday's devotional, is a call or summons to judgment. And frankly, the thought of it unsettles me.

In fact, when I read what the apostle Paul says about the judgment seat of Christ, it is very sobering. He tells us that someday we will all stand before the judgment seat of Christ and give an account for the works done in the body. In 2 Corinthians 5:11, he states this about that day,

Knowing, therefore, the terror of the Lord, we persuade men.

Think about that for a moment. Isn't that unsettling to you?

The apostle Paul who wrote the great majority of the New Testament, who walked the known world three times to establish churches and to preach the gospel where it had been previously unpreached, who gave his life, and according to church history, was even martyred for the cause of Christ, refers to the judgment seat of Christ as "the terror of the Lord."

Wow! That is just unnerving.

Someday I really want to hear, "Well done, good and faithful servant." I'm taking God's call seriously. Now, I am enjoying life to the max, but there is always that serious edge knowing that I am going to have to stand before Jesus someday.

My prayer for you today is that you, too, would take your call before the judgment seat of Christ seriously. Someday you will stand before our Lord and give an account of every part of your life.

May you hear, "Well done, good and faithful servant."

Day 66

No Plan B

Have you ever thought of the fact that in eternity past God planned for you, me, and every other believer to be His Plan "A" to take His salvation to the world?

Read the words of Jude 1:3,

> *Beloved, while I was very diligent to write to you concerning our common salvation, I found it necessary to write to you exhorting you to contend earnestly for the faith which was once for all delivered to the saints.*

In this verse, Jude is telling those to whom he is writing, "I have written to exhort you, to call you near to God, and that you might contend (literally fight) for the faith which was once for all delivered to the saints."

He is referring to the doctrine of Jesus Christ: His crucifixion, His suffering for our sins, His resurrection from the dead, His ascension to the right hand of the Father, and His imminent return.

Notice his words, though, that it "was once for all delivered." In other words, God is not changing His plan now. It was delivered to us to both defend and to declare, once and for all. There is no Plan B. We are it.

This means the gospel has literally been entrusted to you and to me as the Church...the body of Christ. God has chosen that through the foolishness of preaching men would be saved.

The good news of Jesus Christ, God's only method of bringing salvation to a lost and dying world, the only method of changing men and women's eternal destination, has been delivered to us.

Isn't that an awesome thought? That is why my passion is to bring a living Jesus to a dying world. Because there is no Plan B.

Day 67

The Entrance of Error

Jude 1:4 gives us an ominous warning,

> *For certain men have crept in unnoticed, who long ago were marked out for this condemnation, ungodly men, who turn the grace of our God into lewdness and deny the only Lord God and our Lord Jesus Christ.*

Jude is giving us an idea of how the devil brings error into a church. The key phrase is *men have crept in unnoticed.* That phrase literally means to come alongside by stealth. It pictures someone creeping in and coming alongside, like coming in through a side door.

The folks Jude is talking about look like everyone else, they talk like everyone else, but they are not like everyone else.

That is the way the devil brings error and false doctrine into the Church. It looks like the truth, sounds good, seems like the truth, and it may even be partially true. But there is enough poison in it to kill you.

It's like the guy who wanted to break into a used car lot to steal a bunch of auto parts. The only problem was the two guard dogs. So for the next week he showed up every night with some pieces of meat.

At first the dogs would bark like crazy, but after the man left, they would eat the meat. By the end of the week, they didn't bark at all, they just wanted the meat. So, having become familiar with the dogs, knowing that they wouldn't "sound the alarm," he approached them one last time—with poisoned meat. The dogs ate, and he was able to get into the lot and steal all he wanted.

That is the way the devil does it a lot of times. He sends someone among the believers in order to distract and detour them from the truth. But it is calculated and happens by degrees. Do not let your "inner alarm system" go silent through familiarity.

Beware of those who would move you away, even subtly, from the clearly revealed truth of God's Word.

Day 68

The True Grace of God

Yesterday we read Jude 1:4 which states,

> *For certain men have crept in unnoticed, who long ago were marked out for this condemnation, ungodly men, who turn the grace of our God into lewdness and deny the only Lord God and our Lord Jesus Christ.*

Before we move away from this verse, I want to point out a phrase that I believe is very dangerous ground for the Church in America today. It is the phrase, "Ungodly men, who turn the grace of our God into lewdness."

Lewdness literally means unrestrained lust, wickedness, and immorality. These people believed that once you were saved, you could live however you wanted.

There are people in the Church today with this type of thinking. They believe that if you are saved by grace, and good works do not merit salvation, then you can do whatever you want.

You can sleep around, commit adultery, get drunk, the sky's the limit. It's grace, baby! Your works don't have anything to do with it. You can live however you want!

One of the things that I have heard throughout the years is, "Hey, it doesn't matter. It's grace. God will forgive me, so I'm going to go ahead and do this anyway."

You do not want to live that way. Believe me, something begins to break down inside of you, and you will pay the piper eventually.

If you are turning the grace of God into lewdness through immorality, or any other sin, I challenge you to stop today. Confess your sin to God, turn from whatever it is that you have been doing, and ask God to help you live for Him. If you do, you will experience the true grace of God, which teaches us that *we should live soberly, righteously and godly in this present age* (Titus 2:11-12).

Day 69

Six Times We Should Seek God

But from there you will seek the LORD your God, and you will find Him if you seek Him with all your heart and with all your soul (Deuteronomy 4:29).

In today's devotional, I want to show you the first three of six times we should seek the Lord:

1. When we have sinned.

   If My people who are called by My name will humble themselves, and pray and seek My face, and turn from their wicked ways, then I will hear from heaven, and will forgive their sin and heal their land (2 Chronicles 7:14).

If you sin, do not run *from* God, run *to* Him. Do not allow shame to keep you away.

2. When we are feeling dry spiritually.

   O God, You are my God; early will I seek You; my soul thirsts for You; my flesh longs for You in a dry and thirsty land where there is no water (Psalm 63:1).

When you sense a distance between you and God, or if you feel dry spiritually, do not delay! Seek Him early.

When my potted plants feel dry, I water them. I do not wait until they turn brown and are almost dead. If the soil is dry and the leaves begin to droop, they are in need of water right then, and so it is when you are feeling spiritually dry.

One of the keys to keeping potted plants—and our spiritual lives—healthy is to tend to them early.

3. When we are fearful.

   I sought the LORD, and He heard me, and delivered me from all my fears (Psalm 34:4).

When you are fearful or anxious, it is time to seek the Lord. When you seek Him you can expect to be delivered from all of your fears!

Day 70

Six Times We Should Seek God (Part Two)

In yesterday's devotional, we looked at three times we should seek God. Today we will look at three more:

4. When we are in trouble.

   In the day of my trouble I sought the Lord; my hand was stretched out in the night without ceasing; my soul refused to be comforted (Psalm 77:2).

In Hosea 5:15 the Lord says, "*...in their affliction they will earnestly seek me.*"

I don't like to admit it, but the truth is that at times I have sought God more earnestly when I have been in trouble. Problems have a way of getting us on our knees. If you are in trouble today —seek Him!

5. When all is well.

   Seek the LORD and His strength; seek His face evermore! (Psalm 105:4).

If you will carefully read the preceding verses of this psalm, you will find that the context is one of blessing and not trouble.

This may be the most important time of all to seek Him. May we never become smug and think that we do not need God when all is well.

6. Continually.

   Seek the LORD and His strength; seek His face evermore! (1 Chronicles 16:11).

The word *evermore* in this verse means *continually* or *at all times*.

When you have sinned, when you are dry, when you are afraid, when you are in trouble, when all is well, and in any other situation —you need to seek God!

Day 71

True Satisfaction

Isaiah 14:12-15 records the fall of Satan. Created as God's archangel, we read about the dissatisfaction that got him in trouble,

> *"How you are fallen from heaven, O Lucifer, son of the morning! How you are cut down to the ground, you who weakened the nations! For you have said in your heart: 'I will ascend into heaven, I will exalt my throne above the stars of God; I will also sit on the mount of the congregation on the farthest sides of the north; I will ascend above the heights of the clouds, I will be like the Most High.' Yet you shall be brought down to Sheol, to the lowest depths of the Pit."*

Clearly his problem was pride. "I will, I will, I will...I am going to be like God." He wasn't satisfied with being the archangel that God had created him to be. He wanted to take God's place.

The root of Satan's pride was his discontent with the post and station that the supreme Monarch of the universe had assigned and allotted him. He thought he deserved better.

We all have our sphere of influence, and we all have our gifting from God. Your sphere of influence and gifting are different than mine, and mine are different than yours. It is unwise to desire something that someone else has rather than exploring what God has given you and developing that to its highest potential.

When you look over the fence, it looks like the grass is greener on the other side, but when you hop over, you find out it is spray-painted!

You will only be satisfied if you will develop what God has put inside of you and take that to its highest level possible. That is what you will be rewarded for.

Day 72

True Redemption

The passage of Scripture I want to call your attention to today is Ephesians 4:8-10,

> *Therefore He says: "When He ascended on high, He led captivity captive, and gave gifts to men." (Now this, "He ascended"—what does it mean but that He also first descended into the lower parts of the earth? He who descended is also the One who ascended far above all the heavens, that He might fill all things.)*

Before Jesus ascended, what did He do? He descended. I didn't write that. The Bible says that. And when He descended, what did He do? He led captivity captive. That refers to the Old Testament saints who were in what is called "Abraham's bosom" or Paradise.

Jesus went down there. They were in captivity in the sense that they could not go to heaven until Christ's sacrifice. But after Christ died, having paid the price for our sins, He went and emptied Paradise and He led captivity captive. He brought those saints up to heaven.

Here is what I want you to picture. Jesus, through His death and resurrection, defeated hell and death. He took the keys away from the devil, stripped him of his power and his authority, and won redemption for the human race. Then He went to Paradise and there He saw Abraham, David, Moses, Ezekiel, Joshua, Esther, Ruth—all of the people who served the Lord under the Old Covenant.

He threw the door open and said, "Hey, guys! Time to come home! It's been done! The thing the prophets prophesied about, here I am! I am the reality. Time to leave this place and come to heaven with me!"

Then He who descended, ascended, leading all of those Old Testament saints to heaven with Him! And He sent back the Holy Spirit on the Day of Pentecost to empower us to tell the story of His resurrection and His victory.

Let us make that our passion! To proclaim the resurrected Jesus who has paid the price for our redemption.

Day 73

Search the Scriptures

After Paul preached the gospel to the Bereans, they did something that others had not done—they searched the Scriptures.

> *These were more fair-minded than those in Thessalonica, in that they received the word with all readiness, and searched the Scriptures daily to find out whether these things were so* (Acts 17:11).

According to the next verse, the result of their search was that many of them believed.

Jesus said in John 5:39, "*You search the Scriptures, for in them you think you have eternal life; and these are they which testify of Me.*"

I once heard a Jewish believer share his testimony. His daughter, who had become a Christian, challenged him to read through the New Testament.

He began in Matthew and was astonished to find so many Old Testament references to the Messiah being fulfilled by Jesus.

His initial reason for searching the Scriptures was to prove that his daughter was wrong, but instead, he ended up giving his heart to Christ. The Scriptures testified of Jesus!

Look for Him as you read the Holy Scriptures, and encourage others to do the same.

Day 74

God in Nature

God has made Himself known to mankind in a powerful way people often ignore...His creation. Romans 1:18-20 tells us,

> *For the wrath of God is revealed from heaven against all ungodliness and unrighteousness of men, who suppress the truth in unrighteousness, because what may be known of God is manifest in them, for God has shown it to them. For since the creation of the world His invisible attributes are clearly seen, being understood by the things that are made, even His eternal power and Godhead, so that they are without excuse.*

God speaks to people through nature...through His creation. I am confident that there is a point in every person's life where there comes an awareness of God. Whether it is looking at a shooting star, or at a sunset, or at a blade of grass, the thought occurs to them, "This didn't just get here. This didn't just happen. There must be a God."

Creation speaks to us of the Godhead. It is a revelation of God. The book of Psalms says, *Night unto night shows forth knowledge.* And it says the heavens declare the glory of God. The firmament shows His handiwork. Creation speaks to us of God.

But notice what this passage says. This revelation of God has come to men, but some have wanted to suppress it. They came to that point and thought, "You know what? If I find out about this, then I'm going to become responsible. So I don't think I want to know."

The natural bent of men and women is to suppress the truth, but God is speaking loudly and clearly of His greatness and reality through His creation. Praise Him today for revealing His beauty and power through nature, and use it to point people to Him.

Day 75

No Unbelievers in Hell

In Luke chapter 16, Jesus tells a very sobering story,

> *"The rich man also died and was buried. And being in torments in Hades, he lifted up his eyes and saw Abraham afar off, and Lazarus in his bosom... Then he said, 'I beg you therefore, father, that you would send him to my father's house, for I have five brothers, that he may testify to them, lest they also come to this place of torment'"* (Luke 16:22b-23 and 27-28).

Everyone in hell believes in evangelism. They are crying out lest their loved ones end up with them.

Two thousand years have passed and this rich man has had no relief. A billion years from now he will just be getting started in his torment and pain. Listen to his cry, "My brothers! Send someone to my family!"

Hell is for unbelievers but there are no unbelievers in hell!

Several years ago a man came weeping to the altar of our church. A message had been preached that night from these very Scriptures. After giving his heart to Christ (and after a long time of almost uncontrollable weeping), he told us this story:

He said, "I died twice on the operating table during heart surgery. Each time I died, I left my body and went to hell. It was so horrifying that I tried to put it out of my mind. As the message was preached tonight, all the details of my experience came flooding back into my mind."

He did not need to be convinced that hell was real. That night he accepted Christ and was liberated from the fear of returning to that place of torment.

Jesus alone can rescue us from the terrors of hell and bring us safely to heaven. Shouldn't we be telling people there is a heaven to gain and a hell to shun? Shouldn't we be warning them and encouraging them to accept Christ—while there is still time?!

Day 76

Inwardly Compelled

It was love that motivated the Father to send His Son Jesus to redeem mankind. That same love has been poured out into the heart of every believer.

> *Now hope does not disappoint, because the love of God has been poured out in our hearts by the Holy Spirit who was given to us* (Romans 5:5).

God's love in us calls and compels us to do something about the plight of lost people. Even as Paul says in 2 Corinthians 5:14, *For the love of Christ compels us.*

A few years ago, late at night I would hear what seemed to be a very faint chime or bell. Several times I got out of bed to try and find the source of the sound, but it always stopped before I could discover it.

Finally, one evening, I found out what it was. It was an old watch I had, tucked away in a drawer under some junk. Every evening, the alarm would go off at the same time.

The call of God's love in your heart can be like that. Sounding regularly but seldom heard. Buried under personal ambitions, cares and problems, daily routines and the general busyness of life. But it is unmistakably there!

The same love that moved Jesus to heal the sick and minister God's life to broken people is in you! Listen to it. Get in touch with it and express it to someone in need.

Day 77

"Come Over and Help Us"

And a vision appeared to Paul in the night. A man of Macedonia stood and pleaded with him, saying, "Come over to Macedonia and help us." Now after he had seen the vision, immediately we sought to go to Macedonia, concluding that the Lord had called us to preach the gospel to them (Acts 16:9-10).

The world is in need and they are calling! I can hear Africa, Asia, voices from South America and Europe calling out. China and Australia, New Zealand and Indonesia, Japan and the Philippines... voices from around the globe crying out, "Come over and help us!"

The call may be coming from down your street or from the next aisle in the grocery store. "Help me! I'm lost. I want to find God. I have problems I can't cope with. I have an aching void in my heart that I don't know how to fill. Is there anyone out there with answers?!"

Who will go to them if not you and me?

To say, "I don't feel called to go to them," is equivalent to a strong swimmer standing on the shore of a lake saying he doesn't feel called to save the man drowning before his eyes.

Ask God today to direct you to someone whose heart has cried out for answers and help. Chances are you won't have to go too far to find them.

Day 78

Resist the Devil

In Jude 1:9 we are told how Michael the archangel dealt with Satan.

> *Yet Michael the archangel, in contending with the devil, when he disputed about the body of Moses, dared not bring against him a reviling accusation, but said, "The Lord rebuke you!"*

My concern is that some people have tried to use this Scripture to say that we do not have authority over the devil. They believe we have no recourse other than to pray that the Lord will do something about him.

But that is not the point he is making here at all. Jude was referencing the previous verse where some would "speak evil of dignitaries." He used Michael's conversation with the devil to show that this was wrong. To say that we do not have the right to resist the devil and cast him out on the basis of this Scripture is ridiculous. Here are five things to think about:

1. This event between Michael and Lucifer (Satan) happened before New Testament times—before Jesus defeated the devil and broke his power.
2. James 4:7 tells us, *Resist the devil and he will flee from you.* It does not say, "Pray that God will resist the devil for you."
3. Jesus, in the Great Commission, told us to cast out devils (or demons). Jesus wouldn't tell us that if He hadn't given us the authority.
4. In Luke 10:19 Jesus said, "*I give you the authority to trample on serpents and scorpions, and over all the power of the enemy, and nothing shall by any means hurt you.*"
5. In the book of Acts, as the Church carried out their mission, they commanded demons to come out, and they came out in Jesus' name.

My friend, Jesus has broken the authority of the devil in your life. Resist him and he will flee!

Day 79

Criticizer or Encourager?

Verse 10 in the book of Jude talks about those who "speak evil of whatever they do not know."

Criticism, many times, stems from ignorance. People tend to criticize things they do not know anything about.

A number of years ago, a man came up to me after a service. He had never been to our church before, but he was pretty upset. I had taught that particular night about the baptism in the Holy Spirit and what the Scripture had to say about speaking in other tongues.

He told me, "This church is really off-balance. You overemphasize speaking in tongues." I asked, "Really...how many services have you been to at our church?" His reply was, "Just this one."

So I asked him, "How many of my recorded messages have you listened to?" His response was, "None." I told him, "That seems a little imbalanced. Why don't you stick around for a while and find out what we're about, then see if you feel the same after staying here for a few months."

He said, "Okay, I will." He ended up staying and loving the church.

Too often we are quick to criticize, even when we don't know the whole story. Be careful about criticizing others. Too often what you hear is just rumor.

Do not be a criticizer. Be an encourager. Be a person who is known for always seeking to lift and bless, not speaking evil of whatever you do not know.

Day 80

Clean and Committed

But the LORD said to Samuel, "Do not look at his appearance or at his physical stature, because I have refused him. For the LORD does not see as man sees; for man looks at the outward appearance, but the LORD looks at the heart" (1 Samuel 16:7).

When God looks at us, the first thing He sees is the state of our heart. In the next few devotionals we are going to look at several different aspects of the heart—things that must be present in order to experience the richer blessings of God.

- A clean heart. Psalm 51:10 says, *Create in me a clean heart, O God, and renew a steadfast spirit within me.*

Every once in a while I have to clean out the drains throughout our house. It is amazing how quickly they become clogged. If I do not clean them, before long, the sinks get stopped up and the water will not flow through anymore.

If we don't periodically take time before God to have our hearts purified and cleansed, pretty soon His blessings can no longer flow to us or through us.

- A committed heart. 2 Chronicles 16:9 (NIV) says, "*For the eyes of the LORD range throughout the earth to strengthen those whose hearts are fully committed to him.*"

I believe it is important to be committed to God *before* seeking His blessings.

God told Moses to tell Pharaoh, "Let my people go, that they may serve me." Most people want to be delivered from their captivity, but they are not so keen on the "serving God" part of the deal.

The Lord is looking for committed hearts. Does your heart belong fully to Him? If not, commit it to Him today!

Day 81

Sharper Than a Serpent's Tooth

In yesterday's devotional we began looking at different conditions of the heart—conditions that are necessary in order to experience the richer blessings of God. Today we will continue looking at those conditions.

- A grateful heart. Deuteronomy 28:45-47 (Amplified) says,

  All these curses shall come upon you and shall pursue you and overtake you till you are destroyed, because you do not obey the voice of the Lord your God, to keep His commandments and His statutes which He commanded you. They shall be upon you for a sign [of warning to other nations] and for a wonder, and upon your descendants forever. Because you did not serve the Lord your God with joyfulness of [mind and] heart [in gratitude] for the abundance of all [with which He had blessed you].

William Shakespeare said, "How sharper than a serpent's tooth it is to have a thankless child." Do you express gratitude to God for all the things He has blessed you with, or do you take His blessings for granted?

Many years ago, when I was serving in a small church, one of my duties was to take groceries to families in need. I was shocked at the ingratitude of some that received the gift of food delivered to their homes. While some were truly grateful, others acted as if it was somehow owed to them—even complaining because their favorite foods were not included!

Hopefully you have taken time recently to thank God for the blessings He has bestowed on your life. If not, take time today to express your gratitude to Him who is the source of every good thing you enjoy.

Day 82

Listening and Believing

For the last several devotionals we have been looking at heart attitudes that are conducive to receiving God's blessings. Today we will discuss a few more.

- A listening heart. Luke 5:15 says, *However, the report went around concerning Him all the more; and great multitudes came together to hear, and to be healed by Him of their infirmities.*

The people came to *hear* and then be healed. Some did not want to take the time to listen, they just wanted the blessing so they could be on their way.

Listen to what the apostle Paul said to some people in Acts 28:27, *For the hearts of this people have grown dull. Their ears are hard of hearing, and their eyes they have closed, lest they should see with their eyes and hear with their ears, lest they should understand with their hearts and turn, so that I should heal them.*

We must have listening, receptive hearts if we are going to experience healing or any other of God's blessings.

- A believing heart. Proverbs 3:5 says, *Trust in the LORD with all your heart, and lean not on your own understanding.*

Many years ago I was hiking up a canyon with one of my sons. He was about eight years old at the time. We reached a place where he could only get up by trusting me.

I dropped him a rope and pulled him up to where I was. He needed to believe that I would not let go. Because he did, and put actions with his belief, my strength was made available to him and he reached a place he could not have gotten to on his own.

God's strength is made available to the believing heart, and as we believe He brings us to places we could never reach on our own.

Day 83

Unless They Are Agreed

Can two walk together, unless they are agreed? (Amos 3:3).

In order to walk with God, one must agree with Him. In order to experience the fulfillment of His promises in our lives, we must agree with what those promises say—whether we understand how they could ever come to pass or not.

When the angel Gabriel appeared to Mary and told her she would give birth to a son, she asked, "*How can this be, since I do not know a man?*" (Luke 1:34).

A pretty fair question, don't you think? It seemed impossible to Mary. She could not get her mind around how Gabriel's announcement could ever come to pass.

I love the angel's response to her question, "*The Holy Spirit...*" (Luke 1:35). That is the answer to your impossibilities as well. When you can't understand how a promise from God could ever be fulfilled, the answer is "The Holy Spirit!"

At this point Mary could have said, "No way! This makes no sense to me. I don't accept it!" But she didn't. She said, "*Behold the maidservant of the Lord! Let it be to me according to your word*" (Luke 1:38).

Mary agreed with God's promise and accepted it. Then the miracle happened.

Whatever you are facing today, make the decision to agree with God and His promises. The Holy Spirit can bring His Word to pass!

Day 84

Grumbling and Complaining

One of the things I believe grieves the heart of God is when His children grumble and complain. In Jude 1:6 we find some interesting insight into this destructive behavior,

> *These are grumblers, complainers, walking according to their own lusts; and they mouth great swelling words, flattering people to gain advantage.*

The word *complainer* is really two Greek words stuck together. The first word means to blame, and the second word means your fate or lot in life. The point is that complainers blame someone else for their lot in life.

Isn't it always amazing how someone can make wrong choices, and when they have to face the consequences of those choices, it is always somebody else's fault?

I have two pieces of advice for you on this. First, if you are a complainer and grumbler, stop. God is not honored, and you are only showing that you are "walking according to your own lust," not according to God's Spirit.

Second, stay away from people like that or you will end up being like them. Proverbs 22:24-25 says,

> *Make no friendship with an angry man, and with a furious man do not go, lest you learn his ways and set a snare for your soul.*

Their attitudes and mindsets will bleed off on you.

Did you ever throw a pair of jeans in the washing machine with a red shirt? What happened to your blue jeans? They turned pink, didn't they? The red dye bled over into the blue jeans, and the blue jeans were no longer blue. They were pink.

If you hang around with people who grumble and complain, their attitudes will bleed over into your way of thinking. And the last thing you want to be is a grumbler and complainer.

Day 85

Prayer?

In Ephesians 6:17-18, the apostle Paul tells us,

> *And take the helmet of salvation, and the sword of the Spirit, which is the word of God; praying always with all prayer and supplication in the Spirit, being watchful to this end with all perseverance and supplication for all the saints.*

Today I want you to take special note of that phrase, "Praying always with all prayer." In Goodspeed's translation, he puts it this way, *Use every kind of prayer and entreaty; and at every opportunity, pray in the Spirit.*

I believe Paul is pointing you and me to the fact that there are different kinds of prayer. Over the next few devotionals, I want to talk to you about those different types of prayer.

Now, I know you may be thinking, "Well, prayer is prayer. Let's not get so technical." There is a truth there because prayer in its simplest form is just talking to God, and that is something anyone can do.

But to say, "All prayer is prayer," is equivalent to saying, "All sports are sports." It is true in one sense, but you cannot play one kind of sport with the rules that govern a different kind of sport.

I remember when I was coaching Little League. A ground ball was hit into the outfield. When the outfielder got it, he threw it at the kid running to second base and hit him. Then the outfielder started screaming, "You're out! I got you!"

Well, that works in dodge ball, but it doesn't work in baseball. There are different kinds of prayer for different kinds of circumstances, which I look forward to helping you understand in the coming devotionals.

Be diligent to talk to God every day, but along with that commitment, make it your aim to learn the "rules" that govern different kinds of prayer.

Day 86

The Prayer of Dedication

Yesterday we began a journey to understand the different kinds of prayer for the different circumstances we face in life. The first kind of prayer I want to point you to is the prayer of dedication.

Mark 14:32, 35-36 helps us understand this type of prayer,

> *Then they came to a place which was named Gethsemane; and He said to His disciples, "Sit here while I pray."...He went a little farther, and fell on the ground, and prayed that if it were possible, the hour might pass from Him. And He said, "Abba, Father, all things are possible for You. Take this cup away from Me; nevertheless, not what I will, but what You will."*

Here we find Jesus dedicating and consecrating Himself to the will of the Father. He is in agony; He is in distress. This is the eve of His crucifixion. And Jesus is saying, "Lord, if we can redeem humanity some other way, God, please! But Your will is what is important. So I am consecrating Myself to Your will, Father."

This prayer of dedication and consecration is one that believers should pray. In fact, I believe every Christian should pray this prayer in a general sense after they get saved. Just like the apostle Paul on the road to Damascus, "Lord, what would You have me to do?"

Also, when you come to specific crossroads as you follow God, if you are unsure of God's will, or you feel He may be leading you into a specific area that will require sacrifice, reestablish that consecration and dedication to God through this kind of prayer.

Christ was dedicated to do the will of the Father, and yet He reaffirmed that dedication as He prayed, "I am willing to submit Myself to You."

Pray it. Vocalize it. Submit yourself to His will as He reveals it.

Day 87

The Prayer of Faith

Yesterday we learned about the prayer of dedication. Today I want to help you understand the prayer of faith. This kind of prayer is found in Mark 11:22-24,

> *So Jesus answered and said to them, "Have faith in God. For assuredly, I say to you, whoever says to this mountain, 'Be removed and be cast into the sea,' and does not doubt in his heart, but believes that those things he says will be done, he will have whatever he says. Therefore I say to you, whatever things you ask when you pray, believe that you receive them, and you will have them."*

With the prayer of faith, at the moment you pray you are to believe that you receive what you pray for. Not when the circumstances look different, not at some point in the future, *but when you pray.* The Amplified Bible says, *Believe that it is granted to you.*

When you pray, believe that God hears you and that He has sent the answer, whether you feel differently or not. Before you ever get up off your knees, believe that heaven has sent the answer.

1 John 5:14-15 says it this way,

> *Now this is the confidence that we have in Him, that if we ask anything according to His will, He hears us. And if we know that He hears us, whatever we ask, we know that we have the petitions that we have asked of Him.*

The prayer of faith is prayed when you know and understand God's will. Friend, the Bible is a revelation of the will of God. Prayer will not reach beyond the will of God, and God's Word reveals His will to us.

So pray the prayer of faith according to His will, and you can be assured He hears you and heaven has sent the answer to your prayer.

Day 88

The Prayer of Agreement

In the last two devotionals, we have learned about the prayer of dedication and the prayer of faith. Today I want to help you understand the prayer of agreement.

This prayer is found in Matthew 18:19, where Jesus says,

> *"Again I say to you that if two of you agree on earth concerning anything that they ask, it will be done for them by My Father in heaven."*

When I pray with other people, nine times out of ten this is the prayer that I pray with them. And most of the time I will quote this verse to them.

I remember working for a ministry years ago and praying with the folks who called on the phone. When I prayed with someone, I would walk them through this verse before we prayed.

The steps I pointed out were simple:

- There needs to be at least two of us praying.
- We need to agree.
- We need to be on earth (I usually got a laugh out of this one).
- What we are asking God for needs to come under the category of "anything" (which their request always did).
- God will do it.

The only part people ever got hung up on was the agreement. "What does it mean to agree?" they would ask. I would say, "Simple, to agree means to agree." Don't over-spiritualize it. If we decide to get lunch together at a certain time at a certain place, and you say, "Ok, see you there," we have just agreed.

To agree in prayer is no different.

Read this verse again. Look at it step by step, and follow it—in all its simplicity. If we do our part, God will do His.

Day 89

The Prayer of Personal Edification

Today's devotional brings us to the prayer of personal edification. In 1 Corinthians 14:4, Paul writes,

> *He who speaks in a tongue edifies himself, but he who prophesies edifies the church.*

In verse 14, Paul says, *If I pray in a tongue, my spirit prays.* Coupled together with his statement in verse 4, we can see that praying in tongues edifies our spirit.

Edifies is actually an old English word. It means to build an edifice or building higher and higher. The closest modern way to say that would be "charges himself with energy," just like you would recharge a battery.

When I pray in other tongues, I charge my spirit with energy. I build myself up. It is like my cell phone. It needs to be recharged, or before long it will cease to work. Sometimes I keep my phone on and talk on it while it is recharging, but when I do that it takes a whole lot longer to recharge. If I turn it off and plug it in, the charging process happens much quicker.

Sometimes you just need to shut everything down, turn everything off, and go get away with God and pray. Build yourself up in the Holy Spirit, especially praying in other tongues.

Sometimes after a long day I will come home just drained, tired inside and out. Eating a good meal and getting some rest takes care of my physical tiredness, but in order to replenish my inner resources, I need to do something else.

For me, reading His Word is food for my spirit, and praying in tongues brings inward rest and rejuvenation.

Even as the Scripture declares in Isaiah 28:11-12, *For with stammering lips and another tongue He will speak to this people, to whom He said, "This is the rest with which you may cause the weary to rest," and, "This is the refreshing."*

Take the time to get away and recharge your spiritual batteries.

Day 90

The Prayer of Supplication

Today I want to focus your attention on the prayer of supplication. Ephesians 6:18 tells us,

> *Praying always with all prayer and supplication in the Spirit, being watchful to this end with all perseverance and supplication for all the saints.*

When Paul says, *Praying always with all prayer*, the Greek word he uses for *prayer* is just a general term for prayer used throughout the New Testament. But the word he uses translated *supplicatio*n means prayer for definite, specific needs. Most generally, you will find that this is a prayer prayed for others, as is the case in this verse.

In Philippians 1:4, Paul uses this same word for *supplication,* when he says,

> *Always in every prayer of mine making request for you all with joy.*

Both the words translated *prayer* and *request* are the Greek word for *supplication* that we just read in Ephesians 6:18. But here it is translated as *pray*er and *request.*

I want you to notice who he is saying to pray for, *Always in every prayer of mine making request for you all.* It is for someone else.

Recently, I had a pastor friend ask me to pray for his church and their finances. He said things were really tight. So several times I brought the issue before God and made specific requests about it...or supplications.

Now, I did not pray, "I believe I receive it." That is not my place. What I did do was pray for God to help them. I prayed that God would give them wisdom, that God would inspire the people in the church to give, that people would have a heart for souls, and a number of other specific requests over the following several days.

That is the prayer of supplication...praying specific requests for specific people.

Day 91

The Prayer of Intercession

Today I want to help you understand the prayer of intercession…the sixth and last of the kinds of prayer we have been covering over the last week of devotionals.

1 Timothy 2:1 points us to this type of prayer,

> *Therefore I exhort first of all that supplications, prayers, intercessions, and giving of thanks be made for all men.*

Intercession, as we find it here, is a technical term for approaching a king on behalf of another. In a general sense, related to prayer, intercession is seeking God on the behalf of others. But, more specifically, it is coming to God for one who has no standing with Him.

A number of years ago, I was ministering in Nigeria, speaking at a large conference in the city of Onitsha. While there, we were invited to go meet the king of Onitsha.

It was pretty exciting driving in a motorcade with little flags on all the cars. I felt like a big shot! But when we got to the palace, we had to have someone go on our behalf in order to meet with the king. I had no standing with the king, and neither did anyone else in our party.

The person who brought us to the king of Onitsha was an intercessor. And that is the idea of this word *intercession*. You are coming to the King of kings on the behalf of someone who presently has no standing with Him.

Do you remember when Abraham went before God for the city of Sodom—desiring that God would spare Sodom? What was Abraham doing? He was acting as an intercessor. He was coming between God and someone who had no standing with God.

We all should be praying prayers of intercession. You and I are to make intercession for the lost.

Day 92

Regaining Your Cutting Edge

Over the next several devotionals, I want to focus your attention on something that affects every Christian at one time or another: Losing our spiritual edge.

God wants us to stay spiritually sharp. Consider Ecclesiastes 10:10,

> *If the ax is dull, and one does not sharpen the edge, then he must use more strength; but wisdom brings success.*

God is using this analogy to illustrate a very important truth: If you lose your edge spiritually, you lose your effectiveness as well.

Maybe you feel that way today. Though you are exerting strenuous effort, you are making little progress in your spiritual life. God wants you to go forward. He wants you to progress and not become stagnant in your spiritual life.

I have a friend whose father was a logger many years ago. It was a time when they cut all the timber by hand with just an ax.

One day his father shared about the way he would operate. After he chopped down a tree, he would sit on the stump of the tree he had just chopped down, take out a file he kept on his belt, and he would sharpen the edge of the ax. He would sit there until the ax was very sharp again, then he would go after the next tree.

Each time he chopped down a tree he would do exactly the same thing. But he said most of the other guys didn't do that. They just wanted to keep going, never stopping to sharpen their axes.

Without fail, he said, he always got more done than they did, and he used a lot less effort. They had to exercise more strength, yet they got less done.

Over the next several days, we will look at what it takes to regain that spiritual edge.

Day 93

Are You Listening?

Yesterday we began a series of devotionals focusing on how you can regain your spiritual edge. As we think about how to do that, it is important to consider those things that would indicate we have become spiritually dull.

I believe the number one characteristic you find in someone who has lost their cutting edge spiritually is that the voice of the Holy Spirit is no longer recognized. Those impressions that the Spirit makes upon your heart, through which He guides you, are no longer clear.

In Matthew 13:14-15, Jesus talks about this in a pretty plain way,

> *"And in them the prophecy of Isaiah is fulfilled, which says: 'Hearing you will hear and shall not understand, and seeing you will see and not perceive; for the hearts of this people have grown dull. Their ears are hard of hearing, and their eyes they have closed, lest they should see with their eyes and hear with their ears, lest they should understand with their hearts and turn, so that I should heal them.'"*

This concern is echoed in Hebrews 5:11, where the writer, in talking about the priesthood of Christ, says,

> *Of whom we have much to say, and hard to explain, since you have become dull of hearing.*

Have you lost the edge? Have you lost that sensitivity to the voice of God? Hearing with the physical ears, but not understanding in the heart; seeing with the physical eyes, but not perceiving what God is doing?

Jesus said that happens when the heart becomes dull. When someone loses that edge spiritually, it results is an insensitivity to the voice of God.

If this describes you today, ask God to open your eyes to see and your ears to hear. Begin now to regain your spiritual edge.

Day 94

Instruments in the Hands of God

Yesterday we saw that the first sign a person has lost their spiritual edge is that he or she no longer recognizes the voice of the Holy Spirit and His leading.

The second characteristic of someone who has lost their edge spiritually is they lose their usefulness as an instrument in the hands of God.

Revelation 14:14-16 tells us,

> *Then I looked, and behold, a white cloud, and on the cloud sat One like the Son of Man, having on His head a golden crown, and in His hand a sharp sickle. And another angel came out of the temple, crying with a loud voice to Him who sat on the cloud, "Thrust in Your sickle and reap, for the time has come for You to reap, for the harvest of the earth is ripe." So He who sat on the cloud thrust in His sickle on the earth, and the earth was reaped.*

The One sitting on the cloud with a crown on His head is the Lord Jesus Christ. The harvest on the earth is the salvation of lost humanity, men and women who do not yet have a relationship with God.

Then what is the sharp sickle? It is the Church. It is you. It is me. If God is going to reap the harvest of lost humanity, it is going to be through His people.

You and I are to be a *sharp* sickle in God's hand in His great plan of mankind's redemption. That means the housewife, the doctor, the businessman, the student, the truck driver...every one of us. We are to be setting our hand to whatever practical work we have been gifted to do to see people being saved and being discipled.

Let us determine to be an effective instrument—a sharp sickle—in the hand of our God.

Day 95

No Exemption

2 Kings 6:1-7 gives us some important insight into how to regain our spiritual edge,

> *And the sons of the prophets said to Elisha, "See now, the place where we dwell with you is too small for us. Please, let us go to the Jordan, and let every man take a beam from there, and let us make there a place where we may dwell." So he answered, "Go." Then one said, "Please consent to go with your servants." And he answered, "I will go." So he went with them. And when they came to the Jordan, they cut down trees. But as one was cutting down a tree, the iron ax head fell into the water; and he cried out and said, "Alas, master! For it was borrowed." So the man of God said, "Where did it fall?" And he showed him the place. So he cut off a stick, and threw it in there; and he made the iron float. Therefore he said, "Pick it up for yourself." So he reached out his hand and took it.*

There are a number of principles I want to draw from this story.

Although we will be focusing on the one man who experienced the loss of his ax head, for today's devotion I want to draw your attention to the majority.

As we see from this Scripture, this school for the prophets was needing to expand, to build a bigger building. And notice that everyone had a part to play in what God was doing. It says "Let **every man** take a beam from there, and let **us** make there a place where **we** may dwell."

In God's Kingdom plan, being spiritually sharp is not for just a few people. We all have a responsibility to grow. There is no exemption.

God has a role for you to play. You have not been given an exemption from being a part of God's Kingdom plan. He has a part for you to play in His great plan to reach the world!

Day 96

Be Watchful

We started in yesterday's devotional to look at the lessons we can learn about regaining our spiritual edge from the story in 2 Kings 6. In verses 4-5 we are told about the guy who loses his cutting edge,

> *...when they came to the Jordan, they cut down trees. But as one was cutting down a tree, the iron ax head fell into the water; and he cried out and said, "Alas, master! For it was borrowed."*

Notice this guy is working hard, cutting down a tree. But, in the midst of this effort, he loses his cutting edge. His ax head falls into the water.

Now you might think, "Well, you wouldn't end up in a state like that, you wouldn't lose your edge, unless you were out of God's will."

But if you read yesterday's devotional, you will see these guys were in the will of God. They were moving by divine permission. The prophet not only said go, he went with them, showing just how much this was the right thing to do.

Or you might think, "Well, a spiritual man or a spiritual woman wouldn't have lost their edge." No, there is no indication that the guy who lost his cutting edge was unspiritual. Every indication tells us he was spiritually strong.

So what does this teach us? Be careful not to think we cannot lose our spiritual edge. It can happen to you, and it can happen to me. We all can lose our cutting edge if we are not careful.

My friend, it is vital to take care not to lose your spiritual edge. This is something you have to work at to maintain. Just because you have it today doesn't mean you will have it tomorrow.

The good news is that if you have lost your spiritual edge, you can regain it!

Day 97

Are You Just Swinging the Handle?

As you look at your life today in honesty and transparency, perhaps you would have to say that you have lost that edge, that excitement, that zeal, that spiritual passion you once had.

If indeed you have lost your edge, how can you get it back? Over the next seven days, I will help you understand how to regain your spiritual edge based on 2 Kings 6.

The first principle I want to focus on is based on the man who lost his ax head, as we learn in 2 Kings 6:4-5,

> *...when they came to the Jordan, they cut down trees. But as one was cutting down a tree, the iron ax head fell into the water.*

Now, it would have been senseless for him to have kept chopping with a wooden handle with no ax head on it, wouldn't it?! He would make no progress.

And yet that is what a lot of Christians do today. They have lost their cutting edge, and they are just going through the motions, making no progress at all.

They are chopping away with just a wooden handle!

They think, "Well, I know I'm supposed to go to church, so I will go. As long as I keep busy, maybe nobody's going to know the state of my heart." And they will do this not just for weeks or months, but some people have been doing this for years.

No progress, no growth. They are just swinging that handle without an ax head.

If this is you, do not just keep swinging the ax handle. If you are not making progress, admit it. Until you are willing to face up to the fact that you have not been growing, you can never regain your spiritual edge.

Day 98

Looking to the Master

In 2 Kings 6:5, we read the second in our series of seven principles to regain our spiritual edge. It is the response of the man who lost his cutting edge,

> *But as one was cutting down a tree, the iron ax head fell into the water; and he cried out and said, "Alas, master! For it was borrowed."*

When this man lost his ax head and it fell into the water, he cried out and said, "Alas, master!" He went to the prophet.

The prophet was God's representative in that day. He was the mouthpiece of God. If you wanted to hear from God, you went to the prophet, and the prophet would give a word from God.

Today, thank goodness, we have direct access to God as individuals. We can go directly to the Lord Jesus Christ who is our Master. And that is the second principle to regaining your spiritual edge. You need to realize the only One who can restore your edge once it is lost, is the Lord Jesus Himself.

You need to get your eyes off of men and get your eyes on the Master. Some people make a great mistake because they have their eyes on men. You will always be disappointed if your eyes are on men instead of on the Lord Jesus Christ.

There is only One who can help you regain your spiritual edge, and that is Jesus Christ. No man or woman can take His place.

So today, put your eyes on the Master. Cry out to Him to help you regain your spiritual edge.

Day 99

Taking Responsibility

Today we are on the third key to regaining your cutting edge. The first was to admit you have lost your edge, and the second was to put your eyes on the Master. The third is to take responsibility if you have lost your spiritual edge.

I want to take you back to 2 Kings 6:5,

> *But as one was cutting down a tree, the iron ax head fell into the water; and he cried out and said, "Alas, master! For it was borrowed."*

It is important to understand that ax heads do not just fall off. They fall off because they are not properly maintained.

I have spent endless hours chopping wood, and I have owned a number of fine axes in my time. But in all the years I have chopped firewood, I have never had an ax head fly off.

The only reason an ax head would fly off is if the one using the ax has not been taking care of it. This must have been the case for the guy in 2 Kings 6 who lost the ax head. He was responsible to make sure the ax head would stay on.

The point is this: If you have lost your cutting edge, you need to take responsibility. If it is something that you did, or neglected to do, repent. Take responsibility and stop blaming other people.

As much as you might like to point the finger at the last church you went to, or your spouse, or your boss, or whatever it might be, no one can take your cutting edge away from you. Only you can cause it to be lost.

Stop blaming others, and take responsibility if you have lost your edge. It is a necessary step toward regaining your spiritual sharpness.

Day 100

Where Did it Fall?

The fourth key to regaining your cutting edge is found in verse 6 of 2 Kings 6,

> *So the man of God said, "Where did it fall?" And he showed him the place. So he cut off a stick, and threw it in there; and he made the iron float.*

The words I want you to focus on are, *Where did it fall?* That is quite a question. And look at the response, *And he showed him the place.*

That is the fourth key, to know where you lost your cutting edge. Unless you go back to that place, you cannot retrieve it; and unless you are willing to deal with whatever issue caused you to lose your cutting edge, you will never regain it.

Did you notice that the man knew right where he lost his cutting edge? If you will be honest, you can probably point right to the time you lost, or began to lose, your edge spiritually.

Perhaps it was when you became offended because of what someone did. Or maybe it was when you started watching too much television, or when you began hanging around with a certain person.

If when asked, "Where did it fall?" you cannot immediately point to the place, take some time to commune with your own heart and be still. It won't be long before your answer comes.

This is essential because if you are to regain your edge, you need to start where you lost it.

Day 101

The Cross is Enough

Key number five to regaining your spiritual edge is also found in 2 Kings 6:6,

> *So the man of God said, "Where did it fall?" And he showed him the place. So he cut off a stick, and threw it in there; and he made the iron float.*

Why a stick? What does a piece of wood have to do with it?

Please remember that this story is in here for our benefit, and every part of it is significant. I believe this piece of wood is a type of, or points to, another piece of wood where something happened that is very significant to us.

I believe it points to the cross, that piece of wood where Christ was crucified for you and for me, and that God wants us to realize that Jesus' sacrifice at Calvary was enough to take care of all our problems, and restore us no matter our spiritual state.

It is enough to cleanse us and restore our spiritual edge. In fact, it is the only thing that has the power to do it.

If you have lost your zeal for God and you have become spiritually dull, repent and say, "Jesus, I believe that Your work on the cross was enough to restore me."

If you apply what He did on that piece of wood, it is enough to restore you, no matter how far you have fallen away from where you should be. He took your failure, and He nailed it to that cross. He rose from the dead victorious on the third day, and He offers that victory to you!

If you have lost your cutting edge, the cross of Christ and the blood shed upon that cross are enough to take care of everything.

Day 102

A Miracle-Working God

Once again I want to take us back to 2 Kings 6:6, which provides for us the sixth key to regaining your cutting edge.

So the man of God said, "Where did it fall?" And he showed him the place. So he cut off a stick, and threw it in there; and he made the iron float.

Perhaps you are wondering just what other principle for regaining your spiritual edge can come from this verse. Well, there is one more, and it is critical to understand because it points to God's part in the process of restoration.

I want you to look at the words, *And he made the iron float.*

I don't know about you, but I have never seen an iron ax head float. Clearly this was a miracle. God worked a miracle when the man did his part, looking to the master, taking responsibility, and going to the place where the ax head was lost.

You do your part; God does His part. I like the King James Version as it says, *...the iron did swim.* It was against that ax head's nature to swim, but God made it swim.

God brings the restoration. He brings the healing. He brings back that sensitivity and usefulness to Him. I pray that right now God is at work in your heart, and you are responding, making adjustments...regaining your cutting edge.

As you admit to those areas where you have lost your spiritual edge, God is going to restore it. God's part is to make that ax head float once you have admitted where you have failed!

He can restore what has been lost, even if it takes His miracle power to do it.

Day 103

Take It!

The seventh and final key to regaining your cutting edge is found in verse 7 of 2 Kings 6, the passage we have been looking at over the last several days. Here is what that verse says,

> *Therefore he said, "Pick it up for yourself." So he reached out his hand and took it.*

The sixth key was something that only God could do, and that is to make the ax head float; that is, to restore your cutting edge.

Now we see what we must do in response. You and I must receive what God is offering. Unless you take hold of what God is offering, your spiritual edge will never be restored.

Perhaps over the last several days, as we have looked at how to restore your spiritual edge, God has been speaking to you. Maybe you have come to realize that you are not where you should be in your relationship with God.

Maybe you have lost that sensitivity. Maybe you have lost your cutting edge. I am telling you, you can reach out and take what God is doing to restore your cutting edge.

I want to challenge you to take some time today to search your heart. If you have lost your cutting edge, stop swinging an empty handle and just going through the motions.

Be honest and admit you have lost that edge, determine where it fell, look to the Master, listen to His voice, take responsibility, know that the cross of Christ is completely sufficient to restore you, and then take hold of what God is doing to restore your edge.

God can work that miracle in your life if you will only do your part!

Day 104

Created for a Purpose

Many Christians today are not living the successful life God intends because they have missed the purpose for which they were born.

Ephesians 2:10 tells us,

> *For we are His workmanship, created in Christ Jesus for good works, which God prepared beforehand that we should walk in them.*

If you are going to live successfully, you have to know what you are all about. Any tool that is used for something other than what it was created for will not be effective. And it is liable to get damaged.

At times I have needed a hammer to pound in a nail, but I have been too lazy to go out in the garage to get one (don't get too self-righteous, you've done it too!). So I have ended up using whatever I had handy, like a wrench.

Well, you can get the nail in, but you are not going to be very effective. You are liable to dent the wall, and you are liable to damage the wrench.

Too many Christians today are not functioning or flowing in the thing they were created for, and consequently, they are not effective. And sometimes they get hurt and damaged.

You do have a purpose. In fact, the word in Ephesians 2:10 translated *workmanship* literally means you are handcrafted by God. The Greek word is the same word we derive our English word *poem* from.

In other words, your life is not to be without order or symmetry or rhyme or reason. God has some specific things mapped out for your life. You are not an accident. You are not excess baggage. You have a purpose.

Ask God today to show you that purpose, and then develop the gifts God has given you to fulfill that purpose.

Day 105

Keeping Your Focus

Yesterday we discovered that God does have a purpose for each of our lives. Yet even once we discover our purpose, we must remain focused. Luke 4:42-44 says,

> *Now when it was day, He departed and went into a deserted place. And the crowd sought Him and came to Him, and tried to keep Him from leaving them; but He said to them, "I must preach the kingdom of God to the other cities also, because for this purpose I have been sent." And He was preaching in the synagogues of Galilee.*

I want you to notice that statement of Jesus, "*For this purpose I have been sent.*" Jesus knew His purpose. He said, "*I must preach the kingdom.*" But notice the people tried to distract Him from that purpose.

I am sure the people meant well, but they were trying to divert Jesus from His purpose. But Jesus knew His purpose; therefore, He did not stay.

People will innocently divert you from doing what God has called you to do. It is only when you know your purpose that you will not be sidetracked, and you will not be distracted from what you are supposed to do.

The apostle Paul knew his purpose. In fact, he said this in 1 Corinthians 9:26, *So I run straight to the goal with purpose in every step* (The Living Bible). He was not about to get distracted from God's purpose for his life.

Our lives are not to be aimless, but they are to have purpose and direction, and we are to stay focused on that purpose, running straight at that goal. Keep focused on the purpose for which God has created you.

Be able to say like Paul, "I am running straight to the goal with purpose in every step."

Day 106

Living with Passion

I want to focus your attention today on two passages. The first is Ecclesiastes 9:10,

> *Whatever your hand finds to do, do it with your might; for there is no work or device or knowledge or wisdom in the grave where you are going.*

The second passage is Colossians 3:23,

> *And whatever you do, do it heartily, as to the Lord and not to men.*

Do you see the common theme? God desires us to live our lives full out, with passion. Whether you are a preacher, a writer, a teacher, or a singer, whatever you do, you are to do it with passion. You are to throw yourself into it.

People are attracted to passion. They want to see someone who is burning with a fiery zeal for whatever they do!

In my opinion, the greatest example of a passionate person is Jesus. Remember the story when Jesus threw the money changers out of the temple? That was a passionate act. In fact, the end of that passage says, "*Zeal for Your house has eaten Me up.*"

Zeal is just another word for passion. "Passion for Your house has eaten Me up!" Have you ever tried to imagine Jesus doing that? I have a very clear image of what that must have been like.

He is whipping these guys and they are running, covering their heads. He is throwing over these big tables and the disciples are watching with their mouths wide open, when they remember the verse, "*Zeal* (passion) *for Your house has eaten Me up.*"

Let me ask you a question: When is the last time you were eaten up with zeal for anything? When is the last time you were utterly passionate about anything?

Don't just sleepwalk through life. You need to decide you are going to live!

Day 107

Contagious!

In yesterday's devotional, I challenged you to live life with passion. Today I want to give you one other perspective on that.

Take a look at 2 Corinthians 9:2 where Paul writes these words,

> *For I know your willingness, about which I boast of you to the Macedonians, that Achaia was ready a year ago; and your zeal has stirred up the majority.*

Did you notice those last eight words, *and your zeal has stirred up the majority*? Passion is contagious.

What do you think might happen if a community saw a church that was utterly on fire? Where all the members in that church were passionate about their worship, passionate about their relationship with God, passionate about serving one another, passionate about real deal Christianity where the rubber meets the road?

I believe there is a divine attraction to that! And I believe that it would transform a community.

Sadly, most communities witness just the opposite—compromise, apathy, and boredom—not passion.

Now, rather than complain, I want to challenge you to live life with real passion. Go all out for God. It only takes one person to ignite the fire of passion in others.

I heard the story of a man who came to hear D. L. Moody preach. While sitting there the man next to him asked, "Do you come out here because you believe the things he's preaching?"

His response was, "No. I come out because *he* believes it."

Passion is contagious! Are people catching it from you? Is your zeal for Christ stirring up those who come in contact with you? If not, ask God to put that passion into your heart today and watch what happens!

Day 108

Peace

One of the great truths of the Christian life is that you and I can know the peace *of* God in our lives because we have peace *with* God. As believers, we need not live our lives without God's peace.

Are you worried right now about anything? Finances? Kids? Marriage? Job security? Your health? What somebody said about you? How a situation is going to turn out?

If you are worried about anything, here are some instructions for you found in Philippians 4:6-7,

> *Be anxious for nothing, but in everything [that means in every circumstance] by prayer and supplication, with thanksgiving, let your requests be made known to God; and the peace of God, which surpasses all understanding, will guard your hearts and minds through Christ Jesus.*

Talk to the Lord about your problems, offering thanks along with your requests. He promises to give you peace if you will.

Let me leave you with these words from Dr. Stanley Jones:

> *"I am inwardly fashioned for faith, not for fear. Fear is not my native land; faith is. I am so made that worry and anxiety are sand in the machinery of life; faith is the oil.... A Johns Hopkins University doctor says, 'We do not know why it is that worriers die sooner than non-worriers, but that is a fact.' But I who am simple of mind think I know; We are inwardly constructed...for faith and not for fear. God made us that way. To live by worry is to live against reality."*

Day 109

The Value of Play

I think we would all agree that the Christian life is one to be taken seriously. But in our desire to go all out for Christ, we can get to a place where we are physically, emotionally, and spiritually drained.

God does not intend for us to live our lives that way. In fact, in 1 Timothy 6:17, Paul tells us,

God, who gives us richly all things to enjoy.

You and I need to take time to enjoy the things God gives us. In fact, Jesus said this to His disciples in Mark 6:31, "*Come aside by yourselves to a deserted place and rest a while.*"

It is so easy to live our lives believing that somehow it is more spiritual to be on the edge of exhaustion all the time. But God clearly tells us that we are to take time to rejuvenate and to enjoy the things He has put into our lives.

When I was a young minister, I had the chance to meet with a seasoned minister who had literally changed the world for Christ. I thought, "Man, this is my golden opportunity. I'm going to ask him some questions."

So I said to him, "Look, I'm a young man in ministry. You have had decades more experience than me. You have impacted the world. What is the best advice you could give me as a young minister?"

And he said, "Well, Bayless, you have a nice golf swing. My advice is that you get some lessons. And whatever it costs you, join a country club and play golf regularly." Then he looked at me and said, "Golf is the only thing that's kept me alive."

It was some of the best advice I had ever received.

You need to make sure you live a balanced life. Take time for rest and for play. Recharge your batteries. You are in this thing for the long haul.

Day 110

The Ten Commandments of Marriage

Good marriages don't just happen. It is not just because you married the right person and got lucky. Good marriages are built on more than passion. They are built on principle.

In the Scriptures, we find the best guidelines and principles for a healthy marriage. God's words and God's principles are never ever outdated...never! They are just as applicable today as they were to ancient Jews living in Israel.

What I want to do over the next couple of weeks of devotionals is point us to principles God has given us in a place you might not think was intended for marriage. That place is the Ten Commandments, found in Exodus 20.

Today, let me give you those Ten Commandments. What I would like you to do is spend time reading these carefully, and then take time to pray over each one. Ask God to begin to open your heart to see how these commands could be looked at as principles for marriage. I had a friend who challenged me to do the same, and I was amazed at what I discovered.

"You shall have no other gods before Me.
You shall not make for yourself a carved image...
You shall not take the name of the LORD your God in vain...
Remember the Sabbath day, to keep it holy.
Honor your father and your mother, that your days may be long upon the land which the LORD your God is giving you.
You shall not murder.
You shall not commit adultery.
You shall not steal.
You shall not bear false witness against your neighbor.
You shall not covet your neighbor's house; you shall not covet your neighbor's wife, nor his male servant, nor his female servant, nor his ox, nor his donkey, nor anything that is your neighbor's."

Day 111

The First Commandment of Marriage: Exclusivity

The first of the Ten Commandments is simply this, as found in Exodus 20:3,

"You shall have no other gods before Me."

What is God saying in this commandment? That He wants to have an exclusive relationship with you. He wants to be your one and only. He will not settle for flavor of the month.

And how appropriate in marriage as well. We are to have an exclusive relationship with our spouse.

It's been said that Henry Ford, on his golden wedding anniversary ...50 years of marriage...was asked, "What's the secret of your success in marriage?" And he said, "The secret of my successful marriage is the same secret that I have in business: I stick to the same model."

In traditional wedding vows, the man and woman pledge their devotion until death parts them. For life. There is no competition.

My wife has no competition. I am not shopping for a new model. I do not want to trade in the old model. I will not be shopping in the future. One is all I need.

When God made man, He said it is good. But then He said, "It is not good that he is alone. I am going to make a helper suitable for him." And the Bible says God took one of Adam's ribs, and He formed a woman, Eve, and brought her to the man.

God did not take four or five ribs and say, "Okay, Adam, here is Eve, and here is Lois, and here is Samantha, and here is Rachel." No, it was just one. And to have a healthy marriage relationship, that is it.

I am committed for life. An exclusive relationship. I am not shopping, not even window-shopping. One God. One wife. That is enough.

Day 112

The Second Commandment of Marriage: Don't Love a Substitute

In the second commandment recorded in Exodus 20:4-6, we are given the second principle for a strong marriage,

> *"You shall not make for yourself a carved image—any likeness of anything that is in heaven above, or that is in the earth beneath, or that is in the water under the earth; you shall not bow down to them nor serve them. For I, the LORD your God, am a jealous God, visiting the iniquity of the fathers upon the children to the third and fourth generations of those who hate Me, but showing mercy to thousands, to those who love Me and keep My commandments."*

God commanded that there be no carved images, whether in heaven, in earth, or in the sea. He wanted to make sure everything was covered. And He said not to bow down to them and worship them. God said, "Do not make images of Me and then worship them. Do not love or worship a substitute for Me. Love Me."

Religion has made pictures, statues, and idols and then called them holy. They are all imitations. They are all substitutes. And in marriage we should have no substitutes either.

Love your husband only. Love your wife only. Do not look for fulfillment in some other relationship or in some other thing. Find your fulfillment in that relationship.

Pornography is a substitute. When a man watches pornography, he is loving a substitute. He is directing his passion and his sexuality toward those images. That is a substitute, and he is robbing his wife of that intimacy.

Do not allow any substitute, no matter what it might be, to take the place of intimacy with your spouse.

Day 113

The Third Commandment of Marriage: Speak Well of Your Mate

Exodus 20:7 gives us our third commandment of marriage,

> *"You shall not take the name of the LORD your God in vain, for the LORD will not hold him guiltless who takes His name in vain."*

Many misunderstand the term *in vain.* It means empty, meaningless, insincere, not showing due respect.

When we speak flippantly or lightly about someone, we erode our respect for that person. Some people are just far too casual in the way they speak of their spouse, and it erodes your respect for him or her.

In marriage, few things can affect the relationship like words. Words are containers. They can contain love; they can contain hate; they can contain joy; they can contain bitterness.

The book of James says that our tongue is like a rudder on a ship. It will send the ship of your marriage in whatever direction your words go. Some people are on the brink of divorce because they talk divorce. Just listen to the words they say. Are they negative or positive? Critical or encouraging?

One night I was out with a couple of friends diving for lobster. Some guys were out in one of those big, long speedboats drinking and zooming back and forth at 60 miles an hour. All of a sudden, BANG! The boat hit the rocks.

But it did not hit the rocks by itself. It was steered into the rocks. Just like the driver of that boat, some people are steering their marriage into the rocks of divorce, into the rocks of heartache, by the words they speak.

Think about what you say. Are you building up your partner? Learn to speak well of your mate. Build them up with your words. Be lavish with your praise. You will be pleased with where those words will take your relationship.

Day 114

The Fourth Commandment of Marriage: Spend Exclusive Time Together

Over the last few devotionals, we have been working through the principles behind the Ten Commandments…and how they form the basis for a strong and vibrant marriage. Today we come to the fourth commandment, found in Exodus 20:8-11,

> *"Remember the Sabbath day, to keep it holy. Six days you shall labor and do all your work, but the seventh day is the Sabbath of the LORD your God. In it you shall do no work: you, nor your son, nor your daughter, nor your male servant, nor your female servant, nor your cattle, nor your stranger who is within your gates. For in six days the LORD made the heavens and the earth, the sea, and all that is in them, and rested the seventh day. Therefore the LORD blessed the Sabbath day and hallowed it."*

Sabbath means an intermission. It means to put down your work and rest. Take a break. And *holy* means separate to the Lord. "If you want a long-term relationship with Me," God says, "we have to have time together. I want special time, exclusive time. I want a whole day."

In the same way, in order to have a healthy, growing marriage, husbands and wives need time together…special time, exclusive time, sometimes extravagant time. And I think we all know that if we do not schedule it, it will not happen.

My wife, Janet, once did a little research. She found that surveys showed the average couple spends 37 minutes or less in face-to-face conversation every week. I bet before you were married you spent a lot more time together in a week, didn't you?

If your marriage is to thrive, you need to spend exclusive time together. You can't build a relationship and not spend time together. It is just not possible.

Day 115

The Fifth Commandment of Marriage: Honor Your Spouse by Showing How Grateful You Are

The fifth commandment gives us our next principle for a healthy and vibrant marriage. It is found in Exodus 20:12,

> *"Honor your father and your mother, that your days may be long upon the land which the LORD your God is giving you."*

Among other things, God is saying we must be grateful. Generally, parents spend a lot of time, labor, and money…sometimes to the point of radical sacrifice…to give their kids an edge in life.

And it is a tragedy when a child is ungrateful or unthankful. William Shakespeare said, "How sharper than a serpent's tooth it is to have a thankless child." It is very difficult to have a relationship with an ungrateful, selfish person.

"Thank you" are important words to your parents, and an incredibly important phrase in marriage. It is difficult to live with someone who takes you and all of your efforts for granted.

You may be thinking, "I don't say it, but I am grateful in my heart. I truly am!" Well, hooray for you. You are blessed because in your heart you know you are grateful. But it does your spouse no good if you do not vocalize it.

If you do not demonstrate your gratitude, I doubt if you are really grateful because Jesus said, *"Out of the abundance of the heart the mouth speaks."* If it is not being expressed, chances are it is not truly there.

Maybe you think you don't have a lot to be grateful for. But there must be something you can say "thank you" for. There is something you can praise your mate for. Look for those things, and accentuate the positive.

Take time today to express thanks to your spouse in some way… through an action, through a card, through words. That is how you honor your mate.

Day 116

The Sixth Commandment of Marriage: Don't Destroy Your Spouse But Learn to be Gentle

Today we are going to look at the sixth commandment of marriage, based on the sixth commandment God gave to Israel in Exodus 20:13,

"You shall not murder."

While you might think this commandment is not too applicable, I believe it is vital. It is telling you not to destroy your spouse!

Jesus helps us understand this principle in Matthew 5. He said, "*You have heard that it was said to those of old, 'You shall not murder, and whoever murders will be in danger of the judgment.' But I say to you that whoever is angry with his brother without a cause shall be in danger of the judgment.*"

Jesus went right to the root of murder: anger and hatred. If you are going to have a good, healthy, lasting marriage, you need to learn to be gentle. People who are easily angered...who are violent or have an explosive temper...destroy relationships.

If you are dating someone who blows up easily, you ought to take it as a warning sign. If they get mad at things at the drop of a hat, that anger can be turned on you very easily.

Another way anger is expressed is by going stone cold...using silence and angry moodiness to punish your mate. Again, not a healthy thing for a marriage. If you anger quickly and forgive slowly, you are a hard person to live with. Work at being quick to forgive, and make the controlling of your anger a serious matter of prayer. God will help you.

If you do not master your temper, it will master you. And it will not only decay and destroy a marriage relationship, it will harm every other meaningful relationship you have in life.

Day 117

The Seventh Commandment of Marriage: Do Not Commit Adultery

The seventh commandment brings us to one of the most vital principles of having the marriage God intends. Exodus 20:14 simply says,

> *"You shall not commit adultery."*

In a marriage, you would be hard pressed to imagine anything more damaging than your spouse being unfaithful. But being faithful is not only being faithful in action, but also in thought.

Again, Jesus expanded on this in Matthew 5, and I want you to read these words very carefully. He said, "*You have heard that it was said to those of old, 'You shall not commit adultery.' But I say to you that whoever looks at a woman to lust for her has already committed adultery with her in his heart.*"

Having a lustful, exploitive disposition has no place in marriage. Love gives; lust takes. Love serves; lust demands. Love nourishes; lust chokes.

What a wonderful gift God has given us in this thing called sex. It was His idea. It is just as holy as when you lift your hands in church and worship Him. It is God's idea within the context and the confines of marriage. It should be enjoyed.

But lust has no place in marriage. It is a poison that will destroy the fabric of your relationship with your spouse.

Men, do not even entertain the thought of allowing pornography into your life. It can destroy your marriage. You are committing heart-adultery when you look at pornographic images and lust after another woman. Do not let the devil have that ground in your heart and life.

This is such a vital command, over the next few devotionals we are going to stay on this subject. I will share with you three ways to affair-proof your marriage.

Day 118

Affair-Proof Your Marriage with Positive Affirmation

The first way to affair-proof your marriage is to season your marriage with affirming communication.

In Song of Solomon 7:1-6 we read of how Solomon affirmed his bride,

> *How beautiful are your feet in sandals, O prince's daughter! The curves of your thighs are like jewels, the work of the hands of a skillful workman. Your navel is a rounded goblet; it lacks no blended beverage. Your waist is a heap of wheat set about with lilies. Your two breasts are like two fawns, twins of a gazelle. Your neck is like an ivory tower, your eyes like the pools in Heshbon by the gate of Bath Rabbim. Your nose is like the tower of Lebanon which looks toward Damascus. Your head crowns you like Mount Carmel, and the hair of your head is like purple; a king is held captive by your tresses. How fair and how pleasant you are, O love, with your delights!*

Solomon knew it was vital for him to compliment his bride's body, because, as you read in chapter 1, it is evident that it was an area of insecurity for her.

This Shulamite was a country girl. She said, "Do not look on me for I am dark." She was tan from working out in the vineyards. And compared with the fair-skinned, pampered ladies of the court, she felt very insecure.

So Solomon very wisely builds her up in the area where she feels most insecure.

Speak affirming words to your mate rather than tear him or her down. If your spouse is starved for positive affirmation, and it does not come from you, it opens a door of temptation. The devil will send someone to give insincere compliments, and if a person is starved for it, they gravitate towards it.

Praise one another lavishly. It is an important thing to do.

Day 119

Affair-Proof Your Marriage with Companionship

Today I want to give you the second way to affair-proof your marriage. And that is by being a companion to your spouse, spending time together just enjoying each other's company.

Back in Song of Solomon 7 we read this in verses 10-13,

> *I am my beloved's, and his desire is toward me. Come, my beloved, let us go forth to the field; let us lodge in the villages. Let us get up early to the vineyards; let us see if the vine has budded, whether the grape blossoms are open, and the pomegranates are in bloom. There I will give you my love. The mandrakes give off a fragrance, and at our gates are pleasant fruits, all manner, new and old, which I have laid up for you, my beloved.*

Notice that Solomon and his bride just hung out together. It was a vital part of their relationship. And so must it be for any thriving marriage.

If you have drifted apart, I suggest you each make a list of things you like to do, or things that you might like to try. It could be anything from antique hunting, going to garage sales, taking walks, bicycling, fishing, going to museums, watching football, shopping, gardening, snorkeling, reading, sky diving, cooking, hiking, puzzles, photography, whatever.

Once you have made your lists, compare them and see where things overlap. Then find two or three things, and endeavor to do those things together. Have fun together.

Set time apart to do at least one activity together every couple of weeks. If you have kids, get a babysitter so it is just the two of you. It will be the best gift you could give your children.

If you do not do things together, you will find yourselves drifting apart.

Day 120

Affair-Proof Your Marriage Through Intimacy

In the last two devotionals, we have learned that we can affair-proof our marriages through positive affirmation and companionship. The third way to affair-proof your marriage is by making intimacy a priority.

Let me take you back to the Scripture we read yesterday, Song of Solomon 7:10-13,

> *I am my beloved's, and his desire is toward me. Come, my beloved, let us go forth to the field; let us lodge in the villages. Let us get up early to the vineyards; let us see if the vine has budded, whether the grape blossoms are open, and the pomegranates are in bloom. There I will give you my love. The mandrakes give off a fragrance, and at our gates are pleasant fruits, all manner, new and old, which I have laid up for you, my beloved.*

These verses paint a beautiful picture of intimacy between a husband and wife. Couples need to have physical intimacy. In fact, the New Testament commands the husband and wife not to deprive one another except by mutual consent, and then only if they are going to fast and pray.

So how do you create an atmosphere of intimacy? It starts with affirming your spouse. Notice that Solomon has been affirming his wife, complimenting her, building her up. Guys need to understand that women are wired differently. In order for a woman to be intimate, she needs to speak and be spoken to. You have to create an atmosphere for intimacy.

For most husbands, they just catch a glimpse of their wife in the shower and they are ready to go. But for women, it starts differently than that. She is aroused by words, sincere words, and it usually starts around breakfast time.

Take time today to create an atmosphere of intimacy. If you do, you will be on your way to experiencing true intimacy, as we will see in tomorrow's devotional.

Day 121

Affair-Proof Your Marriage Through Intimacy—Part 2

Yesterday we learned the first step in experiencing intimacy in marriage…by creating an atmosphere for that intimacy. Today, I want us to see the results of that deliberate effort.

As we mentioned yesterday, Solomon has been complimenting his wife and affirming her. Look at her response to that affirmation in Song of Solomon 7:10,

I am my beloved's, and his desire is toward me.

She is digging it! She is saying, "He really loves me!" Solomon's affirmation of his bride has created this atmosphere of intimacy. And look what she says next in verse 11,

Come, my beloved, let us go forth to the field; let us lodge in the villages.

She is grabbing Solomon's hand and saying, "Let's get a hotel room!" Then there are verses 12-13,

Let us get up early to the vineyards; let us see if the vine has budded, whether the grape blossoms are open, and the pomegranates are in bloom. There I will give you my love. The mandrakes give off a fragrance, and at our gates are pleasant fruits, all manner, new and old, which I have laid up for you, my beloved.

Friend, catch what is going on. Solomon has affirmed his wife saying, "Honey, you are beautiful! I am so glad I married you. I married out of my league. You are wonderful. Your body is great. I am so happy!"

Her response? "Wow, he loves me. I'll tell you what, let's go away and have a little love vacation. Let's take a few days off." That is enough to get any husband inspired to rent a hotel room!

If you want to affair-proof your marriage, make intimacy a priority!

Day 122

The Eighth Commandment of Marriage: Be a Person of Integrity

Exodus 20:15 gives us the eighth commandment for marriage,

"You shall not steal."

You may be wondering how stealing applies to marriage. Simple. Not to steal is to be a person of integrity.

If you are always cheating or cutting corners, it will be hard for your spouse to respect you. Your uprightness should make your marriage partner feel proud. Your spouse and your family ought to testify of your integrity. This is really one of the things at the heart of a good marriage.

If you are married to somebody, and you know they cheat their customers, it is just hard to respect that person. You cannot respect someone who does not have integrity.

This is a big issue that many people fly right by. But it is vital to a healthy and vibrant marriage because it is hard to fully give yourself to someone who does not have integrity.

If you find that your spouse is holding back, if you feel like he or she does not respect you, take a look inside and see if you are compromising with your integrity. Do you cheat on your taxes? Do you tell that "little white lie" to protect yourself or gain an advantage?

Do you represent yourself one way, when in fact in your heart you believe something totally different? Are you like the man Solomon speaks of in Proverbs 23:7?

> *For as he thinks in his heart, so is he. "Eat and drink!" he says to you, but his heart is not with you.*

If this is an issue in your life, take it to God today. He will help you become the person of integrity He desires you to be. And when you do, you will find your spouse will come to respect you, and your marriage will be strengthened!

Day 123

The Ninth Commandment of Marriage: Be Truthful

The ninth commandment for marriage speaks to the heart of any marriage, trust. It is found in Exodus 20:16,

"You shall not bear false witness against your neighbor."

Someone who would lie about their neighbor, for whatever reason, is not going to make a good marriage partner. Honesty and trust are at the heart of a good marriage.

If you take advantage of people for your own gain, speaking untruthfully to get ahead, you are not a person to be trusted. And you ultimately are the loser.

I am reminded of the guy who was in a fender bender, and he feigned an injury, pretended like he hurt his arm and his shoulder. As a result, the poor little lady who had run into his car was subjected to a truly horrible situation. She was grilled by attorneys, had to give depositions, and ended up in court.

But this guy continued trying to take her for all she was worth. He didn't care because he knew she had money. He didn't care if she had to give up her house. He was looking at an opportunity to get rich.

The attorney for the lady's insurance company put him on the stand and said, "I would like to know, since the accident, since you injured your arm and your shoulder, how far can you now raise your arm?"

With great pain etched on his face, he said, "Well…'bout here. That's it. Just to here." Then the attorney asked, "Well, how far could you lift it before the accident?" The guy responded, raising his arm with ease, "I could lift it up to here."

Needless to say, he lost.

Anyone who is not truthful will ultimately lose. And if your spouse will lie to someone else, he or she will lie to you.

Day 124

The Tenth Commandment of Marriage: Be Content with What You Have

Today we come to the final commandment for marriage. That commandment is based on the tenth commandment given to the nation of Israel in Exodus 20:17,

> *"You shall not covet your neighbor's house; you shall not covet your neighbor's wife, nor his male servant, nor his female servant, nor his ox, nor his donkey, nor anything that is your neighbor's."*

This command is very direct. *Do not covet.* Don't be discontent with what you have. Do not make what you don't have the focus of your life. Accentuate what you do have and what God has blessed you and your spouse with.

You do this by celebrating your husband's or wife's strengths and giftings rather than thinking, "Oh, I wish he was this way," or, "I wish she had that."

If Janet compared me to her brothers, I would be in big trouble. Her brothers are these "Mr. Fix-It" guys who can do anything mechanical. If you are with me and our car breaks down on a desolate road, we are going to be in some serious trouble. I can pray, but do not expect me to fix the car.

Her brothers are another story. One just built a house from the ground up; and if anything mechanical breaks down, he can fix it.

While I am not a Mr. Fix-It, there are other things I am good at. I am so grateful that Janet wants to pull those out of me and give wings to those gifts. And I want to do the same thing for her.

You will always get into trouble if you think the grass is greener on the other side of the fence. Just water your own grass. Because on the other side of the fence, it's just Astroturf anyway.

Day 125

God's Eyes

In Hebrews 4:13, there is a powerful statement concerning God,

> *And there is no creature hidden from His sight, but all things are naked and open to the eyes of Him to whom we must give account.*

In this verse, we are taught that God sees what we do, and He sees the intent of what we do. That leads to one thing: total accountability.

There is no getting out of giving an account for our lives before God. We will all stand before Him. And at that time, there will be no shifting; there will be no saying one thing and thinking something else inside. Everything will be laid bare.

God sees everything all the time. Everything is open and laid bare before the eyes of Him to whom we must give an account. You just can't get away from God.

The Scripture says in Proverbs 15:3, *The eyes of the LORD are in every place, keeping watch on the evil and the good.*

But God also sees the very intent of our heart. When Samuel was sent by God to anoint a new king over Israel, and he was at the house of Jesse, Jesse had his big strapping son pass by. As Samuel looked at this guy he thought, "Surely this is the Lord's anointed."

But God said, "I rejected this one. For the Lord does not see as man sees. Man looks on the outward appearance. But the Lord looks upon the heart."

Our intent can be right, but we can really mess up. God looks on our heart, and if our intent is right, He judges us according to our intent, not according to the mistakes we may have made. But, if the intent of our heart was not pure, God judges us according to that.

Live today...and every day...knowing that the Lord looks on the heart.

Day 126

God's Heart

It is easy for us to think of Christ as this majestic, powerful figure in the heavens, unfazed by what is going on in our lives. But Hebrews 4:15 paints a very different picture,

> *For we do not have a High Priest who cannot sympathize with our weaknesses, but was in all points tempted as we are, yet without sin.*

Have you ever thought about the fact that Jesus sympathizes with you? The King James Version says He is *touched with the feeling of our infirmities*. God is not aloof, distant, and unconcerned, and He does not look at you through some clinical, cold eye. He is moved; He is touched!

I want to show you a verse that, to me, is quite amazing. It is Isaiah 63:9, and it is talking about God and His people. It says,

> *In all their affliction He was afflicted, and the Angel of His Presence saved them; in His love and in His pity He redeemed them; and He bore them and carried them all the days of old.*

When you suffer, God suffers. He is not untouched; He is not unmoved; He is not unsympathetic.

Then there is Jeremiah 31 where God says (speaking of Israel as one single person), *I earnestly remember him still; therefore My heart yearns for him. I will surely have mercy on him, says the LORD.*

Finally, look at Psalm 145:8-9,

> *The LORD is gracious and full of compassion, slow to anger and great in mercy. The LORD is good to all, and His tender mercies are over all His works.*

God feels and sympathizes. He is moved and touched and afflicted as you walk through the difficulties of life. He understands. And He yearns to give you tender mercy.

That is the compassionate and gracious heart of God!

Day 127

God's Provision for Your Failure

Psalm 37:23-24 states,

> *The steps of a good man are ordered by the LORD, and He delights in his way. Though he fall, he shall not be utterly cast down; for the LORD upholds him with His hand.*

When you first read these verses, it is easy to focus on the truth that God orders the steps of a good man, someone who is following God. That is certainly a comforting, motivating, and powerful truth.

But I want to point you to the second sentence, *Though he fall, he shall not be utterly cast down; for the LORD upholds him with His hand.*

What an amazing statement! Even when your steps are being ordered by the Lord, you can still goof up! God affirms that you may be seeking to walk with Him and you can still mess up, there is always that human factor.

Our flesh gets in the way. Sometimes we make wrong decisions. Sometimes we can be a bit stubborn. And sometimes we blow it, even when that is the last thing we want to do!

Here is what I want you to grasp today: Even if you mess things up, even if you stumble and fall, God will not utterly abandon you. He will support you, and He will lift you up with His hand.

The Bible says in the book of Deuteronomy that God is our refuge and our strength and that underneath us are His everlasting arms. That brings me a lot of comfort.

You and I may stumble, you and I may fall, but we are not going to stay down, because God's arms and His hands are underneath us, and they will uphold us.

Thank God for that!

Day 128

The Source of Your Success

There is no question we live in one of the most prosperous of ages. And many Christians today live in tremendous prosperity.

It is pretty easy to look at all we have accomplished, and the wealth we have accumulated, and feel pretty good about ourselves.

Today, I want you to read Psalm 44:1-3. It contains a powerful truth and reminder,

> *We have heard with our ears, O God, our fathers have told us, the deeds You did in their days, in days of old: You drove out the nations with Your hand, but them You planted; You afflicted the peoples, and cast them out. For they did not gain possession of the land by their own sword, nor did their own arm save them; but it was Your right hand, Your arm, and the light of Your countenance, because You favored them.*

Any good thing that you and I possess is the result of God's hand and nothing less. It is not because we are something special or because we are so intelligent.

When everything is said and done, we are not going to be able to point to our own arm or our own intelligence or our own ability. We will only be able to stand back and say, "Look what the Lord has done."

If you are prosperous today, I want you to know that it is the result of God's hand and God's arm working on your behalf.

As you look to the future, if you are going to experience the fullness of what He has for you, it will indeed be the result of the power of His Spirit working in your life. Not your ingenuity, not your human striving, not the power of your flesh, but the power of His Spirit.

Day 129

Gaining the Victory

We live in a society of addictions, of bondage to so many things. Maybe you are in bondage to cigarettes, or alcohol, or pornography, or anger, or any number of other things.

Whatever the condition that has you in bondage today, God's hand and God's arm can lift you up and untangle you and set you free. In Psalm 98:1 we are told,

> *His right hand and His holy arm have gained Him the victory.*

We find repeatedly throughout the Old Testament how, through God's mighty hand and His outstretched arm, He redeemed His people out of slavery and out of bondage.

Now here is the question. Does it just sort of randomly happen? Do we have to wait and see if we are one of the lucky ones God will choose to extend His mighty arm to help? Or, is there anything that we can do to cooperate with God to see His arm extended in our behalf?

The answer is yes, we can, and we must cooperate with God.

In Isaiah 51:5 God tells us,

> *"My righteousness is near, My salvation has gone forth, and My arms will judge the peoples; the coastlands will wait upon Me, and on My arm they will trust."*

The way we cooperate with God is to trust in His arm; not in our own arm, but in His. If you want to see God's mighty arm move on your behalf, then trust Him alone! Do not trust your intelligence, your ingenuity, your education, your status in life, your wealth, or any other thing.

Trust in God alone. And you will have the victory.

Day 130

T-R-U-S-T

In our last devotional, we talked about the need to trust God. You may wonder, what does trust really mean? Let me help you understand by using the word T-R-U-S-T as an acronym.

"T" stands for *trust*...which means that if you are going to trust Him, you have to take Him at His word. Even if it seems like it is not true, you take Him at His word. If we will take Him at His word, He will guide us through the course of life and bring us across the finish line safely.

"R" stands for *rest*. The Bible tells us to rest in the Lord. 1 Peter 5:7 says, *Casting all your care upon Him, for He cares for you*. Do not worry. Worry is like a rocking chair. It gives you something to do, but you don't get anywhere.

"U" stands for *understanding*. Proverbs 3:5 says, *Trust in the LORD with all your heart, and lean not on your own understanding*. Sometimes things just won't make sense to your understanding.

"S" stands for *speech*. Our speech is an expression of our faith. In Mark 11, Jesus said, "*Have faith in God*." And then the very next thing Jesus said is, "*Whoever says to this mountain, 'Be removed and be cast into the sea,' and does not doubt in his heart, but believes that those things he says will be done, he will have whatever he says*." Our faith in God is expressed through our speech.

The final "T" stands for *thanksgiving*. We offer thanks to God in advance. Philippians 4:6 says, *Be anxious for nothing, but in everything by prayer and supplication, with thanksgiving, let your requests be made known to God*. When we offer thanks to God, it is an expression of our faith.

That's T-R-U-S-T!

Day 131

The Power of Humility

One of the greatest dangers of the Christian life is spiritual arrogance.

When pride wells up in our heart, it can absolutely take our spiritual legs out from under us, and keep the strong arm of the Lord from being revealed in our lives.

In 1 Peter 5:6, we are given the antidote to pride. It says,

> *Therefore humble yourselves under the mighty hand of God, that He may exalt you in due time.*

It is unfortunate, but there are some who emphasize the message of faith that at times do so with a touch of arrogance rather than humility. The result is that it has really turned some people off to the whole message of faith.

Our faith always needs to be coupled with humility.

There are only two people in the Bible Jesus said had great faith. One of them was the Roman centurion whom we find in Luke 7. When you study his story, you find that because of his good works, the elders of the Jews said he deserved Jesus' help. But the centurion had a far different view of himself. He said he was not worthy for Jesus to enter under his roof.

The other person that Jesus said had great faith was the woman with the possessed daughter in Matthew 15. Two elements stand out about her as we read her story. She was persistent and she was humble.

Great faith cannot be divorced from great humility. Humility is a necessary ingredient for the soil of our heart, without which a healthy faith cannot grow.

Day 132

The Face of God

The psalmist says in Psalm 30:7,

> *You hid Your face, and I was troubled.*

One thing we should never want to experience is for God to hide His face, because the face of God represents His favor, friendship, and fellowship.

Now there is only one thing that causes God to hide His face from us. It is found in Isaiah 59:1-2,

> *Behold, the LORD's hand is not shortened, that it cannot save; nor His ear heavy, that it cannot hear. But your iniquities have separated you from your God; and your sins have hidden His face from you, so that He will not hear.*

Sin is the one thing that causes God's face to be hidden. The Bible says we have all sinned and come short of the glory of God, which means the sin of mankind had hidden God's face.

But that is not the end of the story, thank goodness! In Isaiah 50:6 we are told,

> *"I gave My back to those who struck Me, and My cheeks to those who plucked out the beard; I did not hide My face from shame and spitting."*

Because Jesus did not hide His face from shame and spitting, because He took your place and died for your sins, God's face can shine upon you.

He could have hidden His face; He could have avoided the whole crucifixion, but He didn't. He bore a shame that was not His as God the Father laid the sin of the world on Him.

Because Jesus did not hide His face, the face of God need not be hidden from any of us. The light of God's countenance can shine upon every one of us, and we can indeed be the friends of God.

Thank you, Jesus, for what You did!

Day 133

Showers of Blessings

In Ezekiel 34:26, God is speaking, and He says,

> *"I will make them and the places all around My hill a blessing; and I will cause showers to come down in their season; there shall be showers of blessing."*

In this passage, God is certainly speaking of natural rain when He talks about the showers He will send. Those are rains He promised to Israel which would water the land and cause it to increase and be fruitful and bring an abundant harvest.

But, more than that, when God says there will be showers of blessing, He is talking about bringing blessings into the lives of His people. The rain is symbolic of more than just the rain that falls to the earth. It symbolizes the good things that God wants to bring into the lives of those who serve Him.

God wants to bring showers of blessings into your life. Not just a blessing or two, but ***showers** of blessings*. An abundance of blessings.

You may feel like you are in a season of drought rather than experiencing showers of blessings. So over the next few devotionals, I will help you understand:

- The three ways God brings blessing into the lives of people
- The things that can cause a spiritual drought
- How you can break such a drought in your life

For today, what I want you to begin to see is God's desire to rain blessings into your life. If you are feeling a spiritual drought, I pray God will use the coming devotionals to help you break that drought, and experience the refreshing rains of His blessing.

Day 134

The Blessing of God's Spiritual Influence

In the beginning of Isaiah 55, God invites His people to come to Him and fellowship with Him. In verses 3 and 6 God says,

> *"Incline your ear, and come to Me. Hear, and your soul shall live.... Seek the LORD while He may be found, call upon Him while He is near."*

In verses 10-11, we are told what happens to those who respond to this invitation, to God's call to come and seek Him and listen to Him,

> *"For as the rain comes down, and the snow from heaven, and do not return there, but water the earth, and make it bring forth and bud, that it may give seed to the sower and bread to the eater, so shall My word be that goes forth from My mouth; it shall not return to Me void, but it shall accomplish what I please, and it shall prosper in the thing for which I sent it."*

In the same way rain brings blessing when it waters the earth (causing it to bring a bountiful harvest and fruitfulness into the lives of the people), so God's spiritual influence brings refreshment and fruitfulness to our lives.

What is God's spiritual influence? It is the impact of His Word and His Spirit upon the hearts of His children.

When you come to God, when you respond to His call to seek Him and incline your ear, He will speak to you. And the effect His Word has when He speaks it into your life, into your heart, is the same effect that rain has on the earth.

His Word, as it penetrates your heart, will bring refreshment, enlightenment, and ultimately, fruitfulness. It will bring revival into your heart causing spiritual growth and progress.

Day 135

God's Plentiful Rain

Psalm 68:6-10 says,

> *God sets the solitary in families; He brings out those who are bound into prosperity; but the rebellious dwell in a dry land. O God, when You went out before Your people, when You marched through the wilderness, the earth shook; the heavens also dropped rain at the presence of God; Sinai itself was moved at the presence of God, the God of Israel. You, O God, sent a plentiful rain, whereby You confirmed Your inheritance, when it was weary. Your congregation dwelt in it; You, O God, provided from Your goodness for the poor.*

When you read various Bible commentators, you will find they agree that this refers to a tremendous rain. The language the psalmist uses refers back to the manna God provided for His children as they wandered in the wilderness.

God sustained them supernaturally. He gave them supernatural provision. He brought them out of bondage into prosperity, and He sent a *plentiful* rain symbolizing His extravagant blessing on their life.

God, out of His goodness, met the needs of those who previously had been poor. And in the same way, He pours blessings into our life. He sustains us, He takes care of us, and He meets our needs.

Take time today to praise Him for His provision and blessing in your life.

Now, if there is a drought in your life in any of these areas, there is a reason for it. In the next few devotionals, I want to talk to you about some potential causes for that drought, and suggest some things you can do to cause the drought to break and bring the rain of God's blessing to fall in your life once again.

Day 136

The Number One Cause for Spiritual Drought

The Scriptures teach that the number one cause for spiritual drought is sin, by far. And the number one cure for drought, according to the Scriptures, is repentance.

In 2 Chronicles 6:26-27, King Solomon is clear in this prayer,

> *"When the heavens are shut up and there is no rain because they have sinned against You, when they pray toward this place and confess Your name, and turn from their sin because You afflict them, then hear in heaven, and forgive the sin of Your servants, Your people Israel, that You may teach them the good way in which they should walk; and send rain on Your land which You have given to Your people as an inheritance."*

Notice that the heavens were shut up, there was no rain, because of sin. But when the people confessed God's name and turned and repented, Solomon prayed, "God, hear and open the heavens once again and send rain."

This prayer is particularly significant because Solomon is praying at the dedication of the temple. Scripture declares to us in 2 Corinthians 6:16, *You are the temple of the living God.*

The Old Testament temple was just a type and a shadow pointing to better things—to the era in which God would no longer dwell in buildings made with mortar and stone, but take up residence in human hearts.

That's you and me! As 1 Corinthians 6:19 tells us, our body is the temple of the Holy Spirit and we are not our own. We have been bought with a price, and God's expectation is that we glorify Him in our bodies. You and I are God's temple.

If there is sin in your life, turn from it and turn to God, so that you can experience the refreshing rain of God's blessing in your life.

Day 137

The Cure for the Drought Brought by Sin

In our last devotional, we talked about sin being the number one cause for spiritual drought. The natural question is, "What is the cure, how do I end that drought?"

One word: *repentance.*

In addition to the passage we read yesterday, 2 Chronicles 7:13-14 is clear and instructive,

> *"When I shut up heaven and there is no rain, or command the locusts to devour the land, or send pestilence among My people, if My people who are called by My name will humble themselves, and pray and seek My face, and turn from their wicked ways, then I will hear from heaven, and will forgive their sin and heal their land."*

True repentance literally means an inward change of heart resulting in an outward change of direction. If there is no outward change of direction, then it is not true repentance.

There is no real repentance even if you are feeling emotional and weeping over your sin. That is not repentance. Feeling sorry is not repentance.

Repentance is the change of heart that results in a change of lifestyle, a change of direction, a turning. So I have a word for you: ***If there is known sin in your life, repent.***

King David gives us a great example in Psalm 32:4-5 when he said,

> *For day and night Your hand was heavy upon me; My vitality was turned into the drought of summer. I acknowledged my sin to You, and my iniquity I have not hidden. I said, "I will confess my transgressions to the LORD...."*

If, because of sin, you are in a drought spiritually, repent. If you do, your drought can be broken and you can experience the blessings of God.

Day 138

Idolatry

The most predominant sin we find in the Bible that stopped the rain of God's blessing from falling was idolatry. Maybe you are thinking, "Well, that's great, but it doesn't really apply. I'm not tempted to go to the nearest pagan shrine and bow down and worship a carved image."

Hold on, though. As you read the New Testament, you begin to realize it has a lot to say to us about idolatry. For example, 1 Corinthians 10:14 says, *Flee from idolatry*, and 1 John 5:21 says, *Little children, keep yourselves from idols.*

Wycliffe in his commentary says, "An idol is anything which occupies the place due to God." An idol is anything in your life that competes with God.

Colossians 3:5 says, *...covetousness, which is idolatry.* In other words, your stuff can become an idol. Greed can become an idol; money can become your idol. If anything becomes the main pursuit of your life, other than God, then that thing becomes an idol.

It can be your job, your boyfriend or girlfriend, your husband, your wife, or even a child. It can be a sport, a hobby, fame, anything that comes before God in your life.

I once saw an interview of one of my favorite golfers. He was a brilliant golfer who had won major tournaments. In the interview he said, "I've had a love affair with the game of golf. But I want to tell you, it cost me my marriage. It's cost me my relationship with my kids. Golf has been my god."

The interviewer asked him, "If you had all of it to do over again, what would you do differently?" He said, "Nothing. I'd do it all the same."

You will never experience God's blessing if there is an idol in your life. Is there?

Day 139

Selfish?

Over the last several devotionals, we have been looking at the cause of spiritual drought. In today's devotional, I want to look at selfishness as a cause of spiritual drought.

Selfishness is where I am focused on my own interests rather than the needs of others or of furthering God's Kingdom.

In Haggai 1:4-6, 9-11, God says,

> *"Is it time for you yourselves to dwell in your paneled houses, and this temple to lie in ruins?" Now therefore, thus says the LORD of hosts: "Consider your ways! You have sown much, and bring in little; you eat, but do not have enough; you drink, but you are not filled with drink; you clothe yourselves, but no one is warm; and he who earns wages, earns wages to put into a bag with holes... You looked for much, but indeed it came to little; and when you brought it home, I blew it away. Why?" says the LORD of hosts. "Because of My house that is in ruins, while every one of you runs to his own house. Therefore the heavens above you withhold the dew, and the earth withholds its fruit. For I called for a drought on the land and the mountains, on the grain and the new wine and the oil, on whatever the ground brings forth, on men and livestock, and on all the labor of your hands."*

They were investing everything in themselves and their homes, but not a thought was given to God's house or God's Kingdom.

Friend, if you want the rain to fall, you need to think about God and His house first, others second, and yourself third. It is like the old saying, "If you want joy, j-o-y, it's Jesus, others, and then you."

Day 140

Rx for Depression

Isaiah 58:10-11 gives you and me a powerful prescription for depression. It says,

> *If you extend your soul to the hungry and satisfy the afflicted soul, then your light shall dawn in the darkness, and your darkness shall be as the noonday. The LORD will guide you continually, and satisfy your soul in drought, and strengthen your bones; you shall be like a watered garden, and like a spring of water, whose waters do not fail.*

Take a moment to think about what God is saying. Think about the promise: If you extend your soul to the hungry and satisfy the afflicted soul, God will satisfy your soul in drought.

If you are a person who is given to depression and you feel like you have this big empty void in your life, I have a prescription for you based on this passage. Are you ready?

Go help somebody else. In fact, find a place in your church, local rescue mission, or The Salvation Army where you can minister to folks who are going through a rough patch. Donate a couple of days a week, and help other folks who are going through a rough time.

God promises that if you will draw out your soul to the hungry and if you will minister to the afflicted soul, He will satisfy your soul in drought.

Rather than being so inwardly focused…"my problems, and I'm so depressed, and why aren't things going right for me?", go help somebody else. Get things in perspective. There are a lot of people who are a lot worse off than you are, and you will find that God will bring the rain into your life when you change your focus.

If your soul is dry, the way to get it watered is to go help someone else. The sooner the better.

Day 141

In a Drought? Ask "Why?"

Perhaps today you are honestly doing all you know to do, but it seems like you are in this season of drought. God's blessing has seemingly dried up in your life.

Let me point you to 2 Samuel 21:1-3,

> *Now there was a famine in the days of David for three years, year after year; and David inquired of the LORD. And the LORD answered, "It is because of Saul and his bloodthirsty house, because he killed the Gibeonites." So the king called the Gibeonites and spoke to them. Now the Gibeonites were not of the children of Israel, but of the remnant of the Amorites; the children of Israel had sworn protection to them, but Saul had sought to kill them in his zeal for the children of Israel and Judah. Therefore David said to the Gibeonites, "What shall I do for you? And with what shall I make atonement, that you may bless the inheritance of the LORD?"*

There was a famine in the land because there had been no rain for three years. So David inquired of the Lord, and God spoke to him. If you read to the end of the story, you see the rain finally did fall, the drought was broken, and the famine was over.

But here is the point. It says, *David inquired of the Lord, and the Lord answered him.*

If there is a drought in your life, ask God why. God will talk to you. Jesus said, "*My sheep hear My voice.*" If you in earnestness will seek God and ask Him why, God will speak to you.

Be willing to take responsibility for whatever He shows you. There just may be something in the past that needs to be corrected.

Just ask. Then act on what He reveals.

Day 142

Praying for the Rain

For the past week we have been seeking to understand what causes a spiritual drought, and then how we can break that drought if indeed we are in one.

Here is what I want you to understand. Even if you earnestly seek God and repent of sin in your life, or you shift your focus and say, "God, I'm putting Your house first, and I'm going to put other people before myself," or perhaps God leads you to do something of a personal nature, you still need to pray for the rain.

Do not just assume God's blessing will automatically fall. You still need to ask for it. Zechariah 10:1 teaches us this truth,

> *Ask the LORD for rain in the time of the latter rain. The LORD will make flashing clouds; He will give them showers of rain, grass in the field for everyone.*

I used to read that and wonder, "God, I don't understand. If it is the time of the latter rain, if it is rainy season, why ask for rain? Won't it just fall automatically? If it is rainy season, why pray for rain?"

Because you cannot assume that it is automatically going to fall.

In James 5:17-18 there is a story about Elijah from 1 Kings 18. James gives us the very, very, very short version. But he tells us something significant,

> *Elijah was a man with a nature like ours, and he prayed earnestly that it would not rain; and it did not rain on the land for three years and six months. And he prayed again, and the heaven gave rain, and the earth produced its fruit.*

What caused the rain to stop? His prayer. What caused the rain to fall again? His prayer.

Ask God today for the blessing of His rain in your life!

Day 143

It's Never Too Late

As we wrap up our series of devotionals on how to break a spiritual drought, I want to focus our attention on Psalm 72:6. This verse contains a very powerful truth that I want to leave with you. It says,

He shall come down like rain upon the mown grass. (KJV)

I remember when I was first saved and read this passage, I would picture somebody out there with a lawnmower. But of course, they didn't have lawnmowers back then!

This verse refers to a field that has been eaten over by locusts, a plague of locusts that has come through and just devoured a field. And God gives a wonderful promise: He will come down like the rain on the mown grass, to revive and to restore that which the locusts have eaten.

Today, as you read this devotional, you may feel like a swarm of locusts has come over your life and eaten your blessing. I think if you seek God and earnestly pray and ask Him to send the rain, you will have an encounter with God beyond anything you could have imagined.

He can restore what the enemy has stolen in your life. You can indeed experience the freshness and revival and fruitfulness in your life again. It is never too late to pray for God's blessing.

No matter the situation, seek God today. Ask, and He will send the rain down on whatever part of your life has been mowed over by the locusts. And you will experience the blessing God desires for you.

Remember, it is never too late.

Day 144

Obedience

To God, obedience is a big deal. And one of the best ways to see just how importantly He regards it is to learn from those who disobeyed.

One of those is King Saul. When he was told by God to make an end of the Amalekites and to destroy all of their property, he did not do it.

Instead of obeying God, he saved the oxen and the sheep, along with some other things, and then claimed he had obeyed God. But when Samuel heard the oxen and the sheep, Saul knew he had been caught. So he changed his story. He said, "Well, these things are just a sacrifice to God."

In response to this act of disobedience, this is what Samuel, the prophet, said. We find it in 1 Samuel 15:22,

> *So Samuel said: "Has the LORD as great delight in burnt offerings and sacrifices, as in obeying the voice of the LORD? Behold, to obey is better than sacrifice, and to heed than the fat of rams."*

God does not want religious lip service. He wants obedience. Obedience is better than sacrifice. One reason for that is because you cannot make up by sacrifice what you lose through disobedience.

Another reason why obedience is better than sacrifice is because it is preventative. In Saul's day, sacrifices were made to cover sin, but if he had obeyed, there would have been no need for sacrifice. Obedience would have prevented his sin.

So do what God desires. Obey what He commands. It is always better.

Day 145

Obey and Honor

Yesterday's devotional helped us understand the importance of obedience. Over the next few devotionals, I want to focus on three areas I believe are critical for you and me to ensure we are obedient.

The first is found in Ephesians 6:1-3. This first category of obedience has to do with family, something God teaches very specifically in His Word. It says,

> *Children, obey your parents in the Lord, for this is right. "Honor your father and mother," which is the first commandment with promise: "that it may be well with you and you may live long on the earth."*

As long as a child is under his parents' roof and under his parents' direct authority, he needs to obey. But throughout your entire life you need to honor your parents.

One time I had a dear lady come to me after a service when I preached on this command and say, "Pastor, I just have to tell you. I just felt I needed to make things right with my dad. I went home that night and called him and said, 'Dad, you need to forgive me because I've been bitter against you for all these years. I'm sorry, and I want you to know that I forgive you for all the past.'"

Then she said, "Pastor, you need to understand, I've had a migraine headache for 15 years, 24 hours a day. I take piles of medication. I go to bed with a migraine, and I wake up with one, but the morning after I made things right with my dad, I woke up, and I had no headache." And she started to cry.

I am telling you, this promise is full of power! It is better to obey and honor your parents!

Day 146

Obedience in Marriage

Ephesians 5:22-24 gives an important area of obedience. While this is not popular in our society today, it is biblical, but is also often misunderstood.

> *Wives, submit to your own husbands, as to the Lord. For the husband is head of the wife, as also Christ is head of the church; and He is the Savior of the body. Therefore, just as the church is subject to Christ, so let the wives be to their own husbands in everything.*

It is important to make clear that before God there is an absolute equality between men and women, between husbands and wives. In fact, this passage does not say, "Women submit to men." It is purely a domestic situation.

Even with that understanding, the Bible says that husbands and wives are heirs together of the grace of life. There is an equality before God between men and women and husband and wife.

What this passage teaches is that God has set up a system of authority in the home that needs to be followed, if it is going to be well with us. In fact, this is even a military term. To submit or to obey means to put yourself in rank under.

Friend, we are in a spiritual warfare, and there are spiritual forces that have been unleashed against homes and against marriages that would love to tear marriages apart.

God has designed a way for the home to function, and that is for the man to take the responsibility of leadership and for the wife to come under that authority. When a husband truly loves his wife, and cares for her like Christ does the church, and the wife respects her husband, things will be well in the home. That couple and that family will be magnets for the blessings of God.

Day 147

An Enemy to Your Enemies

Exodus 23:20-22 says,

> *"Behold, I send an Angel before you to keep you in the way and to bring you into the place which I have prepared. Beware of Him and obey His voice; do not provoke Him, for He will not pardon your transgressions; for My name is in Him. But if you indeed obey His voice and do all that I speak, then I will be an enemy to your enemies and an adversary to your adversaries."*

Israel's success in possessing the Promised Land lay in their obedience. The same is true for us as we endeavor to possess the things promised to us by God.

I like the thought of God being an enemy to my enemies and an adversary to my adversaries, but that hinges on obedience as well.

The difficult thing about obeying God is that it always requires faith. He asks us to do things that sometimes make no sense. Other times He demands that we face seemingly impossible situations armed with nothing but His Word.

But He is faithful. He keeps His promises. And He can be absolutely trusted—in everything and with everything.

So today if you are desiring to enter some aspect of your "promised land," or if you are faced with difficult or seemingly insurmountable obstacles, listen for His voice, search His Word for instructions, and then obey.

He will be an enemy to your enemies, and you will possess the promises.

Day 148

Obeying Civil Authority

In Romans 13:1-3, the apostle Paul gives us some clear instruction on how we are to relate to our civil authorities,

> *Let every soul be subject to the governing authorities. For there is no authority except from God, and the authorities that exist are appointed by God. Therefore whoever resists the authority resists the ordinance of God, and those who resist will bring judgment on themselves. For rulers are not a terror to good works, but to evil. Do you want to be unafraid of the authority? Do what is good, and you will have praise from the same.*

I remember the days before I was saved. If I saw a police car when looking in my rearview mirror, I was struck with instant paranoia. There was a good reason for my fear.

At that time in my life, I would have gotten in a lot of trouble if I had been pulled over. I was constantly high on drugs and alcohol, and there were rarely times I was completely sober.

Thank God I have been saved! Today if I look in my rearview mirror and I see a police car, I may slow down a little bit; but I am not gripped with this feeling of paranoia because I live within the parameters of the laws of the land. And if I do break a law, it is going to be out of ignorance and not out of willful rebellion.

If you live your life in fear of civil authority, it is time to check out why. If you search your heart and find that you are not subject to the laws of the land as you should be, I encourage you to make that change today.

You will be able to live your life without fear, and honor God in the process.

Day 149

Pay Your Taxes!

Yesterday we learned from Romans 13:1-3 that we need to submit ourselves to the laws of the land if we want to live lives free from fear. I want to focus your attention today on the remainder of that passage, Romans 13:4-7,

> *For he is God's minister to you for good. But if you do evil, be afraid; for he does not bear the sword in vain; for he is God's minister, an avenger to execute wrath on him who practices evil. Therefore you must be subject, not only because of wrath but also for conscience' sake. For because of this you also pay taxes, for they are God's ministers attending continually to this very thing. Render therefore to all their due: taxes to whom taxes are due, customs to whom customs, fear to whom fear, honor to whom honor.*

What I want to address today is the need to pay our taxes with honesty, not trying to dodge our responsibility. It is a critical part of obeying the laws of the land as we discussed yesterday.

While I do not like working hard and in the end sending a large portion of every dollar to support the government, it is the right thing to do. I am absolutely amazed when I learn of Christians who try to dodge their responsibility to pay taxes.

Friend, you must be honest and pay your taxes. Certainly take advantage of all that the law allows, and do not pay more than you need to, but don't hide anything. You need to make sure you do this because when you do, you are being obedient to God.

And there are always blessings tied to obedience—even if it is obeying God by paying your taxes!

Day 150

Respecting Your Boss

In Titus 2:9-10, Paul writes a very interesting and important command,

> *Exhort bondservants to be obedient to their own masters, to be well pleasing in all things, not answering back, not pilfering, but showing all good fidelity, that they may adorn the doctrine of God our Savior in all things.*

In our society, it is important to understand that this passage is giving us instructions as employers and employees. And simply stated, as an employee, you are to be obedient to your boss.

One of the ways you do that is by not answering back. It might be hard at times to hold your tongue, but you must. It's not okay when you get to the water cooler to talk to the other employees like, "This idiot that we work for doesn't have a clue what's going on here." I think that comes under the category of answering back.

And *pilfering* means stealing items of small value. I remember this guy I knew in Oregon who did not like the place he worked. In fact, he had a government job, and he would come home quite often with something he had stolen from his office.

Nearly every day he would rip off some small office supply like a stapler, or pens, or a hole punch. While they were always things of small value, he would just keep stealing things.

The Bible says don't do that. And you shouldn't steal time from your employer either by making personal phone calls during office hours. Your employer is not paying you to take care of your business at the office. That is stealing.

I believe that, as Christians, we ought to be the best employees in the world. We should work so hard and bring such a good attitude into the workplace that we set the example to everyone with whom we work.

Day 151

When It Is Right to Disobey

Over the last few devotionals, we have learned the importance God places on obedience to various authorities. And an appropriate question is whether there is ever a time when we draw the line when it comes to obeying men.

In the Book of Acts, Peter and John got in trouble for preaching Christ. In Acts 5:29, when they were told not to preach anymore, Peter answered and said this,

"We ought to obey God rather than men."

That is where you draw the line. If you are ever asked to do something that would cause you to be disobedient to God or that would cause you to violate your conscience (not your preference, but your conscience), that is where you draw the line.

Paul made a statement that he lived in good conscience before God and before men. Your conscience deals with things you truly believe in your heart are morally right and wrong. If you go against your conscience in one of those things, then that is sin.

Stand your ground when it comes to conscience and obedience to God. If people ask you to do something that violates either of these two things—then it is time to take a stand for what you know is right.

For example, in many nations of the world, it is illegal to share your faith. It is illegal to win people to Christ. But Jesus said, "*Go into all the world and preach the gospel to every creature.*" We have an allegiance to a higher authority. And when the authorities are telling us to do something that would cause us to disobey God, we obey God, not men.

Day 152

Are You a "Convenient Christian"?

Some Christians are "convenient Christians." These are believers who seek to obey God, but only when it is convenient.

It is like the men and women of Israel who came to the prophet Jeremiah one day to see if it was God's desire for them to go to Egypt. You find their story in Jeremiah 42-43.

After they asked Jeremiah to ask God on their behalf, they said (Jeremiah 42:6),

> *"Whether it is pleasing or displeasing, we will obey the voice of the LORD our God to whom we send you, that it may be well with us when we obey the voice of the LORD our God."*

Now that sounds pretty good. These folks seem like they have it together spiritually and truly desire to obey God.

But just a few verses later, when Jeremiah tells them, "This is the word of the Lord: Don't go into Egypt. Stay here," they respond this way (Jeremiah 43:2),

> *"You speak falsely! The LORD our God has not sent you to say, 'Do not go to Egypt to dwell there.'"*

Some people's posture is, "God, I'm going to do anything you say...as long as it agrees with my viewpoint." Some will say, "Lord, I'm going to be obedient and give an offering...but I'm not giving ten percent of my income. You can forget that because I just don't see it that way."

Or, "God, I'm going to do whatever You say, but I'm not going to forgive so-and-so because what they did to me is just unforgivable."

Friend, we can't pick and choose. It has to be, "God, I am going to do whatever You say. I'm going to do it whether it rubs the cat's fur the wrong way, whether it plows my field crossways...pleasing, displeasing, I'm going to obey."

Do not be a "convenient Christian."

Day 153

Opening the Door to Calamity

In 1 Kings 13:21-25, God provides us with quite an unusual story,

And he cried out to the man of God who came from Judah, saying, "Thus says the LORD: 'Because you have disobeyed the word of the LORD, and have not kept the commandment which the LORD your God commanded you, but you came back, ate bread, and drank water in the place of which the LORD said to you, "Eat no bread and drink no water," your corpse shall not come to the tomb of your fathers.'" So it was, after he had eaten bread and after he had drunk, that he saddled the donkey for him, the prophet whom he had brought back. When he was gone, a lion met him on the road and killed him. And his corpse was thrown on the road, and the donkey stood by it. The lion also stood by the corpse. And there, men passed by and saw the corpse thrown on the road, and the lion standing by the corpse. Then they went and told it in the city where the old prophet dwelt.

Notice that the lion did something very unnatural. The guy disobeyed, the lion killed him, but the lion didn't go after the donkey. The donkey didn't run away, but the lion didn't try to kill the donkey, nor did it drag the guy off to eat him.

And to top it all off, now people start to walk by. Look, people do not walk by wild lions! But here they are: the donkey, the lion, the dead guy, and people are walking by.

What is God up to here? He is giving a snapshot, something He wants indelibly burned into their understanding: *Disobedience opens the door to calamity.*

If you choose to disobey God, know you have opened your life to calamity!

Day 154

The Cost of Disobedience

In our last devotional, we read the story from 1 Kings 13 about the lion that killed the prophet for his disobedience. We learned how that story illustrates for us the importance of obedience, and how *disobedience* opens the door to calamity in our lives.

1 Peter 5:8 tells us,

> *Be sober, be vigilant; because your adversary the devil walks about like a roaring lion, seeking whom he may devour.*

I believe God wants you to get a snapshot of that lion in 1 Kings 13 imprinted in your mind. He wants you to understand that if you willfully disobey God, your adversary, the devil, is not going to just be roaring at you. Like that lion, he is going to be putting a paw on you.

Frankly, I don't know about you, but I don't want his paw on my finances, on my family, on my health, or on anything else. I don't want him sinking his teeth into my marriage. But disobedience opens the door to that.

James 4:7 says,

> *Therefore submit to God. Resist the devil and he will flee from you.*

You see, you have been given authority in your life over the devil. This verse makes it clear—you can resist him. But your authority in Christ as a believer only operates as you have submitted yourself to God's authority through obedience.

If you are disobedient in areas of your life, knowingly disobedient, your authority in Christ will not work.

So here is the question: Today are you being willfully disobedient to God in any area of your life? If so, confess and repent. Otherwise you can be sure the devil will get a paw on your life.

Day 155

The Reward for Obedience

There are two verses I want to point you to in today's devotional. The first is Isaiah 1:19, where God says,

> *"If you are willing and obedient, You shall eat the good of the land."*

The second is Deuteronomy 28:1, which precedes a chapter of tremendous material blessings,

> *"Now it shall come to pass, if you diligently obey the voice of the LORD your God, to observe carefully all His commandments which I command you today, that the LORD your God will set you high above all the nations of the earth."*

All of the incredible material blessings God promised in the following verses hinged on one thing...obedience.

God will bless you, if you will obey Him. Now, granted, God does not settle up the first and the fifteenth of every month. His blessings do not always arrive on our timetable, but they always arrive.

Sometimes obedience to God will cost you at first. It may cost you friends; it may cost you time; it may cost you embarrassment; but, in the long run, it is well worth it to obey.

Prior to being saved, I was renting a room above a bar in Oregon from a friend of mine. We smoked dope and drank a lot together. But when I was saved, I wouldn't drink or smoke dope any more.

Even though the temptation was there, I knew I needed to obey God. And I would not compromise.

One day my friend said, "You're no fun anymore. You're gone." And that was that. I was out on the street for quite awhile. It cost me. But I look back now and say, "God, You have more than made that up to me. It may have cost me initially, but I'm so glad I obeyed You."

God will reward you for your obedience to Him!

Day 156

The Attitude of Obedience

Over the last several devotionals, we have learned the importance and reward of obedience. Today I want you to see the underlying attitude of obedience modeled by our Lord. It is found in Philippians 2:5-9,

> *Let this mind be in you which was also in Christ Jesus, who, being in the form of God, did not consider it robbery to be equal with God, but made Himself of no reputation, taking the form of a bondservant, and coming in the likeness of men. And being found in appearance as a man, He humbled Himself and became obedient to the point of death, even the death of the cross. Therefore God also has highly exalted Him and given Him the name which is above every name.*

When Jesus coexisted with the Father in eternity past, the Father said, "Son, we need You to go down and be born in a stable, be raised in a poor carpenter's home, and give up Your life."

Jesus could have said no, but He didn't. He said, "Yes, Father."

And as He prayed in Gethsemane, agonizing over the thought of being separated from the bright presence of the Father, He said, "*O My Father, if it is possible, let this cup pass from Me; nevertheless, not as I will, but as You will*" (Matthew 26:39).

He could have said no. But He said, "Yes, Father."

And even hanging upon the cross, having been beaten and disfigured, gasping for every breath, knowing that the end was near—He became obedient to death.

He could have said no. But He said, "Yes, Father."

Through His attitude of obedience, we can receive eternal life. I am so grateful our Savior obeyed the Father!

That is the same attitude of obedience that should be in us.

Day 157

The Supremacy of Jesus

Hebrews 1:1-8 reads,

God, who at various times and in various ways spoke in time past to the fathers by the prophets, has in these last days spoken to us by His Son, whom He has appointed heir of all things, through whom also He made the worlds; who being the brightness of His glory and the express image of His person, and upholding all things by the word of His power, when He had by Himself purged our sins, sat down at the right hand of the Majesty on high, having become so much better than the angels, as He has by inheritance obtained a more excellent name than they. For to which of the angels did He ever say: "You are My Son, today I have begotten You"? And again: "I will be to Him a Father, and He shall be to Me a Son"? But when He again brings the firstborn into the world, He says: "Let all the angels of God worship Him." And of the angels He says: "Who makes His angels spirits and His ministers a flame of fire." But to the Son He says: "Your throne, O God, is forever and ever; a scepter of righteousness is the scepter of Your kingdom."

These eight verses tell us that Jesus is supreme, above any angel, because:

- God speaks to us through His Son.
- Jesus is the heir of all things.
- God made all things through Jesus.
- Jesus is the express image of God the Father.
- He upholds all things with the word of His power.
- He purged our sins.
- Jesus is the Son of God, not a servant as are the angels.
- He is worthy of our worship.
- Jesus is God Himself.

That is the supremacy of Jesus!

Day 158

The Rightful Place of Angels

In our day, angels have become a pretty big thing. In fact, there are some fairly well-known personalities today talking about having their personal angel and needing to "contact your angel."

I believe in angels because the Bible clearly talks about them, but angels have a rightful place, which Paul addresses in Colossians 2:18-19,

> *Let no one cheat you of your reward, taking delight in false humility and worship of angels, intruding into those things which he has not seen, vainly puffed up by his fleshly mind, and not holding fast to the Head, from whom all the body, nourished and knit together by joints and ligaments, grows with the increase that is from God.*

Paul is telling us, "If you become so preoccupied with angels that you let go of the head, Jesus Christ, you are off the rails!" In fact, if you are preoccupied with angels in such a way that it takes you away from Jesus Christ, I'm telling you, you are in error. The body grows; the body is nourished; we get our life and direction from the head, Jesus Christ.

If God wants to have an angel intervene in my life, that is wonderful. But I don't need to contact my angel because I have constant communion with the Son of God, who, as we learned yesterday, is superior to angels!

Jesus is the One who created the universe! He is our Lord and our Savior. He is the Vine, we are the branch. We have communion with Him. Why would we want to contact an angel when we can contact the Son of God whom angels fall down and worship!

Angels are under the lordship of Jesus. That is their rightful place.

Day 159

A Better Covenant

There are two verses for your reading today. Hebrews 7:22, which says,

By so much more Jesus has become a surety of a better covenant.

And Hebrews 8:6, which tells us,

But now He has obtained a more excellent ministry, inasmuch as He is also Mediator of a better covenant, which was established on better promises.

We have a better covenant; we have better promises. And Jesus is the One who makes it sure. He is the guarantee. He has personally pledged Himself to make it good.

As far as I am concerned, that takes away all reason for doubt, all reason for stressing out. Jesus, Himself, is the pledge, the guarantee that this covenant we have called the New Testament will be good and will be fulfilled in our lives.

And He is not only the guarantee, He is the mediator. He is the go-between to what is truly a better covenant, established upon better promises.

Let's say your employer came to you and said, "We're going to give you a better contract. While the old contract was good, we're going to give you one that's better. This better contract will increase your hours, decrease your pay, eliminate your health and dental benefits, you will no longer get reimbursed for your mileage and your auto expenses, and you're going to have a shorter lunch break and no more Christmas bonuses."

Let me ask you, is that better? No! That is not better! And I will never understand how people can say, "We know God healed people and worked miracles and intervened in people's lives under the Old Testament, but He doesn't anymore."

The covenant Christ bought and sealed in His blood is a better covenant, established upon better promises. Praise God!

Day 160

God Leads from Within

In our last devotional, we talked about the new covenant being better than the old covenant. One reason is found in Hebrews 8:8-11 which says,

> *…"Behold, the days are coming, says the LORD, when I will make a new covenant with the house of Israel and with the house of Judah—not according to the covenant that I made with their fathers in the day when I took them by the hand to lead them out of the land of Egypt; because they did not continue in My covenant, and I disregarded them, says the LORD. For this is the covenant that I will make with the house of Israel after those days, says the LORD: I will put My laws in their mind and write them on their hearts; and I will be their God, and they shall be My people. None of them shall teach his neighbor, and none his brother, saying, 'Know the LORD,' for all shall know Me, from the least of them to the greatest of them."*

In the Old Testament, God had to lead His people externally. When fleeing Egypt, God led them by night with a pillar of fire and by day with a pillar of cloud. They did not intuitively know where God wanted them to go or what God wanted them to do.

But under the new covenant, God leads His people from within because He has now taken up residence within. I believe that is why on the Day of Pentecost God chose to manifest the coming of the Holy Spirit in tongues of fire that sat upon each person individually.

God was saying that while under the old covenant, He led His people by a pillar of fire, and now He is coming to dwell and lead from the inside of each believer!

Day 161

No More Remembrance

Today I want to point you to another reason the new covenant in Christ is better than the old covenant. Hebrews 10:1-3, 15-17 tells us,

> *For the law, having a shadow of the good things to come, and not the very image of the things, can never with these same sacrifices, which they offer continually year by year, make those who approach perfect. For then would they not have ceased to be offered? For the worshipers, once purified, would have had no more consciousness of sins. But in those sacrifices there is a reminder of sins every year... But the Holy Spirit also witnesses to us; for after He had said before, "This is the covenant that I will make with them after those days, says the LORD: I will put My laws into their hearts, and in their minds I will write them," then He adds, "Their sins and their lawless deeds I will remember no more."*

Under the old covenant, God remembered the sin of Israel every year. This meant that each year the priest would have to go into the Holy of Holies and offer the blood of an animal to cover the people's sins.

Under the new covenant, God does not remember.

Boy, am I glad that when I accepted Christ, my past was erased on God's ledger. I had a pretty checkered past before I came to Christ. But if today you enter my name in God's computer up in heaven... Bayless...past...push enter...push print...God's big printer prints out nothing but blank sheets.

Why? He doesn't remember my sins anymore. In fact, if you and I talk to Him about our past before we were saved, He says, "Sorry, it doesn't exist as far as I am concerned."

That is truly good news!

Day 162

Removed, Not Just Covered

Today I want to give you another reason why the new covenant is better than the old covenant. I want you to read Hebrews 10:11 first, then Hebrews 9:25-26,

> *And every priest stands ministering daily and offering repeatedly the same sacrifices, which can never take away sins.*

And then talking about Jesus,

> *Not that He should offer Himself often, as the high priest enters the Most Holy Place every year with the blood of another—He then would have had to suffer often since the foundation of the world; but now, once at the end of the ages, He has appeared to put away sin by the sacrifice of Himself.*

Under the old covenant, sins were merely covered. In the new covenant, Jesus removes our sin. In fact, John the Baptist declared, "*Behold! The Lamb of God who takes away the sin of the world!*" Jesus doesn't just cover it, He takes it away!

I want to tell you, friend, we are not just some patched up old sinners. We have been made new creations in Christ Jesus.

I know a horse trainer who trains beautiful thoroughbred horses. If I took a mule over to this guy and said, "Look, I want this mule to run with the thoroughbreds," he could feed it, brush its coat every day, and trim its tail and ears to look like a quarter horse. But when the gun fires and the gates go up and the horses start to run, it is just a mule. That is all it is!

Religion dresses up the mule, but God changes the mule into a thoroughbred. He takes away your sin and makes you a new creature in Christ Jesus when you embrace salvation.

Our sin is not just covered, it is gone, and we have been made into new people.

Day 163

Not Guilty

The new covenant provides cleansing for a guilty conscience. In talking about the old covenant, read Hebrews 9:9,

> *It was symbolic for the present time in which both gifts and sacrifices are offered which cannot make him who performed the service perfect in regard to the conscience.*

Then verse 14 about the new covenant,

> *How much more shall the blood of Christ, Who through the eternal Spirit offered Himself without spot to God, cleanse your conscience from dead works to serve the living God?*

At the point of conversion, not only is sin taken away, but the burden of guilt is lifted. The conscience is cleansed.

Even if you sin as a believer, thank God for 1 John 1:9, *If we confess our sins, He is faithful and just to forgive us our sins and to cleanse us from all unrighteousness.*

If you are still grappling with a guilty conscience after you have from your heart repented of sin and confessed it to God, then one of three things is happening:

1. The devil is accusing you. He is called the accuser of the brethren. He will run by your kitchen window with flash cards which say, "Remember when you did this? Remember when you did that!" Do not listen to the devil.
2. You have not forgiven yourself. You are forgiven by God, but you have not forgiven yourself. If God Almighty has forgiven you, you need to forgive yourself.
3. It may just be that you need to make restitution. That is something you will have to work out between you and God. Sometimes when you have injured a party through your sinful act, your conscience is going to bother you until you make things right with that person.

Under the new covenant there is cleansing from a guilty conscience, and it makes an awfully soft pillow at night.

Day 164

Access

In talking about the Holy of Holies...that second part of the tabernacle behind the veil where the presence of God dwelt under the old covenant...Hebrews 9:7 says,

> *But into the second part the high priest went alone once a year, not without blood, which he offered for himself and for the people's sins committed in ignorance.*

Only the high priest could go into this part of the tabernacle, into God's presence. And he could go only one time each year to offer the blood of an animal to cover the sins of the people.

But look with me at Hebrews 10:17-19,

> *Then He adds, "Their sins and their lawless deeds I will remember no more." Now where there is remission of these, there is no longer an offering for sin. Therefore, brethren, having boldness to enter the Holiest by the blood of Jesus.*

You have access into the very presence of God. In fact, Hebrews 4:16 says, *Let us therefore come boldly to the throne of grace, that we may obtain mercy and find grace to help in time of need.*

You do not have to go through a priest. You do not have to go through Pastor Bayless. You have immediate, constant access. In fact, God not only welcomes you, He desires you to come into His presence.

You know, my kids just barge into my office all the time. I can be in there having a meeting when the door just opens, "Hi, Dad! Got anything in your refrigerator?" They just come in like they belong there...and they do. I'm their father.

Your heavenly Father is the same way. He is not going to put you off and say, "You know what? You have to come through an angel. I'm sorry, but you cannot talk directly to Me."

Nope. You have direct access!

Day 165

Once for All!

As we have been learning in the last few devotionals, the new covenant is better than the old covenant. Hebrews 9:18-24 shows us another way it is better,

> *Therefore not even the first covenant was dedicated without blood. For when Moses had spoken every precept to all the people according to the law, he took the blood of calves and goats, with water, scarlet wool, and hyssop, and sprinkled both the book itself and all the people, saying, "This is the blood of the covenant which God has commanded you." Then likewise he sprinkled with blood both the tabernacle and all the vessels of the ministry. And according to the law almost all things are purified with blood, and without shedding of blood there is no remission. Therefore it was necessary that the copies of the things in the heavens should be purified with these, but the heavenly things themselves with better sacrifices than these. For Christ has not entered the holy places made with hands, which are copies of the true, but into heaven itself, now to appear in the presence of God for us.*

The old covenant was based on the blood of animal sacrifices; but under the new covenant, we are cleansed by the blood of Christ and His sacrifice.

Jesus went into that heavenly Holy of Holies with His own blood. And the Father declared that the blood of Jesus satisfied the payment for sin for all eternity.

Oh, thank you, Jesus! That is why the Scripture declares we are accepted in the Beloved. When God accepted that blood sacrifice in heaven, He accepted all of us who believe, because Jesus went as our representative.

Praise God today for the provision of the sacrifice of Jesus...once for all!

Day 166

For All People

In today's devotional, I want to give you the seventh reason why the new covenant in Jesus is better than the old covenant. The old covenant was only for one nation—only one people—the Jews.

The new covenant is for the whole world. It is for every nation, every people...anyone who will accept the free gift of salvation, by placing their faith in Jesus Christ. Hebrews 7:25 tells us,

> *Therefore He is also able to save to the uttermost those who come to God through Him, since He always lives to make intercession for them.*

Or, as one old preacher said, "He saves to the uttermost and to the guttermost."

That may sound crass, but it is true! Through Jesus Christ, God has made a way of salvation for every person, no matter your race, or what religion you were brought up in, or what you may have done in your life.

John 3:16 says,

> *For God so loved the world that He gave His only begotten Son, that whoever believes in Him should not perish but have everlasting life.*

That means no one has ever done anything so bad that it could make God stop loving them. I don't care where they have been, how dark their past has been, or how burdened down their conscience is today with guilt for the things they have done—no one will be cast out if they come to Him.

His blood has the power to wash anyone clean if they will come to God through Jesus. His sacrifice takes away the sin of the world, the burden of guilt, and the shame of sin. He can make anyone into a new person. Only the blood of Jesus can do that...only the blood of Jesus. Hallelujah!

Day 167

The "Good Old Days"

Hebrews 11:13-16 contains a powerful truth, a perspective I want to encourage you to embrace. These verses are talking about the great heroes of the faith from the Old Testament,

> *These all died in faith, not having received the promises, but having seen them afar off were assured of them, embraced them and confessed that they were strangers and pilgrims on the earth. For those who say such things declare plainly that they seek a homeland. And truly if they had called to mind that country from which they had come out, they would have had opportunity to return. But now they desire a better, that is, a heavenly country. Therefore God is not ashamed to be called their God, for He has prepared a city for them.*

These heroes of the faith sought a better homeland. In verse 15 it talks about calling to mind the country from which they had come, but the word *country* is just added by the translators. It really has the intent of saying if they had constantly thought about from where they had come, there would have been a great temptation to return there.

As you read this passage, it is easy to see why some people struggle so much with past sins. As verse 15 says, *Truly if they had called to mind that country from which they had come out, they would have had opportunity to return.*

The reason some people constantly struggle with returning to their old life, finding a multitude of opportunities to return, is because they keep calling it to mind. They keep rehearsing the "good old days." Perhaps you struggle with that as well.

If you do, seek to remember the "good old days" as they really were. Don't forget about all the pain. Don't forget about the way you struggled, the reason you came to Christ in the first place. Stop rehearsing the past. If the "good old days" were so good, you would not have gotten saved.

Day 168

The Right Perspective

In today's devotional, I want to take you back to the Scripture we looked at yesterday, Hebrews 11:13-16,

> *These all died in faith, not having received the promises, but having seen them afar off were assured of them, embraced them and confessed that they were strangers and pilgrims on the earth. For those who say such things declare plainly that they seek a homeland. And truly if they had called to mind that country from which they had come out, they would have had opportunity to return. But now they desire a better, that is, a heavenly country. Therefore God is not ashamed to be called their God, for He has prepared a city for them.*

Yesterday we talked about how it is so easy to remember "the good old days," but with selective memory, not really remembering the pain and struggle.

Today, I want you to see an important perspective the heroes of the faith in Hebrews 11 provide for us. What did they do? They looked to the future. These men and women of God walked as strangers and pilgrims on this earth because they looked for a better homeland, a better place, which God would prepare for them.

I'm telling you, there is a better homeland than our world today. There is a city called the New Jerusalem. There is a place that does not need the light of the sun nor the light of the moon because the Lamb—Jesus Christ—is its light.

In that city, every tear is wiped away. There is no more sin, no more sickness, no more pain, and no more suffering.

Like the heroes of old, I have my eye on that heavenly city. It is better than anything we have here! I pray that this will be your perspective today...and every day...as well.

Day 169

Mercy! Forgiveness! Acceptance! Pardon! Welcome!

In Hebrews 12:22-24, we are given a powerful word on how the blood of Jesus speaks such better things than the blood of Abel. This is a great insight, so bear with me,

> *But you have come to Mount Zion and to the city of the living God, the heavenly Jerusalem, to an innumerable company of angels, to the general assembly and church of the firstborn who are registered in heaven, to God the Judge of all, to the spirits of just men made perfect, to Jesus the Mediator of the new covenant, and to the blood of sprinkling that speaks better things than that of Abel.*

You can read the story of Abel and his brother, Cain, in Genesis 4. What we learn is that Cain became jealous of Abel, and as a result, Cain rose up against Abel in the field and killed him.

God said, "Cain, the blood of your brother, Abel, cries out to Me from the ground." What did the blood of Abel say? "Vengeance! Judgment!"

The blood of Jesus cries better things. The blood that soaked the cross and made it red, the blood that soaked the ground below the cross at that place called Calvary, the blood that today is in the heavenly Holy of Holies, that blood cries out day and night into the ears of God.

The blood of Jesus today does not cry out, "Vengeance! Judgment!" Instead, it cries out, "Mercy! Forgiveness! Acceptance! Pardon! Welcome!"

The question is: How will you respond? Hebrews 12:25 issues a stern warning,

> *See that you do not refuse Him who speaks. For if they did not escape who refused Him who spoke on earth, much more shall we not escape if we turn away from Him who speaks from heaven.*

If you have yet to accept Jesus as your Savior, do so today.

Day 170

Where Have You Pitched Your Tent?

Genesis 13:12 (KJV) says,

> *Abram dwelled in the land of Canaan, and Lot dwelled in the cities of the plain, and pitched his tent toward Sodom.*

Notice that Lot pitched his tent *toward* Sodom. Every day his attention was placed on that city. Here is what the Bible says about those that lived there.

> *But the men of Sodom were wicked and sinners before the LORD exceedingly* (Genesis 13:13, KJV).

What we focus our attention on will influence us. It will try to draw us in like a magnet. The next time we read about Lot he is living in Sodom.

> *And they took Lot, Abram's brother's son, who dwelt in Sodom, and his goods, and departed* (Genesis 14:12, KJV).

Next we find him even further entrenched among the people of Sodom. Genesis 19:1 declares that Lot was sitting in the gate of Sodom.

In Eastern cities, the "gate" was a place devoted to business transactions, the administration of justice, and the enjoyment of social discourse and amusement. Lot was right "in the thick of things"—but it happened by degrees. It was a process.

What you view and listen to, and the company you keep, will influence you—sometimes in very subtle ways—and will play a role in shaping your values and character.

So be careful where you pitch your tent!

Day 171

Better Than Life

In Psalm 63:1-4, the psalmist makes an incredible statement,

> *O God, You are my God; early will I seek You; my soul thirsts for You; my flesh longs for You in a dry and thirsty land where there is no water. So I have looked for You in the sanctuary, to see Your power and Your glory. Because Your lovingkindness is better than life, my lips shall praise You. Thus I will bless You while I live; I will lift up my hands in Your name.*

What does the psalmist mean when he says that God's lovingkindness is better than life? Let me try and explain.

First, *lovingkindness* literally means *merciful love.* It is God's unfailing, merciful love.

And this is the love the psalmist says is "better than life." This merciful and unfailing love of God is better than life at its best without that love.

When I think of my life without Christ, I can remember many high times, laughter I shared with people, and great relationships. But the least of God's mercies far outweighs the best of those times.

My life before coming to know Christ was chasing shadows. It was doing the best with a counterfeit because I had never experienced the reality. It was eating freeze-dried food when the Master Chef had prepared this sumptuous feast with the finest ingredients.

His lovingkindness is indeed better than the best of life without it. The natural response to such merciful love, to such an abundant life, is praise. Which means that every day, until your dying day, should be a thanksgiving day.

Day 172

A Picture of God's Lovingkindness

Yesterday we learned about God's merciful and unfailing love. 2 Samuel 9:3-7 provides us with a picture of that love,

> *Then the king said, "Is there not still someone of the house of Saul, to whom I may show the kindness of God?" And Ziba said to the king, "There is still a son of Jonathan who is lame in his feet." So the king said to him, "Where is he?" And Ziba said to the king, "Indeed he is in the house of Machir the son of Ammiel, in Lo Debar." Then King David sent and brought him out of the house of Machir the son of Ammiel, from Lo Debar. Now when Mephibosheth the son of Jonathan, the son of Saul, had come to David, he fell on his face and prostrated himself. Then David said, "Mephibosheth?" And he answered, "Here is your servant!" So David said to him, "Do not fear, for I will surely show you kindness for Jonathan your father's sake, and will restore to you all the land of Saul your grandfather; and you shall eat bread at my table continually."*

David made a blood covenant with Jonathan to show Jonathan's offspring the lovingkindness of God. After Jonathan died, Mephibosheth was the only offspring who remained, and he hid in the wilderness in fear of David. But David found him and elevated him to be one of his own sons, set him at his table, and restored everything he lost.

This is such a beautiful picture of the covenant God made with His Son Jesus, a covenant sealed by the blood of Christ. Because of what Jesus did, God shows us His lovingkindness, elevating us to the position of sons or daughters, and inviting us to break bread with Him at His own table.

That is the lovingkindness of God!

Day 173

Cherishing the Presence of God

Psalm 84:10 gives us an important perspective of God's presence,

> *For a day in Your courts is better than a thousand. I would rather be a doorkeeper in the house of my God than dwell in the tents of wickedness.*

When the psalmist talks about "a day in Your courts," he is not talking about being in some building or admiring some bit of religious architecture. He is talking about enjoying the presence of God. As verse 2 of this psalm says,

> *My soul longs, yes, even faints for the courts of the LORD; my heart and my flesh cry out for the living God.*

God is so good that just one day with Him is better than a thousand anywhere else. Just to be on the threshold, just to be on the doorstep, just to feel the slightest fringes, if you would, of the presence of God, is better than spending a thousand days anywhere else.

I think *The Message* Bible conveys the idea of verse 10,

> *One day spent in your house, this beautiful place of worship, beats thousands spent on Greek island beaches. I'd rather scrub floors in the house of my God than be honored as a guest in the palace of sin.*

Not long ago, I was walking through the neighborhood (I do this from time to time) just having a prayer walk. I walked for maybe 45 minutes and just prayed and worshiped God.

As I started thinking about all of the good things He has done for me, I began to sense His presence, and I started to cry. Now, I don't know what the neighbors thought if they happened to look out their window, but I didn't care, because I so appreciate His presence in my life.

I encourage you today to learn to cherish the presence of God!

Day 174

Protecting The Children

Matthew 18:1-6 is our reading for today,

At that time the disciples came to Jesus, saying, "Who then is greatest in the kingdom of heaven?" Then Jesus called a little child to Him, set him in the midst of them, and said, "Assuredly, I say to you, unless you are converted and become as little children, you will by no means enter the kingdom of heaven. Therefore whoever humbles himself as this little child is the greatest in the kingdom of heaven. Whoever receives one little child like this in My name receives Me. But whoever causes one of these little ones who believe in Me to sin, it would be better for him if a millstone were hung around his neck, and he were drowned in the depth of the sea."

This is a powerful truth God desires you and me to understand. He takes very seriously the protection and nurture of children.

First, it is important to understand that the word *sin* in this verse means to entrap. It means to set a snare for someone. Jesus was talking about someone who purposely entices an innocent child to do wrong.

Second, the millstone He refers to was about five feet across and would take an ox or a donkey to turn it. Get the picture?! Better for that millstone to be tied around a person's neck and to drown in the depths of the deepest sea than to entice a child to do wrong.

The exploitation or abuse of children is not overlooked or taken lightly by God. We read in Scripture that some sins incur a worse judgment from the Almighty. Causing children to sin is one of the worst. Never take their exploitation lightly.

Day 175

Dealing with Sin

Matthew 18:8-9 provides an important insight into how to deal with sin,

> *"If your hand or foot causes you to sin, cut it off and cast it from you. It is better for you to enter into life lame or maimed, rather than having two hands or two feet, to be cast into the everlasting fire. And if your eye causes you to sin, pluck it out and cast it from you. It is better for you to enter into life with one eye, rather than having two eyes, to be cast into hell fire."*

The eye represents the thought life, where sin is conceived. The hand represents that sin actually being carried out. And the foot is where it becomes a walk, a pattern, an entrenched habit of life, a sinful lifestyle.

When Jesus says, *"Cut it off,"* He is speaking of ruthless self-judgment. And He didn't stop there. He said, *"Cut it off and cast it from you."* In other words, get as far away from the source of your sin as you can.

I remember one day I walked right into a spider web. As I did, I caught a glimpse of this huge orange-colored spider out of the corner of my eye. As I hit the web, I felt it get on my neck. I started doing a war dance, hitting myself and ripping my shirt off, trying to get that thing off me.

And you know what? The moment a sinful thought lands in your mind, you ought to do the same thing, go on the warpath! Start batting that thing away! Start quoting Scriptures.

Do whatever you can to keep it from sinking its teeth into your life. As Jesus said, it will be better for you if you do!

Day 176

Far Better!

In Philippians 1:21-23, the apostle Paul says this,

> *For to me, to live is Christ, and to die is gain. But if I live on in the flesh, this will mean fruit from my labor; yet what I shall choose I cannot tell. For I am hard-pressed between the two, having a desire to depart and be with Christ, which is far better.*

Wow! Did you see what Paul said? *To live is Christ, and to die is gain.* If I die, I am going to be with Christ. And that is not a little better. It is *far* better.

While the following is a somewhat silly example, I think it makes the point.

My wife and I recently visited some friends in Washington, and it rained virtually the whole time we were there. It was just a series of gray, drizzly, dreary, rainy days. My friend is an avid golfer, so I asked him, "How long has it been since you have been able to go golfing?" He said, "Four months." I thought, "Wow! That's a long time!"

Now, the day Janet and I got back to Southern California it was a stunning Southern California day, about 70 degrees out. My son said, "Dad, you want to go golfing?" I said, "Sure. Throw the gear in the car."

As we were driving to the golf course, it hit me…Southern California is a place that is *far better* for a golfer than Washington! It is gain to be absent from the gray and rain, and present in the sun!

To be absent from the body is gain, because it means to be present with the Lord in the brightness of His glory! Don't feel sorry for believers when they go to be with the Lord. For them it is gain that is *far better*!

Day 177

No Regrets

In yesterday's devotional, we saw from Philippians 1:21-23 how it is far better to depart from this life and be with the Lord. Today I want to follow up with this question: Are you unable to abide thoughts of death?

If you answered "yes" to that question, chances are you are not ready to meet our Lord. But you need to be ready because everyone here is going to die. There are only two exceptions in all of history: Enoch and Elijah, and it is not likely you are going to be the third exception.

Death visits both kings and commoners. Its approach is sure. The Bible says in Psalm 89:48,

> *What man can live and not see death? Can he deliver his life from the power of the grave? Selah.*

That Hebrew word *selah* means to pause and calmly think about that, and that is the problem with some. They never think on it. They push every thought of their own mortality from their mind. But how can you prepare for eternity if you never think about it?

When the time comes and we have finished our course for God, let us face death like men. Let us look it in the eye. Let us not rebel against the cutting of the cords that loose us from the mooring of these earthly shores; but, rather, unfurl the sails and take that blessed journey to a better country!

As we read yesterday, *To live is Christ; and to die is gain.* To depart and be with Christ is far better.

Until then, squeeze every drop of life you can out of every single day. Live with all of your heart and all of your strength for God, and leave no regrets behind. Because life is a short day even at its longest. And when its sun has gone down, it leaves us in eternity.

Day 178

The Best Safeguard Against Adultery

It grieves my heart, as I look across the country, at the number of Christian marriages being destroyed by adultery. It should not be that way!

In 1 Corinthians 7:1-5, the apostle Paul gives us a safeguard against adultery. He says,

> *Now concerning the things of which you wrote to me: It is good for a man not to touch a woman. Nevertheless, because of sexual immorality, let each man have his own wife, and let each woman have her own husband. Let the husband render to his wife the affection due her, and likewise also the wife to her husband. The wife does not have authority over her own body, but the husband does. And likewise the husband does not have authority over his own body, but the wife does. Do not deprive one another except with consent for a time, that you may give yourselves to fasting and prayer; and come together again so that Satan does not tempt you because of your lack of self-control.*

Now, if these verses are saying anything, they are telling us that married couples should enjoy sexual intimacy. In fact, the more they enjoy it, the better safeguard it is against immorality.

Notice Paul even goes so far as to say the wife does not have authority over her own body; and the husband does not have authority over his body. As husband and wife, you belong to one another. It says do not deprive one another unless you are going to be fasting and praying, and then only with consent.

I want to challenge you to make sexual intimacy a priority in your marriage. Don't consider it as unimportant, or leave it to your spouse. Take the responsibility to light the fire of sexual intimacy, and close the door to Satan's temptation.

Day 179

Single?

In yesterday's devotional, we looked at 1 Corinthians 7:1-5 and a word to married couples on the importance of sexual intimacy. Today I want to continue in that passage with verses 7-9 and speak to singles,

> *For I wish that all men were even as I myself. But each one has his own gift from God, one in this manner and another in that. But I say to the unmarried and to the widows: It is good for them if they remain even as I am; but if they cannot exercise self-control, let them marry. For it is better to marry than to burn with passion.*

If you are single, and you long for physical intimacy, and you sometimes struggle with your sexuality, and you want to be married, it is God's will for you to be married. In fact, I can tell you that you do not have the gift to be single that Paul talks about.

On the other hand, you may be single and completely content, with no desire to be married. You need to know that does not mean there is something wrong with you. You just may be operating with a gift God has given you. In fact, Paul says it is better. You can serve the Lord undistracted that way.

If you do not have that gift, I believe it is God's plan for you to get married. If you are tortured with unsatisfied desire, it is better to marry.

That does not mean to go out and marry the first person you would like to have sex with. You have to take this into the context of all of God's counsel. You need to realize marriage should be the highest form of agreement between two people. No marriage should be entered into lightly or just based on physical attraction.

But if you are single and desiring to be married, I believe God does have someone for you.

Day 180

Under Control

In today's devotional I want to follow up on the passage we looked at yesterday, 1 Corinthians 7:7-9,

> *For I wish that all men were even as I myself. But each one has his own gift from God, one in this manner and another in that. But I say to the unmarried and to the widows: It is good for them if they remain even as I am; but if they cannot exercise self-control, let them marry. For it is better to marry than to burn with passion.*

What I want to focus on is verse 9, especially the part about burning with passion. There are way too many young Christians who are out of control in their physical relationship with the opposite sex.

So, mom or dad, here is something you can share with your kids in connection with relating to the opposite sex. Be prepared, I am going to be blunt.

1. Any body part they have that you don't have, don't touch it. Any equipment they have that you don't have, it is hands off!
2. Do not put any part of your body into any part of their body.
3. Do not get horizontal. Don't even sit on the couch watching TV, and lay down in one another's arms. If you do, you know where that can lead.
4. If you are going to kiss, let it be short and meaningful. Don't allow yourselves to get into a wrestling match. Again, it is hard to find the switch to turn it off once you get going.
5. Finally, let things like holding hands or putting your arm around your boyfriend or girlfriend actually be meaningful.

If you are single, apply these rules, and they could save you a lot of grief!

Day 181

Mistreated?

1 Peter 3:13-18 are verses that are a great encouragement,

And who is he who will harm you if you become followers of what is good? But even if you should suffer for righteousness' sake, you are blessed. "And do not be afraid of their threats, nor be troubled." But sanctify the Lord God in your hearts, and always be ready to give a defense to everyone who asks you a reason for the hope that is in you, with meekness and fear; having a good conscience, that when they defame you as evildoers, those who revile your good conduct in Christ may be ashamed. For it is better, if it is the will of God, to suffer for doing good than for doing evil. For Christ also suffered once for sins, the just for the unjust, that He might bring us to God.

Jesus was not guilty. He suffered for things He did not do, and the result is that we came to God. What Peter wants us to understand is the importance of showing forgiveness and a Christlike spirit, even when we are being mistreated.

What it can do is reach the hearts of your persecutors for God. If you keep a Christlike spirit, your good conduct can make them ashamed, even though they are hassling you, and bring them to the place where they will ask you a question for the hope that is in you: Why are you the way you are? What's this deal going on in your life? Why do you react the way you react? And you can tell them about Christ.

But if you lash out, and if you dish out the same kind of abuse that you are receiving, God is not revealed at all.

Patiently endure whatever your mistreatment, and ask God to use it to reach those who need to know Him as Savior.

Day 182

Spirit, Speech and Service

I want to follow up on yesterday's devotional by pointing you to 1 Peter 2:18-23,

> *Servants, be submissive to your masters with all fear, not only to the good and gentle, but also to the harsh. For this is commendable, if because of conscience toward God one endures grief, suffering wrongfully. For what credit is it if, when you are beaten for your faults, you take it patiently? But when you do good and suffer, if you take it patiently, this is commendable before God. For to this you were called, because Christ also suffered for us, leaving us an example, that you should follow His steps: "Who committed no sin, nor was deceit found in His mouth"; who, when He was reviled, did not revile in return; when He suffered, He did not threaten, but committed Himself to Him who judges righteously.*

The Goodspeed translation says, "*He committed His cause to Him who judges righteously.*" Now these verses are pretty clear: God is a righteous judge. And even if you are being mistreated for doing right, if you will commit things to God, He has a marvelous way of turning the tables in your favor.

You have to maintain three things if God is, indeed, going to use you in such a situation.

1. You have to maintain a *right spirit*. You have to keep a good attitude. You cannot get bitter. You have to stay kind.
2. You have to keep *right speech*. Do not dish out the same kind of abuse. Do not start saying things that are going to create division.
3. You have to maintain *right service*. Even if you are being mistreated, continue working hard for the Lord. Do not sabotage things.

If you will do these three things, just watch what God does through your difficulties!

Day 183

What Do You Value?

Psalm 119:72 says,

> *The law of Your mouth is better to me than thousands of coins of gold and silver.*

We understand "the law of Your mouth" to be God's Word. And what the psalmist is saying is, "Lord, Your word is better to me than a pile of silver or a pile of gold."

Let's say you are offered a position at a particular company—offered a great job, great increase of pay, and maybe the housing in that area is less. It is your dream job! But you investigate things, and you find out there is not a good Spirit-filled Bible teaching church in that town where the job is. But you can make a lot more money! Do you go? It depends on how much you value God's Word.

One gentleman who was very involved in my church came to me one day and announced that he was moving. I asked him, "Did you find a church there?" He replied, "No, no. There's not a good church in the town at all. But I'm going to be making a lot more money. We can get a bigger house. It's going to be great."

A year later his teenage daughter was pregnant, his boy was in juvenile hall, he and his wife were getting a divorce, and he was back on drugs. But, hey! He was making a lot more money.

In our society, it is so easy to make decisions based solely on money. And sadly, it is the ruin of many a family and relationship. Value first God's Word. Value it more than anything our world can give you.

If you do, you will never be disappointed.

Day 184

Do You Cherish God's Word?

Psalm 107:20 says,

> *He sent His word and healed them, and delivered them from their destructions.*

God has given us His Word for our benefit, and yet so many Christians ignore it to their hurt.

It is like the story of the woman a preacher went to visit one day. She lived in a dilapidated house. As long as he had known her, she had struggled with poverty. Twenty years earlier she had been the housekeeper for the wealthiest woman in town, but the wealthy woman had died. So this housekeeper moved into an old shack.

As the pastor was visiting her, he noticed a document framed on the wall. He said, "Do you mind if I borrow this for a few days?" She replied, "Well, you can borrow it, but please bring it back. Although I can't read, it is very important to me. It is the only thing that the lady left me when she died. It is very valuable to me. It reminds me of her. So make sure you bring it back."

He took it and had it investigated and authenticated. It was the will of the woman who had died, and in the will she left her housekeeper a fortune. The housekeeper could have had any house she wanted in the whole city and had servants of her own, but due to her ignorance, she lived in poverty and had a rough go of it all those years.

That woman reminds me of a lot of Christians. They don't read their Bible, but they admire it because it reminds them of God. They haven't taken time to find out the inheritance that belongs to them as believers.

God's Word is a light to our path. It is our guidebook for life. It is bread for our spirit. It is our strength. It is our refuge in troubled times.

Cherish God's Word.

Day 185

Whom Do You Trust?

In Psalm 118:8-9, we are told this,

> *It is better to trust in the LORD than to put confidence in man. It is better to trust in the LORD than to put confidence in princes.*

There are a lot of applications to this passage, but let me talk to you about just one. And that is this: You do not want to trust the state of your eternal soul to any man.

Ma'am, maybe your husband prays. Maybe he has a "real deal" relationship with God. Do not expect that to gain you any merit or to somehow get you to heaven. You have to have a relationship with the Lord yourself.

Sir, perhaps you have a praying wife. She is on fire for God. Do not expect that to get you a seat at the marriage supper of the Lamb. You must be born again. You have to be trusting in the Lord yourself. You have to have your own living, breathing, walking, talking, relationship with the Savior, or you will not get in!

When I was in my early twenties, there was a plethora of gurus and eastern mystics people were following. Some of my friends gave up all of their earthly possessions and became disciples of certain "holy" men.

But you know what? If you follow a man, when he perishes, you will perish just like him. Psalm 146:3-4 says,

> *Do not put your trust in princes, nor in a son of man, in whom there is no help. His spirit departs, he returns to his earth; in that very day his plans perish.*

If you put your trust in men, you will perish just like they do. But if you put your trust in God through His Son, Jesus Christ, you will gain eternal life.

Put your trust in God alone!

Day 186

Key #1 to Effective Prayer —Being Specific

Over the next number of devotionals, I want to walk you through the keys to effective prayer. To start, I want to focus today's devotional on Mark 10:46-52 where we find a very intriguing story.

> *Now they came to Jericho. As He went out of Jericho with His disciples and a great multitude, blind Bartimaeus, the son of Timaeus, sat by the road begging. And when he heard that it was Jesus of Nazareth, he began to cry out and say, "Jesus, Son of David, have mercy on me!" Then many warned him to be quiet; but he cried out all the more, "Son of David, have mercy on me!" So Jesus stood still and commanded him to be called. Then they called the blind man, saying to him, "Be of good cheer. Rise, He is calling you." And throwing aside his garment, he rose and came to Jesus. So Jesus answered and said to him, "What do you want Me to do for you?" The blind man said to Him, "Rabboni, that I may receive my sight." Then Jesus said to him, "Go your way; your faith has made you well." And immediately he received his sight and followed Jesus on the road.*

The question Jesus asked, "*What do you want Me to do for you?*", seemed obvious, didn't it? Everybody present knew Bartimaeus needed his eyes to be healed. Why would Jesus ask this question?

He wanted us to understand how important it is to be specific when we ask something of God. Bartimaeus' faith had to become specific before it made him well. It was after he said, "*Lord, that I might receive my sight*," that Jesus said, "*Your faith has made you well.*"

Being specific in what you request of God is the first key to effective prayer.

Day 187

Key #2 to Effective Prayer —Being Connected

By Janet Conley

Yesterday we found that the first key to effective prayer is the need to be specific when we pray. Today, I want to show you the second key: The need to have a close relationship with God.

In John 15:5, Jesus says,

> *"I am the vine, you are the branches. He who abides in Me, and I in him, bears much fruit; for without Me you can do nothing."*

God wants every part of our life to be connected to Him. And He tells us that as that happens, as we have our lives connected with Him, we bear much fruit. A few verses later Jesus directly connected that fruit to prayer.

In John 15:16, Jesus goes on to say,

> *"You did not choose Me, but I chose you and appointed you that you should go and bear fruit and that your fruit should remain, that whatever you ask the Father in My name He may give you."*

If we are connected to God and we abide in Him, Jesus says we will bear much fruit—prayer fruit. Think about a fruit tree for a moment. The leaves come out because the branches are attached to the tree. In the spring the branch will blossom, and from those blossoms comes the fruit.

But if something happens and the branch is not solidly connected to the tree, it will probably not bear any fruit at all. There may be a few leaves, but the blossoms won't come and there won't be any fruit. The blossoms and healthy fruit will only come if the branch is fully connected.

God wants us connected to Him in every part of our lives. When that happens, our prayers will be in line with His desires, and we can be confident that He will answer.

Day 188

How to Stay Connected

By Janet Conley

Yesterday we discovered the second key to effective prayer is to stay connected to God. The critical question is: How do we do that?

While there are many things we can do, I want to focus on two things. First of all, if you want to have a close relationship with God, it is important to realize just how much He desires to have a close relationship with you.

This is an amazing truth when you stop to think about it. He is Almighty God, and yet He wants to have a close relationship with you.

Romans 5:11 in the New Living Translation says, *Now we can rejoice in our wonderful new relationship with God because our Lord Jesus Christ has made us friends of God.*

Through Jesus, God made us to be His friends! So connecting with God starts with remembering He desires to be your closest friend.

Second, you need to practice His presence. Right now God is with you. He is everywhere you go. He is at your job; He is at your home; He is with you wherever you might be, even in the hardest time of your life.

The last part of Hebrews 13:5 says, *For He Himself has said, "I will never leave you nor forsake you."*

There was a monk in the seventeenth century named Brother Lawrence who wrote a book called *The Practice of the Presence of God*. In the monastery there were chimes that rang every hour, and Brother Lawrence would use that as a reminder to connect with God.

If you have a PDA or a wristwatch or a cell phone, you might consider setting it to go off throughout the day to remind you that God is with you. Each time it goes off, spend a few moments communing with Him. Practice His presence. That will help you stay connected to God.

Day 189

Key #3 to Effective Prayer —Praying From the Heart

Today we will look at the third key to effective prayer. This key is found in Romans 10:9-10 where it says,

> *If you confess with your mouth the Lord Jesus and believe in your heart that God has raised Him from the dead, you will be saved. For with the heart one believes unto righteousness, and with the mouth confession is made unto salvation.*

Prayer must come from the heart. These verses in particular teach us that if a person is going to pray a prayer of salvation, the heart and the mouth must get together. It is not good enough to just have the words. Your heart and mouth must be in agreement.

I believe this truth applies to every kind of prayer. It is not good enough to just use eloquent words. There has to be heart behind them if you are going to realize results from your prayers.

I think only those things that burn brightly within our hearts truly touch the heart of God.

When I was young, I would go fishing with my cousins. At night, the bats would come out and my cousins would take a lure, and they would cast it up in the air. Every once in a great while one of the bats would hit the lure and get snagged.

I think when we pray, it is like casting lines up into the heavens. But it is only the prayers that come from our heart that ever hook onto anything in heaven.

Effective prayer comes from your heart.

Day 190

Key #4 to Effective Prayer —Consistent with God's Will

By Janet Conley

In order for your prayers to be effective, they need to be in line with God's Word and will. That is the fourth key to effective prayer.

This means you must have knowledge of God's Word. In John 15:7, Jesus says,

> *"If you abide in Me, and My words abide in you, you will ask what you desire, and it shall be done for you."*

If you abide in God and His words abide in you, your desires will line up with His will. How important it is for us to know the Word of God!

As Hebrews 4 reminds us, the Word of God is living and active and powerful. It is spirit; it is life. It's not just pages on a piece of paper. And as you are in the Word of God, I believe the Holy Spirit will paint heaven's pictures, heaven's thoughts, and heaven's ideas on the canvas of your heart and your mind.

As you read the Word of God, you will have confidence in your prayers because you will have God's heart. And when you have God's heart, He is going to answer your prayers because that is what He desires.

I also want to point you to 1 John 5:14 which says,

> *Now this is the confidence that we have in Him, that if we ask anything according to His will, He hears us.*

His will, of course, is His Word. So if you ask anything according to His Word, He will hear you. And if you know that He hears whatever you ask, you know you have the petitions you have asked of Him.

This means you and I need to know what the Bible says so that our prayers will be answered. Effective prayers are those that are in line with God's Word and will.

Day 191

Key #5 to Effective Prayer —Endurance

The next key to effective prayer is the need to be patient. You need to be willing to endure.

Hebrews 6:11-15 says,

> *And we desire that each one of you show the same diligence to the full assurance of hope until the end, that you do not become sluggish, but imitate those who through faith and patience inherit the promises. For when God made a promise to Abraham, because He could swear by no one greater, He swore by Himself, saying, "Surely blessing I will bless you, and multiplying I will multiply you." And so, after he had patiently endured, he obtained the promise.*

Do you realize that once God gave Abraham and Sarah the promise of having a child, it was 25 years before Isaac was born? There was some patient enduring that took place before they obtained the reality of God's promise in their lives. And so it must be with us.

Perhaps you have been praying for things in your life, and you are getting discouraged. You must remember that God does not always work things on our timetable. He works according to His.

I just want to encourage you today: Be patient. Patience is that long-lasting quality of your faith.

A number of years ago I heard one person say that faith is like your hand and patience is like your arm. When you exercise faith, it is like holding up your hand against the problem, and as you do, things are being worked out. But if you take your patience down, your faith comes down with it.

Patience is the thing that keeps your faith applied until the answer comes.

Patience is a critical key to effective prayer. Whatever you are praying for, patiently endure.

Day 192

Key #6 to Effective Prayer —Humility

Humility is a very important key to effective prayer. In 1 Peter 5:5-6 we read this,

> *Likewise you younger people, submit yourselves to your elders. Yes, all of you be submissive to one another, and be clothed with humility, for "God resists the proud, but gives grace to the humble." Therefore humble yourselves under the mighty hand of God, that He may exalt you in due time.*

God resists the proud. He gives grace to the humble.

Humility, more than anything else, is an attitude of the heart that says, "I recognize I am not self-sufficient. I am open, I am teachable, I am thankful. God, I am willing to bow my heart before You and confess that I am in utter need of Your assistance."

Contrary to what some people say and think, humility is not to be equated with lack of courage. In fact, it takes great courage for a person to admit they have need. Meekness is not weakness. Meekness is a sign of strength.

King David said in Psalm 18:35, *Your gentleness* (or Your meekness) *has made me great.* Moses was called the meekest or the humblest man on the face of the earth, and yet we don't think of him as a weak person. He is one of the greatest leaders to ever step out of the pages of the Bible, and very few people in history have had power with God in the place of prayer like Moses did.

Jesus, our Savior, said, "*Take My yoke upon you, and learn of Me; for I am meek and lowly in heart*" (KJV). Friend, that ought to be one of the hallmark qualities of our lives— especially when we are praying. It is a key to effective prayer.

Day 193

Key #7 to Effective Prayer —The Holy Spirit's Help

By Janet Conley

Today I want to talk to you about another key to effective prayer, and that is the help of the Holy Spirit. I am so glad we have the Holy Spirit to help us, aren't you?

In John 16, Jesus is talking to His disciples, and He is trying to prepare them and let them know that He is going away. In John 16:7 He tells them,

> *"Nevertheless I tell you the truth. It is to your advantage that I go away; for if I do not go away, the Helper will not come to you; but if I depart, I will send Him to you."*

Do you know who the Helper is? It is the Holy Spirit. Earlier in John 14:26 he told His disciples this,

> *"But the Helper, the Holy Spirit, whom the Father will send in My name, He will teach you all things, and bring to your remembrance all things that I said to you."*

The Helper, the Holy Spirit, has been sent to come alongside and teach us all things. He will teach you how to pray; He will teach you things about prayer. The Holy Spirit will help you in that way.

Then He said, "*[He will] bring to your remembrance all things that I said to you.*" The Holy Spirit will help us remember the promises. The things that God has taught us He will bring to our remembrance, so we can pray effectively.

The Holy Spirit is like having a personal assistant. A personal assistant will help you remember your appointments or show you something you do not know. Every moment of every day He is there for us.

Take time to praise God today for His provision of the Holy Spirit. And remember He is there to help you in prayer.

Day 194

Key #8 to Effective Prayer —Forgiveness

An important key to effective prayer is your relationship with others. In Mark 11:24-26 Jesus says,

> *"Therefore I say to you, whatever things you ask when you pray, believe that you receive them, and you will have them. And whenever you stand praying, if you have anything against anyone, forgive him, that your Father in heaven may also forgive you your trespasses. But if you do not forgive, neither will your Father in heaven forgive your trespasses."*

Pretty strong, isn't it? Jesus cited unforgiveness as the number one reason for unanswered prayer. If my prayers were not being answered, this would be the first place I would look—into my own heart, to see whether I had allowed bitterness toward another human being to reside there. Whether I was harboring a grudge or had strife in my heart toward anyone else.

Jesus said if you have anything against anyone, anything—big or small, new or old—or anyone—yourself, your husband, your wife, a family member, a loved one, a neighbor, a co-worker, a relative, an enemy—if you have anything against anyone, it will lead to unanswered prayer.

Sometimes people hold things against themselves. They do not forgive themselves, even after God has forgiven them and after others have forgiven them. They just want to whip themselves for their stupidity for falling into the same stupid sin again, or for whatever they have done, and they don't release themselves!

There are others too, including those closest to us, whom we must forgive. If your prayers are not being answered, then look there.

Perhaps you have searched the Scriptures, filled your heart with the Word, you are praying from the bottom of your heart, and you are expectant of answers; but before you can partake of the fruit of your prayers, you must forgive if you have anything against anyone!

Day 195

Hindered Prayers

1 Peter 3:7 says,

> *Husbands, likewise, dwell with them with understanding, giving honor to the wife, as to the weaker vessel, and as being heirs together of the grace of life, that your prayers may not be hindered.*

Notice it says, "Husbands, likewise," which means, gals, you are not off the hook. The following truth applies to you as much as it does to the boys.

That truth is simply this: If there is bitterness or unforgiveness in your heart toward your spouse, your prayers will be hindered. That word *hindered* literally means to be cut down in the same way one would cut down a tree.

I once had this incredible tree called a cherimoya tree. One of the things about a cherimoya tree is that it is not indigenous to our country, and the insects that pollinate it do not exist here.

In order for the tree to bear fruit, I needed to pollinate it by hand with my little artist paintbrush. I would get pollen on the brush from one flower and pollinate other flowers.

Eventually the little buds I had pollinated began to turn into fruit. I was so excited! They were getting close to the time to be harvested. Then I came home one afternoon to find my whole tree hacked to pieces. Every branch and piece of fruit was in the trash. The gardener had cut my tree down!

I believe that can happen with our prayers. You can be intensely committed spiritually, searching the Scriptures, filling your heart with the Word, praying from the bottom of your heart, but if you are not honoring your spouse or you are treating them in a bad way, the devil has the authority to waltz right in and chop your prayer tree down.

Let's keep the ax out of the devil's hand by honoring and forgiving and valuing our marriage partner.

Day 196

The Power to Forgive

There are times when we need to forgive someone for something they have done. On occasion it can seem so difficult...almost impossible.

But forgiveness is not an option for you and me as followers of Jesus Christ.

Forgiveness is an act of the will. You can forgive. In fact, Jesus said that we even need to love our enemies, those who may not want peace with us.

Jesus said in Matthew 5:44,

> *"Love your enemies, bless those who curse you, do good to those who hate you, and pray for those who spitefully use you and persecute you."*

How can you do that? Because God has done the same thing for you. In Romans 5:10 it says,

> *When we were enemies we were reconciled to God through the death of His Son.*

When you and I embrace salvation through Jesus Christ, that same love of God is poured out in our hearts. (See Romans 5:1 and 5). As a result, we can forgive those who have wronged us.

Once you have forgiven someone, it can still affect your emotions. I like what Corrie ten Boom shared. She went through several sleepless weeks over something that someone had done to her. She tried to forgive the person; but, still, when she would think about it, she would respond emotionally.

When she shared this with her pastor, he had her look up at the bell tower of the church. He reminded her that the bell would continue to ring even after the person ringing it had let go of the rope. But given a little time, the bell would slow down until it was silent.

It may take time for your emotions to settle even when you have let go of the rope. Just let go of the rope and forgive. You can do it!

Day 197

Do You Really Believe It?

Ephesians 2:4-7 says,

> *But God, who is rich in mercy, because of His great love with which He loved us, even when we were dead in trespasses, made us alive together with Christ (by grace you have been saved), and raised us up together, and made us sit together in the heavenly places in Christ Jesus, that in the ages to come He might show the exceeding riches of His grace in His kindness toward us in Christ Jesus.*

There was a time in my wife's life when nothing was going right. It was before we were married while she was attending Bible school. Things were so bad that she was ready to drop out, and she wondered where God was in her life.

It was then that she attended a seminar where a woman was teaching on this passage. As my wife read this, and heard it taught, she saw that God loved her in an amazing way. That He loves everybody so much He sent Jesus Christ, so that He could make us a showpiece of His great love.

She realized He wanted to make her life beautiful and full. He wanted to make it good. He wanted to do things in her life so that she would be a showpiece for Him, and other people would look and say, "What is it about you?" and she could tell them that God made the difference in her life. Since that truth dawned on Janet's heart, she has never been the same.

1 John 4:16 says,

> *And we have known and believed the love that God has for us.*

Do you really believe that God loves you and has good things in store for you? You have heard about God's love, but do you really know it? Are you really believing the love that God has for you?

Well He does love you, and when you believe it, you will never be the same!

Day 198

The Reality of the Battle

Ephesians 6:10-13 provides for us a sober warning,

> *Finally, my brethren, be strong in the Lord and in the power of His might. Put on the whole armor of God, that you may be able to stand against the wiles of the devil. For we do not wrestle against flesh and blood, but against principalities, against powers, against the rulers of the darkness of this age, against spiritual hosts of wickedness in the heavenly places. Therefore take up the whole armor of God, that you may be able to withstand in the evil day, and having done all, to stand.*

Conflict with the enemy is unavoidable. These verses make that eminently clear. There will be a battle if you are part of God's family. We do have a spiritual adversary.

The Bible tells us in 1 Peter 5:8-9,

> *Be sober, be vigilant; because your adversary the devil walks about like a roaring lion, seeking whom he may devour. Resist him, steadfast in the faith, knowing that the same sufferings are experienced by your brotherhood in the world.*

We do have an enemy and we are involved in a spiritual battle. But don't you think if you knew when the devil was going to attack you, that it might give you a bit of an advantage? Well, over the next few devotionals I want to share with you three times that the devil is very likely to bring the battle to your front door.

We are going to find that as we look at the life of Jesus, this pattern was in His life. There were three times that the devil in particular brought the battle to His front door, as it were. And I believe we can expect spiritual battle at the same three times in our lives.

Day 199

Where Satan Will Attack First

Yesterday we began a series of devotionals looking at when we can expect Satan to attack us. Revelation 12:1-5 provides insight into the first time he will attack,

> *Now a great sign appeared in heaven: a woman clothed with the sun, with the moon under her feet, and on her head a garland of twelve stars. Then being with child, she cried out in labor and in pain to give birth. And another sign appeared in heaven: behold, a great, fiery red dragon having seven heads and ten horns, and seven diadems on his heads. His tail drew a third of the stars of heaven and threw them to the earth. And the dragon stood before the woman who was ready to give birth, to devour her Child as soon as it was born. She bore a male Child who was to rule all nations with a rod of iron. And her Child was caught up to God and His throne.*

The child in this passage is the Lord Jesus Christ, the woman represents the nation of Israel, and the dragon that wanted to devour the Child as soon as He was born is our adversary the devil.

It was the devil who was behind King Herod commanding that all of the male children two years old and younger be slaughtered. It was only because Joseph was warned by God in a dream that he, Mary, and Jesus escaped from Herod's clutches.

What I want you to see here is that the battle came to Jesus as soon as He was born. And I think we should expect battle as soon as a person is born again, as soon as someone comes into God's family.

We need to be prepared to help protect and defend those who are new babes in Christ.

Day 200

Protecting New Believers

We have been talking about the devil's attack on newborn babes in Christ. This is something we can expect. But what are the reasons for it?

Look at Isaiah 59:15-16, as it provides us with a clue,

> *So truth fails, and he who departs from evil makes himself a prey. Then the LORD saw it, and it displeased Him that there was no justice. He saw that there was no man, and wondered that there was no intercessor; therefore His own arm brought salvation for Him; and His own righteousness, it sustained Him.*

I want you to think about that. Truth fails, and the person who departs from evil makes himself a prey, in the same way that a lion looks at a wounded gazelle as prey.

To me this is a picture of what happens to some new believers. They depart from evil (get saved) and suddenly it seems like everything is going wrong for them. And God is not pleased about it!

Where it says He *wondered* literally means He was astonished that there was no intercessor. This means that there was no one praying. That is why they became prey!

If we do not pray for those who turn from evil, then they will become the prey of the devil. We have a responsibility to intercede for people who come to Christ. It puts up a barrier of protection around them.

Paul wrote to the Colossians about this when he said, *Praying always for you, since we heard of your faith in Christ.* Paul didn't just pray for them before they were saved, he also prayed for them after they were saved.

Oh, may God not wonder in our day, "Where is the intercessor who should be praying for the new babes in Christ?"

Let's take our responsibility seriously and pray for those who have newly come to the faith.

Day 201

Getting Established in the Faith

If you are a new believer in Christ, or know someone who is, I want to talk to you today. I want to share with you four things that will help you get established in your faith.

1. Read your Bible every day. That's food for your spirit. Psalm 119:11 says, *Your Word I have hidden in my heart, that I might not sin against You.* It is vital you spend time in God's Word.
2. Pray every day. Spend time talking to God and then listening in your heart for His answers. As 1 Thessalonians 5:17 admonishes us, *Pray without ceasing.* This is a vital part of your growth and protection as a believer.
3. Fellowship with other believers. Do not get isolated from the church. Do not get isolated from the rest of the body. Scripture tells us to *not forsake the assembling of yourselves together, as is the manner of some* (Hebrews 10:25). In fact, it is important to get integrated into a smaller circle of fellowship. You need to get connected relationally. There is a real safety in that.
4. Listen to your spiritual leaders. Go to church whenever the doors are open, and go expecting God to speak to you through the teaching and preaching. One translation of Hebrews 13:17 says, *Give ear to your spiritual leaders and be willing to do what they say for their work is to watch over your souls.* Become a part of a strong Bible-believing fellowship and take heed to what is taught.

If you will do those things: read your Bible every day, pray every day, get involved in a smaller circle of fellowship and listen to your spiritual leaders, you will be all right.

Day 202

You Made it This Far!

In the last couple of devotionals, we saw how the devil will attack a new babe in Christ. Hebrews 10:32 sheds some additional light on what we can expect,

But recall the former days in which, after you were illuminated, you endured a great struggle with sufferings.

When it says, *after you were illuminated*, it literally means, "After you came to the light." This verse is talking about when the light of the gospel dawned on you, when you were saved.

And what does it say? You need to recall, to remember, that after you came to Christ, you endured. You went through some battles.

I think we need to remember that. In fact, let me just encourage you today. The fact that you are reading this devotional today says something about you. Did you know there are a lot of people who were saved at the same time you were, but they are not seeking God today?

You made it through the battle! You stood fast. You might feel like you are pretty rickety and ready to keel over, but you are still seeking God! If the devil could get you, he would have gotten you already.

By God's grace you made it this far. Now is no time to quit!

Day 203

Attack at the Point of Spiritual Breakthrough

We have seen in previous devotionals how Satan will attack when a person comes to Christ, when they are a babe in their faith. I believe Scripture shows us that the devil will also attack when you are on the verge of a breakthrough, or at a time of important transition. This is the second battle we must fight.

In Matthew 3, we find Jesus at an absolutely critical time of transition in His life. We have not heard from Him since He was 12 years old. There has been about 30 quiet, unnoticed years where He presumably was working in His father's carpentry shop.

That is when we read in Matthew 3:16-4:1,

> *When He had been baptized, Jesus came up immediately from the water; and behold, the heavens were opened to Him, and He saw the Spirit of God descending like a dove and alighting upon Him. And suddenly a voice came from heaven, saying, "This is My beloved Son, in whom I am well pleased." Then Jesus was led up by the Spirit into the wilderness to be tempted by the devil.*

Jesus is about to enter public ministry. The sick will be healed; the poor will have the gospel preached to them; miracles will be worked; the Father will be revealed. So from this point, the battle is on. And we are given a bird's-eye view of the conflict that occurs between Christ and the devil, which we will look at in more detail in the next several devotionals.

But I want to submit something to you today. If it seems that all hell has broken loose in your life, maybe, just maybe, it's because you are on the verge of a breakthrough in your life.

Maybe it's a time of very important transition where God wants to lift you into a place where there is going to be greater influence and greater impact through your life.

Day 204

The Devil's Seeds of Doubt

As we saw yesterday, Satan will seek to attack when we are on the verge of a major breakthrough. I believe there are three distinct areas of attack in this battle. Today I want to cover the first with you. It is found in Matthew 4:3-4,

> *Now when the tempter came to Him, he said, "If You are the Son of God, command that these stones become bread." But He answered and said, "It is written, 'Man shall not live by bread alone, but by every word that proceeds from the mouth of God.'"*

The devil's first area of attack will be to try to get you to doubt your calling.

Notice that just prior to this encounter the voice of God the Father said to Jesus, "*This is My beloved Son!*" And that is the first thing the devil challenges, "Well, if you are the Son of God...."

He will do the same thing to you.

What is it that God has spoken to you about that He wants you to do with your life? Has He told you that He wants to use you to funnel vast resources into the gospel? Or maybe God said you are to be a teacher, or that you are going to impact the entertainment industry, or that you are going to be a prayer warrior and tip the spiritual scales in critical times.

Whatever it is, the devil will saddle up next to you and say, "Who do you think you are? What God has told you is just a pipe dream. It's just your own head speaking to you." He will try and get you to doubt what God has said to you and to doubt what God has called you to do.

When that happens, you need to go back to that word that God has spoken to you in order to keep your focus and direction right.

Day 205

Where Satan Will Attack Second

Yesterday we saw the first area the devil will attack when you are on the verge of a breakthrough or in a time of important transition. Today, I want to show you the second area, the area of pride.

We pick up the drama of Satan's attack of Christ in Matthew 4:6,

> *"If You are the Son of God, throw Yourself down. For it is written: 'He shall give His angels charge over you,' and, 'In their hands they shall bear you up, lest you dash your foot against a stone.'"*

I believe the devil was appealing to Jesus' pride at this point. He realized Jesus was solid in His own heart about who He was and what He was to do.

So the devil took Him to the most public of all places, and told Him, "Now, hey, You need to prove this to everybody else. If You cast Yourself down, You will have a soft landing because the angels will catch You, and everyone will know that You're the Son of God."

Pride will cause us to do things recklessly, and Satan was doing all he could to get Jesus to act recklessly. But Jesus answered perfectly, "*You shall not tempt the LORD your God.*"

By the way, the verse Satan quoted to Jesus about the angels catching Him had an ending, which he failed to include. It says, "*To keep you in all your ways.*" The Amplified Bible says, "*In all your ways of obedience and service.*"

In other words, you can't do some reckless thing to prove a point to other people and expect God to save you. Don't let your pride get you out on a limb. Instead, resist Satan's attack in the area of pride. Realize it for what it is; it's his temptation to get you to fall!

If you are secure in who you are, you don't have to prove anything to anyone.

Day 206

Compromise

Today, I want to highlight for you the third area where the devil will seek to cause you to fail when you are on the verge of a breakthrough. It is found in Matthew 4:8-11,

> *Again, the devil took Him up on an exceedingly high mountain, and showed Him all the kingdoms of the world and their glory. And he said to Him, "All these things I will give You if You will fall down and worship me." Then Jesus said to him, "Away with you, Satan! For it is written, 'You shall worship the LORD your God, and Him only you shall serve.'" Then the devil left Him, and behold, angels came and ministered to Him.*

If you think about it, the devil offered Jesus exactly what He had come to this world to obtain. Jesus came to win the kingdoms of this world to our God.

And the devil is saying, "Hey, You can take a shortcut. I will give You what You want. You don't have to do it God's way. You may have to compromise Your integrity, but think of how quickly You will succeed! You can even avoid the whole sacrifice thing! You don't have to do it God's way."

Listen, anytime God has set a goal for you, and you are going to obtain something, the devil will always come and try to get you to compromise and offer you substitutes.

He will tempt you by saying things like, "You can get what you want without living by all those narrow, restrictive rules that God puts on people's lives. You can be dishonest; you can be unfaithful; you can compromise; and you can still be blessed, and you can still be happy."

Do not believe him for a moment. His way of compromise leads only to ruin!

Day 207

Sacrifice?

Matthew 16:21-25 shows us another time in our lives when we can expect the devil to strike, or the third battle we must fight,

> *From that time Jesus began to show to His disciples that He must go to Jerusalem, and suffer many things from the elders and chief priests and scribes, and be killed, and be raised the third day. Then Peter took Him aside and began to rebuke Him, saying, "Far be it from You, Lord; this shall not happen to You!" But He turned and said to Peter, "Get behind Me, Satan! You are an offense to Me, for you are not mindful of the things of God, but the things of men." Then Jesus said to His disciples, "If anyone desires to come after Me, let him deny himself, and take up his cross, and follow Me. For whoever desires to save his life will lose it, but whoever loses his life for My sake will find it."*

The cross is a place of sacrifice. It is a place where you die. In this passage Jesus is talking about the sacrifice that He is going to give, laying down His life for our sins.

Peter is being manipulated by the devil to challenge Jesus. The devil is speaking through Peter, telling Christ to back off a bit, that He doesn't need to sacrifice, that He doesn't need to give that much, or to lay His life down.

Friend, when God is leading you to sacrifice for the sake of His kingdom, count on the devil to be right there doing all He can to stop you. He will make you believe you should let your temperature cool down a little bit, that you shouldn't be so on fire for God. That you shouldn't be that sold out!

Do not listen. Instead, heed God's call to sacrifice. You will not regret it!

Day 208

The Impact of Sacrifice

Yesterday we saw how Jesus calls us to sacrifice, and how the devil will do all he can to keep us from that. Read again Jesus' words,

> *"If anyone desires to come after Me, let him deny himself, and take up his cross, and follow Me. For whoever desires to save his life will lose it, but whoever loses his life for My sake will find it"* (Matthew 16:24-25).

The devil will fight to keep you from sacrifice because he knows several things.

1. He understands that sacrifice brings the presence of God. Throughout the Old and New Testaments you will find that whenever men and women sacrificed, God's presence came. The devil doesn't want more of the presence of God in your life. He would love for you to live a mediocre, half-hearted life. But to follow Jesus means self-denial. When Jesus leads you to sacrifice, it will always bring a greater measure of His life and His presence into your life. And the devil understands that.
2. He understands that sacrifice opens a great channel of blessing that otherwise we will not experience. Paul wrote to the Philippians, "I've received your gift. It is a sacrifice, a sweet-smelling aroma to God, and my God will supply all of your need according to His riches in glory by Christ Jesus." That promise of needs being met according to a heavenly standard was directly linked to sacrificial giving.
3. He understands that those who have changed the world were always men and women who sacrificed. You will not find anyone who has changed the world for good that has not been a person of great sacrifice. The devil knows that is true!

Don't let Satan keep you from the sacrifice God is calling you to make.

Day 209

Samson and Jesus—Part 1

For behold, you shall conceive and bear a son. And no razor shall come upon his head, for the child shall be a Nazirite to God from the womb; and he shall begin to deliver Israel out of the hand of the Philistines (Judges 13:5).

And behold, you will conceive in your womb and bring forth a Son, and shall call His name JESUS... And the angel answered and said to her, "The Holy Spirit will come upon you, and the power of the Highest will overshadow you; therefore, also, that Holy One who is to be born will be called the Son of God" (Luke 1:31 & 35).

There are some striking similarities between Samson the Nazarite and Jesus the Nazarine. Here are a few of them.

- Both the birth of Samson and the birth of Christ were announced through angelic messengers.
- Samson's father said, "Let your words come to pass." Mary, the mother of Jesus, said, "Let it be unto me according to your word."
- Samson was born to deliver the Israelites who were in bondage to and oppressed by the Philistines. Jesus was born to deliver the world that was in bondage to and oppressed by Satan.
- The Spirit moved upon Samson. The Spirit descended upon and anointed Jesus.
- Samson was a thorn in the Philistines' side, going about destroying their yoke over Israel. Jesus went about doing good and healing all who were oppressed by the devil and thereby destroying Satan's yoke of bondage.
- Samson's own people rejected him and turned him over to the Philistines. Jesus' own people (the Jews) rejected Him and turned Him over to the Romans.

These similarities between Samson and Jesus are not coincidental. Samson's story is meant to point the way to Jesus. God wants people to know about the blessed Savior. You can point the way to Him as well. Tell someone today about Jesus!

Day 210

Samson and Jesus—Part 2

For behold, you shall conceive and bear a son. And no razor shall come upon his head, for the child shall be a Nazirite to God from the womb; and he shall begin to deliver Israel out of the hand of the Philistines (Judges 13:5).

And behold, you will conceive in your womb and bring forth a Son, and shall call His name JESUS (Luke 1:31).

In yesterday's devotional we examined some amazing similarities between Samson and Jesus. Here are a few more parallels to ponder:

- Samson was betrayed by Delilah. Jesus was betrayed by Judas.
- Samson was taken prisoner and tortured by the Philistines. Jesus was taken prisoner and tortured by the Romans.
- Samson, while being mocked in Dagon's temple, wrought his greatest victory and gave the Philistines their worst defeat—*the dead that he killed at his death were more than he had killed in his life.* Jesus, while being mocked on the cross by his persecutors, wrought His greatest victory and handed hell its ultimate defeat. And He did it through His death.
- It is said that Samson "began to deliver Israel," indicating that his work was to be carried on by others. Jesus has left the work of evangelism to us. Though He paid the price, we are to carry the good news of His victory to the ends of the earth.

As you think about these similarities, I want you to especially consider the last one I presented. Once we receive the gospel, we are then to be carriers of the gospel. Tell someone about Jesus and what He has done for them—today!

Day 211

Prosperity

In Luke 12, Jesus has some very direct and clear teaching on prosperity. For instance, take a look at Luke 12:13-15,

> *Then one from the crowd said to Him, "Teacher, tell my brother to divide the inheritance with me." But He said to him, "Man, who made Me a judge or an arbitrator over you?" And He said to them, "Take heed and beware of covetousness, for one's life does not consist in the abundance of the things he possesses."*

It's easy to read these verses and believe that God is against prosperity. But if you look at what I call the Genesis Principle, I think you can see that prosperity is God's will.

When God created man, He gave him abundance. You can't read the story in the Garden of Eden and think that Adam lacked for anything. And God's plan, His idea, His heart for humanity has never changed.

But God did not give Adam all that abundance so that the abundance itself would be the focus of his life. His focus was to be his relationship with the Father as they walked and talked in the garden. His life did not consist in the abundance of things, but in his relationship to his Creator.

So what is abundance? Abundance, or prosperity, is having all that you need to meet any circumstance, with enough left over to give wherever God might direct you.

Jesus certainly is not against prosperity. In fact, prosperity is what I believe is God's will for all of His children. I don't think God wants any of His kids to be in poverty. Poverty is not a virtue unless you choose it for some reason.

God wants you to be prosperous, but there are some principles to properly understand prosperity, which we will discover in the next few devotionals.

Day 212

The Seduction of Covetousness

One of the verses we read in our last devotional was Luke 12:15, which says,

> *And He said to them, "Take heed and beware of covetousness, for one's life does not consist in the abundance of the things he possesses."*

Jesus begins His teaching regarding prosperity in this passage by saying, "*Beware of covetousness.*" In our society, even in the Church, there are a lot of people whose lives are tied up in "things." The focus of their life is their stuff, and doing whatever they can to acquire even more things.

It is what the Bible calls covetousness.

I want to ask you today, is your heart filled with covetousness? Do you find yourself thinking, "I know the missing ingredient in my life, I just need a little more. If I could just get a little more, I would be happy. If I could just build a bigger house and fill it with a little more stuff...if I could get a nicer car...if I could upgrade...then I would be happy, and then I would be successful"?

A little more, a little more, a little more.

The problem is, however, that desire for more never stops. In fact, as we will see in our next devotional, God called a man a fool because he never realized that riches are only temporary.

If you find your life driven by the need for more things, if you are consumed with stuff, if you define your success by what you have (or do not have), then you have been seduced by covetousness, and you will never find the happiness you are looking for.

Do not be a fool seeking after things. Instead, make the passion of your life seeking after God.

Day 213

It Might Be Today

Over the last few devotionals, we have been looking at Luke 12. Today I want you to read verses 16-21, which will be the basis for our next few days of devotionals,

> *Then He spoke a parable to them, saying: "The ground of a certain rich man yielded plentifully. And he thought within himself, saying, 'What shall I do, since I have no room to store my crops?' So he said, 'I will do this: I will pull down my barns and build greater, and there I will store all my crops and my goods. And I will say to my soul, "Soul, you have many goods laid up for many years; take your ease; eat, drink, and be merry."' But God said to him, 'Fool! This night your soul will be required of you; then whose will those things be which you have provided?' So is he who lays up treasure for himself, and is not rich toward God."*

I want to direct our thoughts to verses 19-20 today.

Sometimes it is easy for people to think they have many years left. But that is a foolish perspective. We need to live like we will meet with the Lord tonight.

That doesn't mean you don't work towards the future; it doesn't mean you don't save. In fact, the Bible says a righteous man leaves an inheritance for his children's children.

But we need to live in such a way that we will not be ashamed because we have left all sorts of unused and undesignated funds sitting in the bank that are not going to do anybody any good.

Someday we will have to stand before Jesus and give an account for all of our stuff. And that may be sooner than later!

Day 214

Living for Whom?

Today I want us to return to Luke 12, but focus on verses 16-19,

> *Then He spoke a parable to them, saying: "The ground of a certain rich man yielded plentifully. And he thought within himself, saying, 'What shall I do, since I have no room to store my crops?' So he said, 'I will do this: I will pull down my barns and build greater, and there I will store all my crops and my goods. And I will say to my soul, "Soul, you have many goods laid up for many years; take your ease; eat, drink, and be merry."'"*

This guy is classic! While he was rich, he was only rich toward himself. He did not have any thoughts about being rich toward the Kingdom of God. He was totally self-centered.

In fact, in the few short verses where this man speaks, verses 17, 18, and 19, he uses six "I"s, five "my"s, and four "I will"s. He says, "My crops, my barns, my goods, my soul." Pretty self-centered!

Yes, his land brought forth an incredible harvest, but who provided the fertile soil? Who provided the rain? Who provided the sunshine? Who gave him his health? Who gave him the ability to think and plan? In fact, for that matter, who gave him his soul?

In Ezekiel 18:4 God says, "*All souls are Mine.*"

This man totally left God out of his plans. Everything he did, he did for himself. And God said he was a fool. On the very same day he made his boast, his soul was required of him.

Instead of a barn, he had a burial; instead of living in the lap of luxury, he had to stand before God and give an account of his life.

Day 215

Ruined by Success

As we continue our consideration of prosperity, I want to turn your attention to Luke 12:31,

> *"But seek the kingdom of God, and all these things shall be added to you."*

This is a simple but powerful principle for life: We have to put God's Kingdom first if we are to realize God's prosperity.

A lot of Christians get caught up in the drive for prosperity and forget that God's greatest desire is for us to pursue His Kingdom. In fact, I think some of God's children today are frustrated as they are endeavoring to prosper. They can see the promise of prosperity in the Word, yet they are coming up short, and they are asking, "God, what's up?"

I really think this is an issue of the heart. God is not prospering them because they may not be mature enough spiritually to handle the degree of prosperity they are seeking. It might do them harm.

This brings to mind a young coworker of mine from a number of years ago. He was a believer but was struggling financially. One night we were in a restaurant after work when he shared a difficult struggle he was going through.

We prayed that God would do something supernatural to help him in his time of need. Two days later, he got an unexpected inheritance. It was huge! And you know what? The next week he wasn't at work. Instead he was out partying. All of a sudden, his church life stopped and he walked away from his relationship with God. He didn't have the maturity to handle the success.

I think success has ruined more people than failure. It has been said that money is the most dangerous thing God can put into your trust.

Seek after God. And when He prospers you, keep seeking after Him!

Day 216

The Secret to God's Provision

In Luke 12:31-32 Jesus tells us,

"But seek the kingdom of God...." (In Matthew 6:33, He said, *"Seek first the kingdom of God...and all these things shall be added to you."*) *"Do not fear, little flock, for it is your Father's good pleasure to give you the kingdom."*

The secret to receiving God's provision is to put God's Kingdom first, then everything else will be added to you. That includes all the things you worry about and strive after. God promises He will add them to you.

I know for some people it is just too simplistic. It is just a childish notion to be brushed aside. But, to do so is a grave mistake. Never underestimate the power of obedience. When we obey God and get our priorities in line, it unlocks and releases incredible blessings in our life.

When we put the spiritual above the material, when we put the cause and the mission of God's Kingdom before our own personal desires, it will cause things to be added to our lives.

I remember reading about J.L. Kraft. He began his business by selling cheese on the streets in Chicago, but failed miserably. One day a Christian friend told him, "J.L., you don't have God first in your life, or in your business. Put Him first in all things you do, and you will see a different outcome."

From that day on, he put God's Kingdom first in every way and he built the largest cheese empire in the world.

First things first. Jesus said, "Do not worry. Just get your priorities in line, and God will take care of you."

Day 217

What Has You?

In Mark 10:17-22, this is what we read,

> *Now as He was going out on the road, one came running, knelt before Him, and asked Him, "Good Teacher, what shall I do that I may inherit eternal life?" So Jesus said to him, "Why do you call Me good? No one is good but One, that is, God. You know the commandments: 'Do not commit adultery,' 'Do not murder,' 'Do not steal,' 'Do not bear false witness,' 'Do not defraud,' 'Honor your father and your mother.'" And he answered and said to Him, "Teacher, all these things I have kept from my youth." Then Jesus, looking at him, loved him, and said to him, "One thing you lack: Go your way, sell whatever you have and give to the poor, and you will have treasure in heaven; and come, take up the cross, and follow Me." But he was sad at this word, and went away sorrowful, for he had great possessions.*

This is an interesting passage, isn't it?! I think verse 22 could probably be read as "great possessions had him," and we wouldn't do too much damage to the text. Possessions possessed him, and he went away from his conversation with Jesus sorrowful.

When Jesus met this guy, He was able to cut right to the heart issue, what controlled his life. Verse 21 could be paraphrased, "Okay, you really want it? Here's your roadblock, baby." It was the guy's attitude toward his stuff.

This man loved possessions, wealth, and the things of this life more than he loved Jesus.

Where are you today, my friend? Have you allowed our world to con you into believing that you should base your life on the stuff you accumulate? Or do you love God the most?

Day 218

Giving When No One Sees

Matthew 6:1-4 gives some important insight into giving,

> *"Take heed that you do not do your charitable deeds before men, to be seen by them. Otherwise you have no reward from your Father in heaven. Therefore, when you do a charitable deed, do not sound a trumpet before you as the hypocrites do in the synagogues and in the streets, that they may have glory from men. Assuredly, I say to you, they have their reward. But when you do a charitable deed, do not let your left hand know what your right hand is doing, that your charitable deed may be in secret; and your Father who sees in secret will Himself reward you openly."*

Jesus points us to a truth that is vital to us as Christians: *Giving is an issue of the heart.*

God will not honor your giving if, when you give, your heart is saying, "I want everyone to know what I'm doing. I want to be noticed when I give. I want everyone to know just how generous and kind I am and what a benevolent heart I have."

We should give with a pure motive. When we give with the right motive, not to be seen by men but out of a right heart, God will reward us openly. That may not exactly translate into dollars and cents, but it will translate into tangible blessings, things that people can see.

If nobody else knows you kicked in the extra hundred bucks, don't worry about it. God sees, and He has a way of rewarding you openly. Everyone will recognize the hand of God is on you. God's blessings will come into your life.

So when you give, check your heart to make sure you are giving with the right motive.

Day 219

A Matter of the Heart

God cares deeply about the motivations of our hearts. Yesterday, we saw that the heart is what matters most in giving. In Matthew 6:6,17,18, we are shown just how important the heart is to God.

First Jesus deals with our heart when we pray,

> *"But you, when you pray, go into your room, and when you have shut your door, pray to your Father who is in the secret place; and your Father who sees in secret will reward you openly."*

Next He deals with our heart when fasting,

> *"But you, when you fast, anoint your head and wash your face, so that you do not appear to men to be fasting, but to your Father who is in the secret place; and your Father who sees in secret will reward you openly."*

Jesus wants you and me to pray with the right heart, not seeking the praise of others. And the same is true with fasting. When you fast, you are not supposed to let everybody know.

When you fast, if somebody says, "Hey, would you like to go to lunch today?" and you reply, "I can't. I'm fasting," they may think, "Wow, he's spiritual!" but that is all the reward you get, right there, so you better enjoy it.

What is Jesus' point? When we give to the poor, when we pray, when we fast, we do not do it to get the applause or recognition of men. We do it out of obedience to God, out of love for our fellow men, and just wanting to help somebody else who is trying to make it through the day on this planet.

That is why we should do it. That is the right motivation of the heart.

Day 220

The Heart of the Issue

Over the last few devotionals, we have learned just how important our heart motivation is in giving, praying, and fasting. In Matthew 6:19-21, Jesus continues to deal with matters of the heart,

> *"Do not lay up for yourselves treasures on earth, where moth and rust destroy and where thieves break in and steal; but lay up for yourselves treasures in heaven, where neither moth nor rust destroys and where thieves do not break in and steal. For where your treasure is, there your heart will be also."*

How do you lay up treasures in heaven? Jesus told the rich young ruler, "*Sell what you have and give to the poor, and you will have treasure in heaven.*" So giving to help people, giving to the poor, giving to ministry, giving to God's work instead of hoarding it up, giving to God—that is the way you lay treasure up in heaven.

But notice that Jesus goes on to say, "*Where your treasure is, there your heart will be also.*" Jesus hasn't really changed the subject. The heart of the issue is the heart. That is the theme of Jesus' teaching.

A right heart attitude—a proper heart motive—is what God cares about most. That is true whether you are giving, you are praying, or you are fasting. He wants you to do these things for the right reasons.

Those right reasons include your desire to help people. Your desire to express your love for God and His Kingdom. Those are the right reasons.

Jesus said, when you are motivated by the right reasons, you are laying up treasure in heaven. He says, "*Where your treasure is* (in heaven with God), *there your heart will be also.*"

His point? The heart of the issue is your heart.

Day 221

God's Guidance System

In Matthew 6:22-24, Jesus tells us the impact when God has our whole heart,

> *"The lamp of the body is the eye. If therefore your eye is good, your whole body will be full of light. But if your eye is bad, your whole body will be full of darkness. If therefore the light that is in you is darkness, how great is that darkness! No one can serve two masters; for either he will hate the one and love the other, or else he will be loyal to the one and despise the other. You cannot serve God and mammon."*

While it may not seem like it, Jesus is talking about the heart.

As we learned in our previous devotionals, if you give to God, and give for the right reasons, God has your heart. Your heart belongs to Him. When God has your heart, He can lead you; because that is how God leads, He leads through your heart.

That's really what this illustration is about. That is what He means by, "The lamp of the body is the eye."

Think about the difference light makes when trying to walk on a narrow, craggy path. When light comes into your eye, you can see your way. Your eyes, when the light is able to come in, are a built-in guidance system, aren't they?

Well, you know what? You have a guidance system God uses to lead you. That guidance system is called your heart. If God has your treasure, He has your heart. But God can't lead you through your heart if He doesn't have your heart.

If God has your heart, then He can begin to lead you. You can go anywhere He tells you to go. And interestingly enough, the loyalty of our heart is expressed through our giving. Giving and guidance tied together? According to Jesus...definitely!

Day 222

When God Has Our Hearts

In Matthew 6:25-26, Jesus applies all we have covered over the last few days,

> *"Therefore I say to you, do not worry about your life, what you will eat or what you will drink; nor about your body, what you will put on. Is not life more than food and the body more than clothing? Look at the birds of the air, for they neither sow nor reap nor gather into barns; yet your heavenly Father feeds them. Are you not of more value than they?"*

Given the context of the preceding verses, Jesus is telling us that if God is first in our giving, then He indeed has our heart. If He has our hearts, He can guide us and meet our needs, and we have no need to worry about provision for our life.

He feeds the birds. He will take care of you. Do not worry. Obey Him, trust Him, and look to Him for your daily bread.

Matthew 6:33 says,

> *"But seek first the kingdom of God and His righteousness, and all these things shall be added to you."*

Day 223

Go Fish

Over the next seven devotionals, I want to talk to you about the number one business of the Church: the business of winning souls. It is what I call "The Seven Cs of Soul Winning."

The first "C"—*commission*—is found in Mark 16:15. These are some of the last words Jesus spoke before He ascended into heaven,

"Go into all the world and preach the gospel to every creature."

Could it be any clearer? Jesus said, "Go." Dare we say, "No"? He said, "Go."

That is the opposite of "stay," isn't it? Go: G-O.

God wants you and me to take the Gospel to Others.

You and I need to get out into the world! Jesus was not crucified between two candles on a church altar. He was crucified out in the byways and highways of humanity, and that is where we must take the message.

Jesus said, "*Follow Me, and I will make you become fishers of men.*" That is a promise. But you know what? You have to get to the water if you are going to catch fish. You have to get out of the four church walls, out to where hurting humanity is, and engage them with the gospel.

A while back, I went backpacking with my two sons in a very remote area. We found a pristine lake where just about every time we would put a line in the water, we would catch a fish.

We also had this incredible camp. But you know what? If we wanted to catch fish, we had to go down to the water. No one could catch a fish sitting in camp.

A lot of Christians just hang around the camp. They form fishing clubs and talk about how important it is to fish. But they don't fish.

God wants us to go fish!

Day 224

Compassion for the Lost

Yesterday we started a series of devotionals I am calling "The Seven Cs of Soul Winning." Today I want to point you to the second "C"—*compassion.* In Mark 16:16 Jesus said,

> *"He who believes and is baptized will be saved; but he who does not believe will be condemned."*

Now, *condemned* is a pretty soft word in the English language. I actually like the King James Version, where it says, "*He that believeth and is baptized shall be saved; but he that believeth not shall be* ***damned.***"

Condemned or damned, it means eternally separated from God with no opportunity of rescue or retrieval. Forever lost. Think about it!

Do you recall the story Jesus told of the rich man who died? It ought to send a shudder through the heart of even the most brazen sinner.

Jesus tells us that the rich man died and was in torment, in flame. Jesus goes on to say that the rich man lifted up his eyes, and begged for mercy. But no mercy came, even as it says in Revelation 14:11, "*The smoke of their torment ascends forever and ever.*"

I know it is not a popular subject in the Church to talk about hell, but Jesus talked more about hell than He did about heaven. It is a very real place. If we would consider just for a moment the end of the man or woman who rejects Christ, it ought to cause our hearts to be stirred with compassion.

When was the last time you and I shed a tear over lost humanity? When was the last time you and I were truly broken with the things that break the heart of God?

Our compassion for the lost ought to move us to do all we can to share Christ with them!

Day 225

Common Ground

The next "C" of "The Seven Cs of Soul Winning" is *common ground*. We need to endeavor to find common ground with people. In 1 Corinthians 9:19-24, Paul says,

> *For though I am free from all men, I have made myself a servant to all, that I might win the more; and to the Jews I became as a Jew, that I might win Jews; to those who are under the law, as under the law, that I might win those who are under the law; to those who are without law, as without law (not being without law toward God, but under law toward Christ), that I might win those who are without law; to the weak I became as weak, that I might win the weak. I have become all things to all men, that I might by all means save some. Now this I do for the gospel's sake, that I may be partaker of it with you. Do you not know that those who run in a race all run, but one receives the prize? Run in such a way that you may obtain it.*

In this passage, Paul is talking about the way he ran—the method he used—to reach people for Christ. Verse 22 in The Living Bible puts it this way, *Yes, I try to find common ground with everyone so that I might bring them to Christ.*

Paul didn't run aimlessly. And like Paul, you have to find a point to relate to people so that you can build a bridge over which the gospel can come.

I encourage you today to find a common area of interest, a common ground, to relate to people in order to share Christ with them.

Day 226

Character Counts

So far we have learned about the first three "Cs" of soul winning in the last few devotionals. Today let me share the fourth "C"—*character*. 1 Corinthians 9:24-27, particularly verse 27, tells us the importance of character in witnessing to others,

> *Do you not know that those who run in a race all run, but one receives the prize? Run in such a way that you may obtain it. And everyone who competes for the prize is temperate in all things. Now they do it to obtain a perishable crown, but we for an imperishable crown. Therefore I run thus: not with uncertainty. Thus I fight: not as one who beats the air. But I discipline my body and bring it into subjection, lest, when I have preached to others, I myself should become disqualified.*

Paul said he was temperate in all things, that he disciplined his body. He would bring it into subjection, meaning he had problems keeping his body in subjection, just like you and I do.

Every one of us has a propensity toward certain sins. It is important, though, that we rein in our flesh and that we are temperate in all things because our lifestyle affects our message.

Take just a moment and do the following exercise. Imagine you are an employer. If you wanted to hire an efficient, competent, trustworthy employee, would you hire yourself at your present salary?

Or let's say that you were going to have to spend the rest of your life with someone just like you. Would you look forward to it as a great opportunity and privilege? Or not?

If your character is out of whack, people are going to have a hard time hearing what you have to say. Character counts!

Day 227

The Comforter

Today we are going to look at the fifth "C" of soul winning, and that is the *Comforter.* Many times when Jesus spoke of the Holy Spirit, He referred to Him as the Comforter.

In Acts 1:4-5, after the resurrection, Jesus said something to the disciples that was very intriguing,

> *And being assembled together with them, He commanded them not to depart from Jerusalem, but to wait for the Promise of the Father, "which," He said, "you have heard from Me; for John truly baptized with water, but you shall be baptized with the Holy Spirit not many days from now."*

He had already told them to go into all the world, but then He said, "Hey, you need to wait for something. There's some equipment you need before you go. Don't go start a Bible study, don't go pass out a tract, don't do anything. You need something first. You need to be baptized with the Spirit."

Then look at what He said in verse 8,

> *"But you shall receive power when the Holy Spirit has come upon you; and you shall be witnesses to Me in Jerusalem, and in all Judea and Samaria, and to the end of the earth."*

The Holy Spirit gives us power to be a witness. There is something beyond even living a life of integrity. There is a supernatural, captivating element when a person is filled with the Holy Spirit that makes the witness of the gospel even more inescapable.

Jesus was so strong on it He said, "Look, don't leave Jerusalem without it." God has given us His Holy Spirit, the Comforter, to empower us to reach our generation for Christ.

Day 228

Convicting and Convincing

In yesterday's devotional, we talked about the fifth "C" of soul winning—the *Comforter*, which is the Holy Spirit. The Holy Spirit is such an important part in witnessing I want to take you to another passage today to help you understand His role more clearly.

The passage is John 16:7-9. Here Jesus is talking to the disciples about the coming of the Holy Spirit, the Comforter,

> *"Nevertheless I tell you the truth. It is to your advantage that I go away; for if I do not go away, the Helper will not come to you; but if I depart, I will send Him to you. And when He has come He will convict the world of sin, and of righteousness, and of judgment: of sin, because they do not believe in Me."*

Jesus is not telling us that we need to pray, "Holy Spirit, go convict this person." Rather, the foundation from which He is speaking is found in John 14. In that passage He says, "When the Holy Spirit comes, He will no longer just be with you, but He will be in you."

In the following verses, He then talks about all the things the Holy Spirit does within us. And here, when He talks about the Holy Spirit convicting people of sin (and, as the Amplified Bible says, convicting and convincing the world of sin), He does that work when we engage them with the gospel.

When we talk to people about Christ, the Holy Spirit then goes to work.

I think about that little boy who told me about Jesus—a Spirit-filled 12-year-old. I had never heard the gospel in my life, yet there was something so captivating, so arresting about him, I could not get him out of my mind.

It was the power of the Holy Spirit working through him. And He wants to work through you as well.

Day 229

Wise Counsel

The sixth "C" of "The Seven Cs of Soul Winning" is *counsel*—the counsel of God. By that I mean the Word of God. It's important we learn to share the Word with people.

Our testimony is powerful and should be shared. But even though that may move people and influence people, folks need to know they are anchoring their trust in the promises of God. Not just in a feeling they have gotten, not just because they feel influenced and moved—even if that is by the Holy Spirit.

Why? Because feelings change. Our feelings can go up and down like a rollercoaster. You may be feeling God today, and tomorrow feel like He is nowhere around. Ever felt that way?

I have had days when I have woken up and not felt God at all, even though I had experienced a good time with Him the night before. In those times, if I would have gone by my feelings, I would have said, "God, You have deserted me this morning."

But I know He hasn't because God's Word makes it clear that He never leaves us nor forsakes us. When a person is saved, they need to be anchoring their faith on the promises of God, not on their feelings.

Promises like Romans 10:9-10,

> *That if you confess with your mouth the Lord Jesus and believe in your heart that God has raised Him from the dead, you will be saved. For with the heart one believes unto righteousness, and with the mouth confession is made unto salvation.*

So when we witness to people, we need to give them the counsel, the promises of the Word of God.

Day 230

The Coming Reward

Today brings an end to our consideration of "The Seven Cs of Soul Winning." The final "C" is the *coming reward*. Let me quote to you from Daniel 12:3, which says,

> *"Those who are wise shall shine like the brightness of the firmament, and those who turn many to righteousness like the stars forever and ever."*

There is a coming reward for those who turn people to righteousness.

The dearest thing to God's heart is winning humanity and bringing them into His family. Nothing is more important to God. He bankrupted heaven and gave His only begotten Son to save humanity.

The Bible teaches us that there will be a reward, my friend: authority in heaven, a place in heaven, honor in heaven. In addition to that, I want to hear, "Well done, good and faithful servant."

Someday there is going to be a joy and a fullness in heaven, but there are some who will not experience that level of joy.

The story is told that Cyrus, the king of Persia who had defeated Babylon and set the captive Jews at liberty, was walking through his garden one day with a visitor. The visitor was looking at all of the beautiful trees and shrubs and exclaimed how much pleasure the garden was giving him.

Cyrus said, "Not nearly the pleasure it gives to me for, you see, I have planted every one of these trees myself."

I think there is going to be something about being in heaven and seeing your fingerprints on people who are there because you shared, because you gave, and because you prayed. I believe there is going to be a greater joy for some because they did more for heaven while on earth than others.

There is a coming reward!

Day 231

Worry About Work

In 2 Corinthians 11:28, the apostle Paul says something very interesting,

Besides the other things, what comes upon me daily: my deep concern for all the churches.

You may be wondering, "Bayless, what does this have to do with my life?" Let me show you.

The phrase "deep concern" literally means anxiety and worry. And that phrase "to come upon" in the original language literally means "it conspires against me in order to overthrow me."

The apostle Paul's job was to oversee the churches that God had used him to establish, and in this verse he is confessing, "I daily have to battle with worry over these churches. How are they doing? Are they being misled by false prophets? Are they staying true to good doctrine?"

He was dealing with worry about those churches. Every day he grappled with that worry, and he had to throw it down.

It is easy for all of us to worry about our job. Some people, even though they are at home, never leave their job. They carry the burden around with them twenty-four hours a day, seven days a week.

They are always worrying about the job, even when they are home with their family. "How are things going at work? I wonder what they're saying. I wonder about the competition. What about sales? What about my job security? What's going to happen tomorrow?"

Consequently, when they get home from work, they are carrying this burden of work around with them, and they are robbing their family. Their own spiritual life is robbed, many times almost to the point of bankruptcy.

Do not let your family be robbed. Do not let your own personal and spiritual life be robbed because you carry the care of your job around with you. Instead, give it to God.

Day 232

An Original

1 Samuel 15:19 and 24 provide us with real insight into an area of anxiety for many people. One that may control your life today.

This is Samuel talking to Saul,

> *"Why then did you not obey the voice of the LORD? Why did you swoop down on the spoil, and do evil in the sight of the LORD?"*

Saul gives his answer in verse 24,

> *Then Saul said to Samuel, "I have sinned, for I have transgressed the commandment of the LORD and your words, because I feared the people and obeyed their voice."*

Hmmm! "I feared the people and obeyed their voice." Saul confessed that he was worried about what other people thought of him and what other people would say about him. As a result, he made a horrible decision that was counter to what God wanted.

Too many people, even good Christians, are eaten up with worry over what other people think and say about them. Let me tell you, the worst place to have your peace is in somebody else's head. As Proverbs 29:25 says, *The fear of man brings a snare.*

Saul is a perfect example. He never fulfilled his destiny, he never fulfilled his purpose in life, because he was too worried about what people thought about him even though God chose him to be king.

Someone wisely said this:

> *"It is not what I think I am that molds me and drives me, and it is not what you think I am that molds me and drives me. It is what I think that you think I am that molds me and drives me."*

Is that your concern today? If so, let me give you some advice: Be yourself. You were created by God as an original, and it would be a shame if you died a copy.

Day 233

The Power of a Word

Proverbs 12:18 gives us some valuable advice,

> *There is one who speaks like the piercings of a sword, but the tongue of the wise promotes health.*

Have you ever known someone who was good at making cutting remarks? They spoke like the piercings of a sword?

Over twenty years ago I was at the house of some friends. We were all just kind of hanging out, and I made a comment to one of the brothers in the family. It was a clever little comment and was basically meant to take a jab at him.

A couple of the family members heard it and snickered and said, "Oh, way to go, Bayless! You got him!" But as soon as I said it, his countenance fell, and my heart just sank. While I looked for an opportunity to apologize to him that night, I didn't do it because he ended up leaving early.

I've regretted that comment ever since. I repented, and the blood of Jesus Christ cleansed me from that sin. But you know what? Those words were out, and I couldn't get them back.

Shortly after that night, he went feet first into a very destructive lifestyle involving his sexuality. I have to think that quite possibly my words pushed him away from God. It may have been that little jab of the sword that pushed him off the edge.

The New Testament says in Ephesians 4:29, *Let no corrupt word proceed out of your mouth, but what is good for necessary edification,* (or for building up) *that it may impart grace to the hearers.*

Are your words imparting grace to those that hear them? Are they building up? Or are they tearing down?

Day 234

No Fear

People tend to worry in these days about world events. In Matthew 24:6-7, Jesus tells us this,

> *"And you will hear of wars and rumors of wars. See that you are not troubled; for all these things must come to pass, but the end is not yet. For nation will rise against nation, and kingdom against kingdom. And there will be famines, pestilences, and earthquakes in various places."*

Jesus said, "When these things happen, don't be troubled. Don't worry. They must come to pass." Think about some of those things.

Earthquakes in various places. I have been told that around the world earthquakes are increasing both in frequency and in size. They are happening more and more, and they are getting worse and worse. It is a sign, my friend.

Jesus mentions pestilences—diseases without cures. Ring any bells? There are certain nations where it is reported that 50 percent of the population is infected with AIDS. It is rampant in many countries of the world. It is an incredible problem even in our own country.

Jesus points to famines. There is drought, which is causing famines, which is causing starvation around the world.

Then Jesus talks about wars, rumors of wars, nation against nation, kingdom against kingdom. You can't turn on the news without hearing about some terrorist attack. There are countries today aggressively pursuing nuclear capabilities. Nations are poised against one another.

The leaders of our nation and other nations make decisions that affect literally the whole world. It seems like the world is on fire! Things are hanging in the balance.

Our response? It should not be fear, but rather recognition that these things must come to pass before Christ returns!

Day 235

Could It Be Today?

In yesterday's devotional, we looked at Matthew 24 and some of the things people worry about today that are going on in our world—earthquakes, famine, pestilence, war, and rumors of war.

Now, it is easy to be concerned about these things, but earlier in that passage—in verse 3—we find out why we should not worry,

> *Now as He sat on the Mount of Olives, the disciples came to Him privately, saying, "Tell us, when will these things be? And what will be the sign of Your coming, and of the end of the age?"*

Jesus was answering the question about the signs of His return, and what will point to the end of the age. That is why He said, "When you see these things begin to come to pass, it is not time to start worrying."

It is time to lift up your head because He is coming soon! Hallelujah!

Think about it. When you open up the paper today and read about the things happening in the Middle East, it seems like Bible prophecy is being fulfilled almost on a weekly basis. What a time we are living in!

Beloved, Christ is going to return, and from the way things are shaping up, it is not far off at all. I want to live like He is coming back today, and I want to plan and work like He won't be back for a hundred years.

But it could be any day.

Jesus is coming soon. Are you ready to meet Him? Think about it. Are you living in a way that you know when Jesus Christ comes, you won't be ashamed at His coming? I pray you will be able to look up with a joyful face and heart and say, "Come, Lord Jesus, come quickly!"

Day 236

Guarding Your Ways

In Psalm 39:1, we are given an important warning,

I said, "I will guard my ways, lest I sin with my tongue; I will restrain my mouth with a muzzle, while the wicked are before me."

The Hebrew word translated *ways* in this passage literally means a well-trodden path. It paints the picture of a pathway that has been walked down so many times that a groove has been worn in that path.

The psalmist is drawing our attention to something that has been repeated again and again, a response that has been so often repeated that it has become engrained in our behavior—a habit.

You have probably heard the saying, "He's set in his ways," meaning it is not likely you are going to change the way a person acts in certain instances. The "ways" are habits, attitudes, and responses that aren't likely to change without a very powerful motivation or without some sort of an encounter with God.

I think virtually every habit we have, initially began with a thought. Sow a thought; reap an action. Sow an action; reap a habit. Sow a habit; reap a character. Sow a character; reap a destiny. It all goes back to a thought that perhaps should have been dealt with, but wasn't.

Take some time today to consider your thoughts. Are you giving way to thoughts that will lead to ungodly habits? If so, give those thoughts to God and ask Him to help you think the thoughts that will lead to godly habits.

Day 237

Uniquely You

Each of us possesses strengths which God has given us. Psalm 18:32 says,

It is God who arms me with strength.

And in Philippians 4:13,

I can do all things through Christ who strengthens me.

And King David said this in 1 Chronicles 29:12,

...in Your hand it is to make great and to give strength to all.

God gives us all strength, yet I believe there are specific things He gives each of us that make you and me strong individually. The book of Psalms says in 33:14-15, *From the place of His dwelling He looks on all the inhabitants of the earth; He fashions their hearts individually.* In the New Testament in 1 Corinthians 12:27 it says, *Now you are the body of Christ, and members individually.*

We are collectively the body of Christ, but God has wired us each differently. God has formed our hearts individually. He has put certain deposits in one person that may not be in another person. He has given one person a certain kind of strength that may not be another person's strength.

Here is what I am getting at. I believe there is something uniquely you that gives you strength and character and presence, something that makes you a person to be reckoned with, something that God has put in you. It is a foundation, a seat of strength that He wants to move through in order to influence and to bless others.

Rather than coveting someone else's unique giftings and strength, discover and develop your own. Remember, God *individually* fashioned you. There is something wonderfully unique about you, through which God wants to bring blessing to others.

Day 238

Promises, Promises

God has given us His promises because He wants to fulfill them. Be they promises of peace, restoration, healing, or for material supply, we must keep in mind that the Lord would not have made the promise if He did not want to do it.

Here are four thoughts to help you when it comes to experiencing the benefit of God's promises:

1. Find a promise from the Bible that covers your need. Faith begins here.
2. Consider the promises.

   Hebrews 10:23 says, *Let us hold fast the confession of our hope without wavering, for He who promised is faithful.*

   And Hebrews 11:11 *says, By faith Sarah herself also received strength to conceive seed, and she bore a child when she was past the age, because she judged Him faithful who had promised.*
3. Act on the promise, fulfilling all necessary conditions. God is not a respecter of persons, but He is a respecter of conditions.
4. Start thanking God and exercising patience.

   Hebrews 10:36 says, *For you have need of endurance, so that after you have done the will of God, you may receive the promise.*

   And Hebrews 6:12 says, *That you do not become sluggish, but imitate those who through faith and patience inherit the promises.*

If you will do these four things, you are on your way to experiencing the fulfillment of God's promises in your life.

Day 239

Builder and Protector

Psalm 127:1-2 says,

> *Unless the LORD builds the house, they labor in vain who build it; unless the LORD guards the city, the watchman stays awake in vain. It is vain for you to rise up early, to sit up late, to eat the bread of sorrows; for so He gives His beloved sleep.*

These verses have been favorites of mine for a long time.

If ever I am tempted to worry about the Church, I remember that it is His house and ultimately only He can build it. My efforts, by themselves, are in vain.

He is not only the builder of the Church, He is the protector of it as well. These truths take a lot of weight off of my shoulders and help me sleep well at night. And I believe that is the way God wants it.

Too many of God's children sit up late, worrying and eating the bread of sorrows. Whether you are a pastor or a business owner or a stay-at-home mom, learn the secret of casting your cares on God.

He is the builder and protector of your life, and He knows the battles you face. Trust Him today and sleep well tonight!

Day 240

God Can Build The Family

Earlier we have looked at Psalm 127:1-2 which says,

> *Unless the LORD builds the house, they labor in vain who build it; unless the LORD guards the city, the watchman stays awake in vain. It is vain for you to rise up early, to sit up late, to eat the bread of sorrows; for so He gives His beloved sleep.*

The Hebrew word for *house* in verse one can actually be translated family. That is one reason why the next few verses (3-5) read like this,

> *Behold, children are a heritage from the LORD, the fruit of the womb is a reward. Like arrows in the hand of a warrior, so are the children of one's youth. Happy is the man who has his quiver full of them; they shall not be ashamed, but shall speak with their enemies in the gate.*

If you have sat up late, worrying about your children or your family, you need to know that God can turn things around.

Trust Him to build and protect your family. Do your part, but look to Him for guidance and strength. And trust Him to do what you cannot do.

He can cause your "arrows" to be effective against the enemy instead of wounding your own heart.

May you be happy with your quiver of "arrows," and may God be glorified in your family.

Day 241

Tithing

In Matthew 23:23, Jesus speaks about the issue of tithing in this way,

> *"Woe to you, scribes and Pharisees, hypocrites! For you pay tithe of mint and anise and cummin, and have neglected the weightier matters of the law: justice and mercy and faith. These you ought to have done, without leaving the others undone."*

Jesus tells us, "*These you ought to have done, without leaving the others undone.*" Yes, they should tithe, but the things He lists are the most important issues.

While we will touch on these issues in later devotionals, I want to point out the fact that Jesus does say we should tithe.

The Living Bible paraphrase of this verse is helpful, "*For you tithe down to the last mint leaf in your garden, and ignore the important things—justice and mercy and faith. Yes, you should tithe, but you shouldn't leave the more important things undone.*"

You should tithe. The first ten percent of your income, or the first ten percent of the increase that God brings to you, is called a tithe. The Bible says in the last chapter of Leviticus that the tithe is holy, and it belongs to the Lord.

So you should tithe. That is very important. In fact, I believe it is the first step in getting God involved in your finances, and an important step in you getting control of your finances.

If you are not tithing, I want to encourage you to open your heart to God's Word in this area and consider the possibilities that He sets before you.

Day 242

Tithing Today?

In Malachi 3:10-11, God says:

> *"Bring all the tithes into the storehouse, that there may be food in My house, and try Me now in this," says the LORD of hosts, "If I will not open for you the windows of heaven and pour out for you such blessing that there will not be room enough to receive it. And I will rebuke the devourer for your sakes, so that he will not destroy the fruit of your ground, nor shall the vine fail to bear fruit for you in the field," says the LORD of hosts.*

Those are pretty amazing promises! God says when we bring the first tenth to Him, He will open the windows of heaven and pour out a blessing we cannot contain. He even invites us to test Him in this area! (As far as I know there is no other place in the Bible where God does that.)

Notice, too, that He says He will rebuke the devourer. While this was written to an agrarian society whose prosperity was measured in vineyards, crops, and their livestock, you can transpose this principle right into the era in which we live. God will still bless us, and He will still rebuke the devourer for our sakes.

Years ago, in a small church in Mexico, a friend of mine was teaching on tithing. A poor man in the church got angry and stormed out. Later that day, he read the verses from Malachi again and decided to put God to the test. "Could God fulfill His promise—even in my circumstance?" he thought.

That poor villager later testified—interrupting a service and demanding that tithing needed to be taught again—"because these people need it!" He told how he had been blessed like never before since he started giving one-tenth of his earnings to the church.

God is not limited by the circumstances that surround us. He can bless us no matter where we are if we will "try Him" and bring all the tithe into His storehouse.

Day 243

Robbing God—of What?

Malachi 3:8-9 gives us a sober warning:

> *"Will a man rob God? Yet you have robbed Me! But you say, 'In what way have we robbed You?' In tithes and offerings. You are cursed with a curse, for you have robbed Me, even this whole nation."*

Now if you think about this statement, you have to ask, "How do you rob God? I mean, really, what does that mean?"

There are two ways we rob God when we refuse to tithe:

1. We rob God of honor that is due Him. In Proverbs 3:9 it says to, ***Honor** the LORD with your possessions, and with the firstfruits of all your increase.* By giving God the first part of our income, we are honoring Him as being first in our lives. We demonstrate faith in His promise to supply our needs as well—and God is honored by our faith.
2. We rob God of the opportunity to bless us. In Malachi 3:10, God promises to bless us if we bring Him the first tenth of our income (the tithe).

The promise in Proverbs is that our barns will be filled with plenty if we will honor the Lord with our firstfruits (Proverbs 3:9-10).

He can bless us. He desires to bless us. Let us not rob Him of the opportunity to do so, nor of the honor that is due Him.

Day 244

What's Your Measure?

In Luke 6:38, Jesus said these words:

> *"Give, and it will be given to you: good measure, pressed down, shaken together, and running over will be put into your bosom. For with the same measure that you use, it will be measured back to you."*

That is a promise of Jesus that you can stake your life on. Give and what happens? It will be given to you good measure, pressed down, shaken together, and running over. Sounds like fun, doesn't it?!

But notice that He also added this, "*The same measure that you use, it will be measured back to you.*" If you take a serving spoon, and that is what you measure out your giving with, you will get an overflowing serving spoon. It comes back to you good measure, pressed down, shaken together, and overflowing from a serving spoon.

The measure you use is what is measured back to you. If you use a shovel, and that is what you measure it out with, that is how it comes back to you.

Wouldn't you rather have a good measure, pressed down, shaken together, running over shovel as opposed to a serving spoon? The measure you use, Jesus said, that is what is used to measure back to you.

I believe many people are using a teaspoon and yet they are praying, "God bless me. I have big needs." I am sure God is saying, "I'm doing all I can. You know, I'm pressing it down as much as I can press it down. It is running over. But a running over teaspoon is just not that much."

Are you using a teaspoon or a shovel? Whatever you use is what comes back multiplied, but it is only according to the measure you use.

Day 245

Giving to Get?

Any time I give, I expect a blessing to return. It is a law that we find in Scripture. It is a promise of Jesus.

But you know what? That is not my main motivation for giving. And that should not be our heart for giving. Jesus says in Luke 6:32-38,

> *"But if you love those who love you, what credit is that to you? For even sinners love those who love them. And if you do good to those who do good to you, what credit is that to you? For even sinners do the same. And if you lend to those from whom you hope to receive back, what credit is that to you? For even sinners lend to sinners to receive as much back. But love your enemies, do good, and lend, hoping for nothing in return; and your reward will be great, and you will be sons of the Most High. For He is kind to the unthankful and evil. Therefore be merciful, just as your Father also is merciful. Judge not, and you shall not be judged. Condemn not, and you shall not be condemned. Forgive, and you will be forgiven. Give, and it will be given to you."*

What is the heart of this whole thing? Jesus said, "Don't love just to get love back; don't do good just so that good might be done back to you; don't lend just hoping to get something back."

He makes it clear that if you do those things for the right motivation, it will come back to you. Your reward will be great.

Do not give with the motivation of just getting something back. Non-Christians have that motivation! How does that set you apart from them? Give out of a higher motivation.

Day 246

The Right Motivation

In yesterday's devotional, we saw how we should not give just to get. That should not be our sole motivation. So the question is, "What is the right motivation?"

All we need to do is look at what motivated God to give. It is found in John 3:16,

> *For God so loved the world that He gave His only begotten Son, that whoever believes in Him should not perish but have everlasting life.*

God so loved that He gave. And, yes, God certainly did reap a harvest when He gave His Son. He reaped a harvest of sons and daughters.

You should give out of love and devotion for God. Give because you do not want people to go into an eternity without God, because you love humanity, because you have mercy and compassion for broken, dying people.

That is the right motivation for giving. When you give with that motivation, your reward will be great. God will see that it comes back to you multiplied.

That is a far cry from what many emphasize when it comes to giving today. It appears to me that a lot of people, when they teach on giving, are just pushing people's greed buttons. It seems that the main motivation that some leaders are teaching for people to give is, "Hey, give because God will bless you." And there is no doubt that God blesses those who give. The Scriptural promises are clear.

But what about the weightier matters? Remember how Jesus rebuked the Jewish leadership in Matthew 23:23 because they, "*Neglected the weightier matters of the law: justice and mercy and faith*"?

God looks at the heart. Our hearts ought to be like that of our heavenly Father, who is merciful, kind, loving, and generous, even to the most thankless and evil among us. That is the right motivation.

Day 247

Where's Your Heart?

I want to have you read and think about Mark 12:41-44 today:

Now Jesus sat opposite the treasury and saw how the people put money into the treasury. And many who were rich put in much. Then one poor widow came and threw in two mites, which make a quadrans. So He called His disciples to Himself and said to them, "Assuredly, I say to you that this poor widow has put in more than all those who have given to the treasury; for they all put in out of their abundance, but she out of her poverty put in all that she had, her whole livelihood."

That is quite a picture, isn't it? Jesus sitting opposite the treasury, watching what people put in and how they put it in. I believe Jesus still watches during offering time. He watches how we give, what we give, and why we give. He said, "Where your treasure is, that is where your heart is also."

Notice He calls His disciples over and says, "This poor widow has put in more than everyone else." Why? Because He wanted them to understand that God measures your gift based on what you have.

Some people could give $1,000, and there is really no sacrifice at all. It never touches their life, never causes any kind of change of priorities. While for other people, $10 or $15 is a great sacrifice.

I believe some of the rich people Jesus points to in this passage were giving out of their abundance, but from heaven's viewpoint, they were putting it in with a teaspoon. But this little widow, who put in less than a penny, walked up with a shovelful—everything she had. It got heaven's attention.

Where is your heart when it comes to giving?

Day 248

Rich or Poor

It is interesting that Jesus, in our devotional yesterday, did not try to keep the widow from giving all she had. It is especially interesting considering what He said a little earlier in Mark 12:38-40,

> *Then He said to them in His teaching, "Beware of the scribes, who desire to go around in long robes, love greetings in the marketplaces, the best seats in the synagogues, and the best places at feasts, who devour widows' houses, and for a pretense make long prayers. These will receive greater condemnation."*

You can hear the protection of God for widows in the voice of Jesus. You can hear His concern, and you can hear the judgment of God on those who manipulate, abuse, and take advantage of defenseless people and widows.

Yet, right on the heels of saying that, this widow gave all she had, which means she probably didn't even have anything left to buy food for a meal that night. With her gift of less than one penny, she had nothing left. And yet, Jesus said she gave more than everybody else.

Jesus did not give the slightest indication that she shouldn't have given an offering. He didn't run after her and say, "Now wait a minute, Ma'am! You shouldn't be doing this. You're a widow. God doesn't want this." On the contrary, it seems that He commended her for it, even calling her gift to the attention of the disciples.

Why do you suppose this lady would have given like that—all she had? I reckon because of her love for God and her love for the work of God.

Which is what Jesus looks for when we give, whether we are rich or poor.

Day 249

The Core Motivation for Giving

I want to return one last time to Mark 12:41-44 and have you consider one final thought about giving,

> *Now Jesus sat opposite the treasury and saw how the people put money into the treasury. And many who were rich put in much. Then one poor widow came and threw in two mites, which make a quadrans. So He called His disciples to Himself and said to them, "Assuredly, I say to you that this poor widow has put in more than all those who have given to the treasury; for they all put in out of their abundance, but she out of her poverty put in all that she had, her whole livelihood."*

In Phillips' translation of these verses, it says that Jesus sat opposite the temple alms box. In other words, where people gave their gifts for the poor. This courtyard area, referred to as the treasury, actually contained thirteen trumpet-shaped receptacles for giving. Some of them were for specifically designated purposes, and one of them was for giving alms to the poor.

If the Phillips translation is right, it makes the story all the more amazing. This poor widow, with less than a penny, put it in to help the poor.

She gave it to touch the life of another. Which is why I hope you will give.

Heaven is too real, hell is too hot, eternity is too long, people are too lost, and life is just too short for us not to be actively engaged—through our giving as well as other means—in reaching people. The only thing we take to heaven with us are the precious souls we reach for Christ.

That ought to be the core motivation for us to give to God's work.

Day 250

The Right Word at the Right Time

Proverbs 15:23 contains a powerful truth,

> *A man has joy by the answer of his mouth, and a word spoken in due season, how good it is!*

Notice that this verse talks about not just a word spoken, but a word spoken in due season—at the proper time. How good it is!

It is critical for words of encouragement, words of comfort, words of counsel, words of wisdom, and even words of correction to be spoken in due season. Timing is just as important as content.

I read once about a lady who invited family and friends over for Thanksgiving dinner. When they received the invitation, they let her know that they were going to come. In fact, they were looking forward to the day.

She really put on quite a spread. She baked pies and bread; she cooked a turkey with all of the trimmings—an incredible meal. When the time came for her guests to arrive, she lit candles and put the finishing touches on decorating the house.

The only problem was, no one showed up.

Then she remembered the calendar she had picked up from a local business. On that calendar it said that Thanksgiving was on the 21st rather than on the last Thursday of the month as it normally is every year. At the time she thought it was strange, but she figured that they must have moved the holiday.

She had prepared her sumptuous banquet a week early! The content was great but the timing was not so great.

So it is with our words. They can be just the right words, perfect for the need of the person, but if not delivered at the right time, they can fall short.

Be sensitive to pick the right time to speak as well as the right words to say.

Day 251

A Word of Encouragement

I want you to look today at a passage of Scripture that helps guide us in what to say, who to say it to, and when and how to say it. Isaiah 50:4-5,

> *"The Lord GOD has given Me the tongue of the learned, that I should know how to speak a word in season to him who is weary. He awakens Me morning by morning, He awakens My ear to hear as the learned. The Lord GOD has opened My ear; and I was not rebellious, nor did I turn away."*

First, we need to be sensitive to the Holy Spirit. He will teach us how to speak a word in season to the person who is weary. As it says, "He will awaken our ear."

Jesus made it very clear in Matthew, chapter 10 verses 19-20, that the Holy Spirit is quite able to give us the right words to say at the right time. In Isaiah 51:16, God says, "*I have put My words in your mouth.*" In Isaiah 57:19, He says, "*I create the fruit of the lips.*"

Chances are there is someone in your world today who needs to be given a word of encouragement. The key is being sensitive and available. Sometimes we are so embroiled in our own struggles that we don't even give a thought to the fact that there may be someone around us who needs encouragement...a coworker, a neighbor, your spouse, your child.

I personally think our children need to be given encouragement every day. Like the little boy said, "Daddy, let's play darts. I'll throw, and you say 'Wonderful!'" Children crave affirmation and encouragement.

There is someone who you either have contact with now, or you will have contact with, who needs encouragement. And you are God's messenger.

Day 252

For Just a Little While

Today's Scripture will start with the very last word of 1 Peter 1:4, just so you know who it is talking about, and go through verse 7,

> *...you, who are kept by the power of God through faith for salvation ready to be revealed in the last time. In this you greatly rejoice, though now for a little while, if need be, you have been grieved by various trials, that the genuineness of your faith, being much more precious than gold that perishes, though it is tested by fire, may be found to praise, honor, and glory at the revelation of Jesus Christ.*

Notice in verse 6 it says, *Though now for a little while, if need be, you have been grieved by various trials*. That phrase "a little while" literally means a season. The King James Version says, *Though now for a season, if need be, ye are in heaviness through manifold temptations.*

I like the phrase "a little while." That tells me the season is going to end. It is not forever. Every season ends. Winter ends. Spring ends. Summer ends. Fall ends. Every season has a beginning, and every season has an end.

If you are in a trial right now and feeling the weight of it, you are grieved because of it, I have good news. It will not be forever. Things are going to change. It may not seem like it, but that season will come to an end.

Even if you are not experiencing a trial today, I am confident you have gone through such a season, and it is likely that you will probably experience such a season again.

When you do, or if you are today, be encouraged. God's Word wants you—and me—to remember it is for just a little while.

Day 253

Keep Trusting

In the passage we looked at yesterday, Peter encouraged us to see the trials we face as temporary, something that only lasts for a while. I want you to read that passage again today, and then I want to point your attention to another truth that is vital to enduring through whatever trial you may be facing.

It says in 1 Peter 1:5-7,

> *Who are kept by the power of God through faith for salvation ready to be revealed in the last time. In this you greatly rejoice, though now for a little while, if need be, you have been grieved by various trials, that the genuineness of your faith, being much more precious than gold that perishes, though it is tested by fire, may be found to praise, honor, and glory at the revelation of Jesus Christ.*

One of the critical things you and I need to do when faced with trials is continue to trust God in the midst of those trials.

No matter how difficult, do not unplug your faith, even when things get rough. Keep trusting God and His promises. Why? Well, look at what verse 5 says: We are "kept by the power of God through faith."

When you keep your faith plugged in, you are then kept by God's power.

That word *keep* means to preserve. It means to protect, to guard. It is used elsewhere in Scripture of a garrison of soldiers protecting something. When you are going through a trial, God will protect you through His power when you trust Him.

That word *power* is the same word in the Bible translated miracle. I take it to mean this: When you or I are in a season of trial, if God has to work a miracle to keep us and protect us, He will do it.

Whatever your trial...keep trusting.

Day 254

Keep Laughing

I want to head back to 1 Peter 1:5-7 again today. Something tells me we could all continue to use the encouragement of Peter's words, especially the advice I want you to focus on today.

1 Peter 1:5-7,

> *Who are kept by the power of God through faith for salvation ready to be revealed in the last time. In this you greatly rejoice, though now for a little while, if need be, you have been grieved by various trials, that the genuineness of your faith, being much more precious than gold that perishes, though it is tested by fire, may be found to praise, honor, and glory at the revelation of Jesus Christ.*

Regardless of what you may be going through today, you need to rejoice. Peter says in verse 6, *In this you greatly rejoice, even if for a season you are experiencing various trials.*

Friend, keep your sense of humor. It will help you outlast your trials.

I read a story once about a guy parachuting when the wind blew him onto a track where they were racing cars...not a good place to land in a parachute. He was trying to get his parachute off when another gust of wind came and started dragging him face first down the track.

He finally got the parachute off and stood up only to see a car racing towards him. He quickly jumped out of the way and said to himself, "Man, I'm glad that's over!" and turned to get off the track. As he did, he stepped in a hole and twisted his ankle.

That was just too much! Even in his pain, he just started laughing!

Keep your sense of humor. Even if you are going through the roughest patch you have ever been through.

Do not let your trials rob you of your joy.

Day 255

Stop the Worry

Over the last few devotionals, we have been talking about trials and how we should respond. Today I have a simple but important word for you directly from God's Word: Don't worry.

1 Peter 5:6-7 tells us,

> *Therefore humble yourselves under the mighty hand of God, that He may exalt you in due time, casting all your care upon Him, for He cares for you.*

Jesus said, "Don't take an anxious thought for tomorrow. Sufficient for the day is the evil thereof." When we worry about tomorrow, we pull tomorrow's clouds over today's sunshine.

I have shared many times in my ministry about the incredible truth of Jesus' command, "*Do not worry about tomorrow.*" It is like we have this 24-hour fuse. We are wired up to deal with the stresses of life one day at a time.

If you worry about tomorrow today, you are putting a 48-hour load on a 24-hour fuse, and something is going to give somewhere.

Some people don't just worry about tomorrow, they worry about next week and next month. No wonder the fuse is blowing!

You see, what the mind cannot contain, it will impose upon the body. If your health is breaking down, worry may just be the problem. The Bible says to cast all of your care, the whole of your care, all your anxieties, on Him, once and for all.

Roll your burden on the Lord. The Bible says be anxious for nothing. And that means nothing. Do not worry about your children, do not worry about your money, do not worry about your future, do not worry about anything.

Your Heavenly Father does care for you, and it is His good pleasure to give you the Kingdom.

Day 256

Your Real Adversary

As we continue to think about the reality of trials in our lives, and the challenge it is to handle those trials, I want to point you to another important teaching about trials in today's devotional.

You need to realize who your adversary is. It is not God; it is the devil. Look at 1 Peter 5:8-9,

> *Be sober, be vigilant; because your adversary the devil walks about like a roaring lion, seeking whom he may devour. Resist him, steadfast in the faith, knowing that the same sufferings are experienced by your brotherhood in the world.*

Some of the trials and sufferings that we experience are the direct result of the adversary's work.

Some people want to blame God for everything, but the Bible says it is the thief—the devil—who comes to steal, kill, and destroy. Jesus came to give us life and more abundantly.

Peter makes this even clearer in verse 10,

> *But may the God of all grace, who called us to His eternal glory by Christ Jesus, after you have suffered a while, perfect, establish, strengthen, and settle you.*

Our God is the God of grace. The devil is seeking to devour.

Frankly, I hate the middle part of this verse, *After you have suffered for a while....* Clearly, God wants us to understand that suffering is going to happen. Trials are going to happen. No matter how much you may say, "I don't receive it!", it is still there! You are going to go through difficult times. It is part of the human experience.

But when you go through that time of trial, remember not to blame God. It is the devil who is your adversary!

Day 257

The Path to Maturity

1 Peter 5:10 provides a very critical principle for those times when we are going through trials, a principle that is easy to miss,

> *But may the God of all grace, who called us to His eternal glory by Christ Jesus, after you have suffered a while, perfect, establish, strengthen, and settle you.*

You need to realize that even though God did not initiate your trouble, He can still use it to work something good in you. What the devil means for evil, God can turn into something good.

Even though the devil's purpose is to destroy you, if you will respond correctly, God can work good things. Notice the verse says after you have suffered a short season, God will perfect. It brings maturity to you.

While we might hate it, how we respond in times of trial makes us who we are—and it fits us to accomplish God's will. I hate some of the things I have gone through! But you know what? I would not be who I am had I not experienced those things. It has fitted me to do the will of God.

And while it may not seem like it, your present difficulty may be instrumental in your future success.

It reminds me of the guy who was shipwrecked on a deserted island. One day he decided to go across the island for food. When he got to the other side he looked back and saw a plume of smoke in the sky. He ran back only to find that his shack burnt to the ground!

It stung him to the core! Except the next morning a ship arrived and rescued him. When he asked the sailors, "How'd you know I was here?" they said, "We saw your smoke signal."

Your present trials just may be fitting you for something you would never expect!

Day 258

Rich Blessings

Let me ask you a question. Do you believe God wants to bless you? You may say, "Yes," but in your heart do you really believe this to be true?

Take a moment to read Ezekiel 34:26,

> *"...I will cause showers to come down in their season; there shall be showers of blessing."*

I believe the Bible teaches us that just like there are seasons of trial, there are seasons of exceptional blessing that come from God. And those seasons of exceptional blessing should not be taken for granted. We should capitalize on them and seize the momentum when those seasons come.

Don't get me wrong. God is good all the time, and He is good to all. His tender mercies are over all His works. He causes His sun to rise on the good and on the evil, and He sends rain on the just and on the unjust. The fact of the matter is, God is good even to people who are not good because it is His nature.

However, there are richer, more frequent blessings that come from the hand of God. And they come to those who do a particular thing.

Tomorrow I want you to look with me in the book of Galatians. As we look at these verses, we will find that though God is good to all, the richer and more frequent blessings come to those who do a particular thing. Together we will see what that thing is.

Today, I just want you to grasp the truth that God does want to bless your life in an extraordinary way.

Day 259

Sow Good...Reap Blessing

As I mentioned in yesterday's devotional, God wants to bless your life, and the richer, more frequent blessings come to those who do a particular thing. We find that thing in Galatians 6:9-10,

> *And let us not grow weary while doing good, for in due season we shall reap if we do not lose heart. Therefore, as we have opportunity, let us do good to all, especially to those who are of the household of faith.*

The seasons of blessing come due more often to those who consistently sow, to those who seize opportunities that are afforded them to do good. Notice again in verse 9, *Let us not grow weary while doing good.* Verse 10 says, *Therefore, as we have opportunity, let us do good to all.*

This same truth is reinforced by verse 7, which states,

> *Do not be deceived, God is not mocked; for whatever a man sows, that he will also reap.*

If we sow good, we will reap good. A season of blessing will come.

What many Christians tend to do is stand before a field in which they planted no seed, and pray, "God, give me a miracle harvest."

Now, God is God, and He certainly can do things out of the ordinary. But He also works according to laws and principles that He has set into motion. One of those laws is the law of sowing and reaping.

Whatever a man sows, that shall he also reap. Therefore, do not grow weary while doing good. In due season, you will reap, if you do not faint. When you have opportunity, do good. Get some seed in the ground.

Because the richer and more frequent blessings come to those who sow good.

Day 260

Real Treasure

Proverbs 15:6 says:

> *In the house of the righteous there is much treasure, but in the revenue of the wicked is trouble.*

Notice that this verse does not just declare there is treasure in the house of the righteous. It says there is *much* treasure in the house of the righteous.

You can also find treasure in the house of the wicked, but Solomon says it is laced with trouble. The income of the wicked has a bunch of trouble with it.

But the same is not true for those who are right with God. When the treasure is found in their house, it does not have the same trouble that it does when it is found in the house of the wicked.

If you read on, the Lord shares two things that must accompany this treasure if it is going to be enjoyed. First, you must have a right relationship with God. Proverbs 15:16 says, *Better is a little with the fear of the LORD, than great treasure with trouble.*

It is better to have almost nothing and have a right relationship with God than to have everything money can buy and not have a relationship with God. We must get our priorities right.

The second thing we need to have is a right relationship with people, lest the treasure become hollow and become a curse. Proverbs 15:17 says, *Better is a dinner of herbs where love is, than a fatted calf with hatred.*

Some people have more prosperity than they know what to do with, but all of their relationships fail. They do not have love. Consequently, there is a vacuum they can never fill with things, that they can never fill by accumulating more possessions.

Pursue your relationship with God, and a right relationship with people. Then you will enjoy the treasure God gives you!

Day 261

Overrated

We read in Proverbs 23:4:

> *Do not overwork to be rich; because of your own understanding, cease!*

First, I want you to notice that this verse does not say don't work. And it does not say don't work hard. It says don't overwork.

There are some people in God's family who are not led, they are driven. They are so focused on reaching their goals and achieving whatever level of success they are going after, that they are making a lot of sacrifices along the way.

But they are making the wrong sacrifices. They are sacrificing their marriage and they are sacrificing their relationship with their kids. Why? Because they overwork. And, friend, that is not healthy.

In fact, I would say that overworking is as unhealthy as not working. You miss out on the grand things in life, the important things in life. With some people, even their relationship with God gets squeezed out because they overwork.

You need to be motivated; you need to work hard; but you don't want to overdo it to the point that you don't have time for your children. You don't want to work so hard that you don't have time for your spouse. And you don't want to so overwork that you don't have time for your God.

You are missing life if you are just after possessions, and you are sacrificing the more important things along the way.

How does your work life measure up today? Are you overworking at the expense of your marriage, your family, and your relationship with God? If so, determine today to get your life back in balance.

Overworking is overrated!

Day 262

Only Temporary

In our last devotional, we looked at Proverbs 23:4. Today I want us to look at the next verse. I will bet you can relate to it. Verse 5 says,

> *Will you set your eyes on that which is not? For riches certainly make themselves wings; they fly away like an eagle toward heaven.*

Does it ever seem to you that your money has wings? That it just flies off more quickly than you would have ever imagined?!

Money can be very temporary, very transitory in nature. Proverbs 27:24 reinforces that truth when it tells us,

> *For riches are not forever, nor does a crown endure to all generations.*

You need to understand that wealth is temporary just like our time here is temporary. What are the implications for how we live our lives? As believers, it is so important for us to have a pilgrim mindset and realize that we are just passing through.

This world is not our home. This life is a vapor that appears for a little time and then vanishes away. If you begin to think that somehow things are permanent, and you plan as if it is all permanent, you are going to get off course in your life with God.

Moses is a great example of someone who made a choice to live life with the right priorities. You can read about it in Hebrews 11. In that chapter, Moses chose to suffer affliction with the people of God rather than to enjoy all the riches of Egypt.

Moses had everything at his fingertips, but he made the right choice. He said, "You know what? There are more important things. My priorities are different than this." And his lifestyle changed pretty radically in a hurry.

But looking back, it's obvious that Moses made the right choice, isn't it? If he had chosen the temporary over the eternal, we wouldn't even know his name today.

Day 263

Untrustworthy

Proverbs 11:28 uncovers a powerful truth,

> *He who trusts in his riches will fall, but the righteous will flourish like foliage.*

Solomon is giving us an important warning: He who trusts in his riches will fall. Why does he tell us this? Because it is our natural tendency, when prosperity comes, to trust in that prosperity and to have that become our source of security.

As Psalm 62:10 says, *If riches increase, do not set your heart upon them.* There is a tendency in every human heart to do just that, and that is why God warns us. If the blessing comes, if prosperity comes, if you achieve a degree of success, do not set your heart on the wealth.

Instead, make sure your trust remains in God because riches are not trustworthy. In fact, if you trust in your wealth, you will fall!

The New Testament echoes this same truth in 1 Timothy 6:17. In this passage, Paul is writing to his son in the faith, Timothy. He is giving him some instructions to pass along to other believers,

> *Command those who are rich in this present age not to be haughty, nor to trust in uncertain riches but in the living God, who gives us richly all things to enjoy.*

Like Solomon, Paul is warning us that riches are uncertain. Do not put your trust in them. Instead, make sure your trust is in God. If riches increase, do not set your heart on them. And I like the last part. He said to put your trust in God, *Who gives us richly all things to enjoy.*

Where is your trust today? Are you trusting in your money and wealth? Or is the object of your trust God? I hope you will answer honestly. If you find yourself trusting in riches, just remember, they are untrustworthy!

Day 264

Guilt-Free Prosperity

Yesterday's devotional showed us how money, riches, and wealth are untrustworthy. So the natural question is, "Is wealth a bad thing?"

Let's go back to 1 Timothy 6:17-19 for our answer,

> *Command those who are rich in this present age not to be haughty, nor to trust in uncertain riches but in the living God, who gives us richly all things to enjoy. Let them do good, that they be rich in good works, ready to give, willing to share, storing up for themselves a good foundation for the time to come, that they may lay hold on eternal life.*

I believe God makes it clear that if you are in a position where He has blessed you, you should enjoy it. And do it guilt-free. If you can take the whole family on a 30-day vacation to Europe, go for it.

Just make sure you pay your tithes first. Make sure you are generous to the work of God, but enjoy what God gives you. It is a gift of God to be able to enjoy the fruit of the work of your hands.

God is all for us enjoying whatever measure of prosperity we have. He just wants us to be generous in proportion to our prosperity. He wants us to be ready and willing to give big. To be sowing extravagantly into the gospel and thereby laying up treasure in heaven.

The point is this: Do not just live with your eye on this world. Rather, live with your eye on the world to come. If you do, you will truly be able to enjoy the wealth God gives you.

Day 265

It's All About Him

I want us to look again at the last two verses from our last devotional, 1 Timothy 6:18-19,

> *Let them do good, that they be rich in good works, ready to give, willing to share, storing up for themselves a good foundation for the time to come, that they may lay hold on eternal life.*

I think it is beautiful the way verse 19 ends, *...that they may lay hold on eternal life.* Paul is writing to believers here, and he is not saying they must do this so that they can get saved.

Rather, I think he is saying that when they are *rich in good works, ready to give, willing to share*, then they will lay hold on what eternal life is all about. It is not about the things you possess; it is not about the blessings God gives you. It is about a relationship with Him. Jesus said in John 17:3, "*This is eternal life, that they may know You, the only true God, and Jesus Christ whom You have sent.*"

If you are blessed, realize the main thing is not your riches and wealth. They can be very transitory.

I have a friend who, years ago, migrated from a country in Central America that had experienced a military coup. Her family was quite well off, having property and wealth that had been passed down through several generations.

But after the coup, the new government seized all of the family's properties and wealth. All was lost overnight.

This story could have turned out badly except that this woman is an exceptional Christian with a great attitude. She has built a successful life here in the U.S. and has chosen not to be bitter or resentful over the past. She has kept her trust in God, realizing that no matter what happens if she still has Him, she will be alright.

Friend, keep your eyes on God and keep your trust anchored in Him. He is what life—real life—eternal life is all about!

Day 266

His Stuff

You have probably noticed that over the last few days of devotionals, we have been focusing on material blessings and how we should view those blessings.

1 Chronicles 29:14-16 is very helpful to see God's perspective,

> *"But who am I, and who are my people, that we should be able to offer so willingly as this? For all things come from You, and of Your own we have given You. For we are aliens and pilgrims before You, as were all our fathers; our days on earth are as a shadow, and without hope. O LORD our God, all this abundance that we have prepared to build You a house for Your holy name is from Your hand, and is all Your own."*

In these verses, King David is actually talking to the Lord as an offering is being received, and resources are being collected for the building of the temple (something his son Solomon is going to achieve).

We see that David recognized that everything he had, everything the people had, literally belonged to God. They were just giving God back something that belonged to Him in the first place.

I am going to let you in on a little secret: You and I are just stewards, and one day the Owner will call us into account for how we handled His stuff. Every one of us will give an account for our stewardship of *His* possessions.

While He gives us richly all things to enjoy, He is going to ask you if you did what He told you to do with His stuff. It is not our stuff.

Material treasure is a stewardship, and we must do what the Owner wants with it. This means we have a responsibility to be listening for the Owner's voice and following His instructions with His goods.

Day 267

Spiritual Treasure

In 2 Corinthians 4:7, Paul tells us,

But we have this treasure in earthen vessels, that the excellence of the power may be of God and not of us.

If you look at this chapter, Paul helps us understand that this treasure is ministry, the gospel, the Word of God, and the light and the glory of God, God's presence.

Paul wants us to understand that God has placed in us an incredible spiritual treasure...a treasure residing in these earthen vessels...our bodies. The treasure is in you and me!

But that treasure needs to be poured out.

I can't help but think that Paul was thinking of two particular earthen vessels that were used in his day. One was the vessel of mercy and the other the vessel of honor.

One place you would find the vessel of honor was around the home. People would use the water to wash their feet after traveling the dusty roads before they would enter your house, or they would use the water to quench their thirst. Like the vessel of honor, we are to wash the feet of our family, to humbly serve them and to help quench their thirst for more of God.

The vessel of mercy looked identical to the vessel of honor, but it was located in public places like the town square, so that any traveler coming through that arid land would be guaranteed to find a fresh drink of water. It was placed where the needs were. We need to take mercy where mercy is needed most—out onto the highways of humanity.

You are an earthen vessel filled with His spiritual treasure, so start pouring it out—in your home and out where the people are.

Day 268

You're Not Stuck

1 Corinthians 10:13 says,

> *No temptation has overtaken you except such as is common to man; but God is faithful, who will not allow you to be tempted beyond what you are able, but with the temptation will also make the way of escape, that you may be able to bear it.*

The word *temptation* in this verse also means test or trial. With that in mind, here are a couple of thoughts to encourage you today.

1. Whatever test, trial, or temptation you are facing today, it is "common to man." That means that you are not the only one who has gone through whatever you are facing.
   It is comforting to know that others have faced similar problems before us and made it through!
2. God makes a way of escape with the trial or temptation. That means you're not stuck! Before your difficulty ever arose, God designed a way of escape. And that means of escape comes *with* the problem.

So if you find yourself embroiled in trials, tests, or temptations today, start looking for God's way of escape—it exists. Trust Him to guide you safely through and out of your difficulties!

Day 269

Agreeing With God's Word

When the twelve spies returned from searching the Promised Land, they said, "*We are not able to go up against the people, for they are stronger than we*" (Numbers 13:31).

That was the report they brought back—at least ten of them that is. The other two, Joshua and Caleb, had this to say,

> *"Only do not rebel against the LORD, nor fear the people of the land, for they are our bread; their protection has departed from them, and the LORD is with us. Do not fear them"* (Numbers 14:9).

They all saw the same things in the land of Canaan, but only Joshua and Caleb chose to agree with God. The Lord had previously told them that He would give them victory and that they would be able to drive out the inhabitants of the land.

The ten spies (along with all Israel) died without ever possessing what God had promised. Only two men from that generation entered into Canaan and possessed the land. I think you can guess who they were—Joshua and Caleb. The only two who agreed with the declarations of God.

Check out what you have been saying. Do your words agree with God or not?

Day 270

Unlikely Vessels

1 Corinthians 1:26-29 says,

> *For you see your calling, brethren, that not many wise according to the flesh, not many mighty, not many noble, are called. But God has chosen the foolish things of the world to put to shame the wise, and God has chosen the weak things of the world to put to shame the things which are mighty; and the base things of the world and the things which are despised God has chosen, and the things which are not, to bring to nothing the things that are, that no flesh should glory in His presence.*

God delights in calling and using those the world passes by and counts as nothing. One old preacher said, "God isn't looking for golden vessels, God isn't looking for silver vessels, God is looking for yielded vessels." I think that is true.

It is amazing what God can do through someone's life who doesn't have to have the credit.

You may feel like you do not have much to offer. If that is the case, then you are perfect! When God does great things through you, then He will get the credit. People will know it was Him and not you!

God is looking for yielded vessels that He can use in a dynamic, community-altering way.

Why not say today, "Here I am Lord, use me;" and after praying that simple prayer, get ready. God may bring some amazing opportunities your way to step out and be used for His glory.

Day 271

The Road to Perfect and Complete

I want us to focus our attention today on James 1:2-4,

> *My brethren, count it all joy when you fall into various trials, knowing that the testing of your faith produces patience. But let patience have its perfect work, that you may be perfect and complete, lacking nothing.*

What I want to look at today is how God seeks to bring us to maturity by building patience into our lives. If there is one thing I have learned in my Christian walk, it is that *God is not in as much of a hurry as I am!*

Now, what is patience? Patience is the long-lasting quality of your faith. If you let go of your patience, your faith falls to the floor.

The end result God is looking for is *that you may be perfect and complete, lacking nothing*. The word *perfect* here means mature. God is developing maturity in us by working on our patience.

I have a dear friend who has a great church. They endeavored to build another building on their property and it ended up being a major undertaking. In fact, it turned out to be the most difficult thing he had ever done. I mean, it took a strip out of his hide.

Eventually it got built, but you know what my friend says about it? He says, "You see that building? I didn't build that building. It built me."

Going through those trials, facing those difficulties, having his faith tested, having to trust God when it seemed like there was a lack of finances, having to hold onto God's Word when he was a laughing stock with some people, all of that built character in him as he stood the test.

I have a question for you: Has anything been building you lately? If so, rejoice, because God is working maturity in you!

Day 272

It Will All Work Out

Ephesians 1:11 is a powerful verse with a vital lesson,

> *In Him also we have obtained an inheritance, being predestined according to the purpose of Him who works all things according to the counsel of His will.*

Over the 30 years of my Christian life, I have come to have great confidence in God's ability to work things out. No matter what is going on or how obscured my understanding of a situation is, I believe God is always working things according to His great sovereign plan.

It is as if there is this giant tapestry that God is weaving, and my life is a part of it. I sometimes get caught up with the temporal things and the stuff that is happening, but God reminds me, "Hey, nothing is taking Me by surprise. I'm weaving all of these things into this great pattern. Your mistakes, the stuff that happens to you, it is all going to turn out alright!"

Has it ever occurred to you that nothing occurs to God? The thing you are embroiled in right now did not take God by surprise. He did not look at your situation and say, "Oh no! I didn't figure on that! Gabriel, do you have any suggestions? What are we going to do?"

I know that sometimes in my microscopic view of things I have said, "Lord, such and such has got to happen." And God has replied, "Well, you don't have the big picture." Then, as time went on, God pulled the camera back, and I got the wide view, and I realized God was up to something very cool—totally apart from what I thought "had to happen."

Whatever your situation, you can rest assured that God has plans to work things out. God is working all things after the counsel of His own will. So relax! Even if your present circumstances have totally taken you by surprise, God saw it coming and made provision far ahead of time.

Day 273

The Remnant

Today, I want you to read Romans 11:2-5,

> *God has not cast away His people whom He foreknew. Or do you not know what the Scripture says of Elijah, how he pleads with God against Israel, saying, "LORD, they have killed Your prophets and torn down Your altars, and I alone am left, and they seek my life"? But what does the divine response say to him? "I have reserved for Myself seven thousand men who have not bowed the knee to Baal." Even so then, at this present time there is a remnant according to the election of grace.*

When Elijah pleads with God, he is physically, mentally, and spiritually exhausted. Jezebel is after his head and he has run into the wilderness. He is sitting down under a tree, and he is crying to God, "I'm the only one. Nobody else is serving You."

But God says, "Hey, wait a minute, Tiger. I have seven thousand more who haven't bowed their knee to the false idol. You're not the only one."

God is saying, "I have a remnant." And then Paul brings it right into present day, and says, "Just like God had a remnant then, God has a remnant today."

A remnant is a small group that has remained. That is where the word *remnant* comes from. It comes from the root "to remain." God always has a remnant. A remnant that remains faithful, committed, on course, obedient to God. That does not get discouraged, quit, or give up because of life's many turns.

Life has its share of setbacks and unexpected turns, and many people give up because of those setbacks. But those who stay on course and remain faithful will experience God's richer blessings.

God blesses all of His children. But those who stay the course are rewarded for their faithfulness.

So stay on track, hold course, stay steady, and remain faithful. Be a part of the remnant.

Day 274

Not There Yet

In Philippians 3:12-13, Paul gives us an important insight into becoming complete or mature in Christ,

> *Not that I have already attained, or am already perfected (or complete); but I press on, that I may lay hold of that for which Christ Jesus has also laid hold of me. Brethren, I do not count myself to have apprehended; but one thing I do, forgetting those things which are behind and reaching forward to those things which are ahead.*

As believers, we must realize that we have a way to go. We have not arrived. There are still some things ahead. We still must press on.

But some people have the idea they have arrived. They don't need to grow anymore; they don't need to study anymore; they don't need to increase anymore.

It is like the true story of a young neighbor who was talking to Albert Einstein at a dinner party. She asked, "What is it exactly that you do as a profession?" Einstein looked at her and said, "I've devoted myself to the study of physics." And in shock she replied, "Studying physics at your age? I finished my studies a year ago!"

Unfortunately, that is the attitude many Christians have today about their spiritual growth. They think they have finished. Instead, our attitude should be like 95-year-old Pablo Casals, considered to be the greatest cellist that the world has ever known.

A young reporter asked him one day, "You're 95. The world considers you to be its greatest cellist; and still, at 95, you practice six hours a day. Why?" To which he responded, "Because I think I'm making progress."

Friend, you have not arrived. Set your goal to be making progress every day. That is how you will become mature in Christ.

Day 275

Prayers and Preaching

Yesterday we talked about how progressing towards spiritual maturity is a process that will never end in this life. There are two things I want to focus your attention on today that will help you in that effort.

The first is found in Colossians 4:12,

> *Epaphras, who is one of you, a bondservant of Christ, greets you, always laboring fervently for you in prayers, that you may stand perfect and complete in all the will of God.*

If you are going to be complete or mature in Christ, you need the prayers of others. In the long haul, I am convinced none of us make it across the finish line without the prayers of other Christians.

The second is found in Colossians 1:27-28,

> *...Christ in you, the hope of glory. Him we preach, warning every man and teaching every man in all wisdom, that we may present every man perfect in Christ Jesus.*

In addition to the prayers of others, you need to be under good preaching and teaching to become complete in Christ. Preaching promotes change while teaching promotes growth, and you need both of them.

Looking back at my Christian life, I can still remember messages that literally shook my world and changed me. I remember one in particular when I had been saved less than a month.

Some new Christian friends took me to hear an evangelist preach. I was blessed so I decided to go back the next night. That night I heard a message that changed my life. It was a message on the parable of the sower, and that night I fell in love with the Word of God. It absolutely shaped me.

To become mature in your faith, make sure you are under solid biblical preaching and teaching, and develop the prayer habit as well as soliciting the prayers of others.

Day 276

Bearing One Another's Burdens

In Galatians 6:1-2, Paul admonishes us,

> *Brethren, if a man is overtaken in any trespass, you who are spiritual restore such a one in a spirit of gentleness, considering yourself lest you also be tempted. Bear one another's burdens, and so fulfill the law of Christ.*

We need to bear one another's burdens. Paul, in this passage, gives us some keen insight into what that looks like.

First, the word *overtaken* means to be taken by surprise, to suddenly fall into. In other words, the sin Paul is referring to is not a premeditated sin, but rather a temptation that suddenly came up, the person stumbled in, and now they are having trouble getting out.

Notice Paul also says, "If you're spiritual, restore that one." The word *restore* actually brings with it the thought of setting a dislocated limb. The role of the spiritually mature person is to skillfully and gently relocate the "limb" that has been knocked out of its socket.

I think this happens most often to baby Christians. They are suddenly invaded, they give in to some temptation, and they feel awful. Then the devil goes to work on them, "Some Christian you are! You hypocrite! You better never go back to church again! You're so wicked. You're probably not even saved."

They do not know how to pull themselves out, and you and I need to help them get back in right relationship with God and the Church.

I had a friend who dislocated a shoulder one time. It took him 45 minutes to work it back in by himself. It would have been easier to have someone help him.

And, that is true for us as Christians. We need to be there to help restore that brother or sister whose spiritual life has been dislocated.

Day 277

God's GPS

Hebrews 13:20-21 are two verses that give me great encouragement,

> *Now may the God of peace who brought up our Lord Jesus from the dead, that great Shepherd of the sheep, through the blood of the everlasting covenant, make you complete in every good work to do His will, working in you what is well pleasing in His sight, through Jesus Christ, to whom be glory forever and ever. Amen.*

These verses teach us that God is working in us all the time to bring us to maturity—our destiny in Christ.

A friend of mine shared a brilliant illustration of this one time. He likened God's guidance to that of the Global Positioning System (GPS), one of those systems they now have in cars that guides you to your destination.

A GPS system uses a satellite to give an aerial view, and its sole function is to get you to your destination, your "destiny."

As you travel to your destination, you have a map on the screen, and this little annoying voice talking to you through the whole trip, "Left turn a quarter mile ahead; left turn 150 feet ahead; left turn 50 feet ahead."

If you miss your turn, it immediately computes a new course for you so you can get back to where you are supposed to be. And if you mess up on those directions, it then computes another new course.

In the same way, God has a destiny for us to fulfill, something that fits into His great master plan. By His grace, He is guiding us all the way, even when we get off track. God just readjusts and says, "This is the next thing you need to do to get back into My plan."

Through His "GPS," He is always working to get us where we need to be. Praise God!

Day 278

An Encouraging Word

A while back I ran into a woman who I hadn't seen in quite some time. Being my friendly self I said, "Hi!"

The moment I said that she replied, "Oh, Bayless!" and proceeded to open her purse and pull out a letter I had written to encourage her three years earlier. She said, "I take this with me everywhere I go."

I wanted to cry! I mean, I was touched. But then I thought, "Is there no one else who comforts you? Is there no one else who speaks encouraging words into your life?" And I wonder the same about you.

Are you needing some encouragement today? I don't know what you may be faced with, but I personally find comfort and encouragement in the following passage. It is 1 Thessalonians 5:9-11,

> *For God did not appoint us to wrath, but to obtain salvation through our Lord Jesus Christ, who died for us, that whether we wake or sleep, we should live together with Him. Therefore comfort each other and edify one another, just as you also are doing.*

Think about this for a moment. As you look into eternity, which is what ultimately matters, you and I are not appointed to wrath! That is good news! That is great news! That is encouraging news! And that is great comfort!

God is storing up wrath against the ungodly. But, just like in ancient Egypt when the death angel passed over every home where the blood of the Lamb was, I thank God the wrath of God passes over us!

It is being stored up, but not for me or for you. As believers in Jesus Christ, we have escaped the wrath of God.

Thank you, Jesus!

Day 279

Forever With Him

1 Thessalonians 4:16-18 gives us powerful prophetic words,

> *For the Lord Himself will descend from heaven with a shout, with the voice of an archangel, and with the trumpet of God. And the dead in Christ will rise first. Then we who are alive and remain shall be caught up together with them in the clouds to meet the Lord in the air. And thus we shall always be with the Lord. Therefore comfort one another with these words.*

Jesus Christ will return, and the Church will be caught away! We will meet the Lord in the clouds and in a moment, in the twinkling of an eye, we will be changed. From that moment on, we will always be with the Lord.

Maybe you are going through a rough patch right now. If so, let me remind you that this earthly life is a vapor that appears for a little time and then vanishes away. But we have eternity in store. Thank God we will ever be with the Lord!

If He tarries and we die before He returns, we get to go to heaven. But I have a feeling, with the way things are shaping up, that we will be the generation that sees His return.

Have you noticed how the eyes of the world are on the Middle East? This is all end times stuff. Also, one of the things that Jesus said would be a precursor to the end is that the gospel of the Kingdom would be preached to every nation, literally, to every language group.

And you know what? That will be completed in our generation.

So keep your eyes fixed on His return, and that day you will meet Him in the air and be with Him forever!

Day 280

Exceedingly Great and Precious Promises

2 Peter 1:2-4 says,

> *Grace and peace be multiplied to you in the knowledge of God and of Jesus our Lord, as His divine power has given to us all things that pertain to life and godliness, through the knowledge of Him who called us by glory and virtue, by which have been given to us exceedingly great and precious promises, that through these you may be partakers of the divine nature, having escaped the corruption that is in the world through lust.*

I want to draw your attention to verse 4 where the Scripture states that through the promises we partake of God's nature.

The promise is the connector, it is the pipeline through which God's nature flows to us.

"What is God's nature?" you might ask. It is the answer to everything you need! His nature is life, it is health, it is peace, it is wisdom, it is abundance. There is an answer in God's nature for every one of mankind's needs.

That is why the promises are called "exceedingly great and precious." Without a promise, there is no pipeline. Without a promise, we cannot partake.

But when you take a promise—an exceedingly great and precious promise—and act upon it in faith, God's nature is released into your situation.

Thank God for His promises!

Day 281

Stay the Course

Jeremiah 23:3-4 says,

> *"But I will gather the remnant of My flock out of all countries where I have driven them, and bring them back to their folds; and they shall be fruitful and increase. I will set up shepherds over them who will feed them; and they shall fear no more, nor be dismayed, nor shall they be lacking," says the LORD.*

As we discovered in one of our earlier devotionals, God gives richer blessings to these who remain faithful (the remnant). A good question to ask is, "What are the blessings for those who remain faithful?"

Jeremiah gives us a good clue,

- They will have no fear.
- They will lack for nothing.
- They will be fruitful.
- They will increase.

Are you interested in increasing? In fruitfulness? In not being afraid? God says those are things that happen to the remnant. These are the rich blessings you will receive if you stay faithful, committed, and obedient.

I once read a story about an old member of the Brooklyn Dodgers, a pitcher named Harry Hartman. In 1918, he was called up from the minors to pitch against the Pittsburgh Pirates. It was his dream come true! On his first pitch, the batter hit a single. No big deal.

The next batter hit a triple. Harry walked the next guy on four consecutive pitches. The next batter hit a single. Harry Hartman walked off the mound, went into the locker room, showered, put on his street clothes, went to a local naval recruiting office, and enlisted. The next day he was in uniform and was never seen again in professional baseball. He got discouraged and quit.

No matter what, do not give up! Remain faithful, because God promises great blessings to those who stay the course.

Day 282

Liberty!

Look at Isaiah 30:21,

> *Your ears shall hear a word behind you, saying, "This is the way, walk in it," whenever you turn to the right hand or whenever you turn to the left.*

The idea this verse is conveying is that if you get off course with God, He is going to let you know you are making a wrong decision or a wrong turn.

The Living Bible puts it this way, *And if you leave God's paths and go astray, you will hear a voice behind you say, "Not this way. Walk here."*

What I have come to realize is that you and I have far greater liberty within the parameters of God's will than I previously thought.

It is important that you stay open and keep things laid out before God. But I have discovered, as I said, that we have far greater liberty than I previously thought. Let me give you an example.

Not long ago, my wife and I were very seriously considering selling our house and moving. Real estate had gone up so much that the equity in our house had more than doubled since we bought it. So we got to thinking that it might be a good time for us to move.

I did not have a word from God about moving. But I just know God well enough to know that I could make a decision like that. If I was getting into an area where we were going to make a mistake, God would let me know!

Some people get so uptight about everything. But as long as you stay open to God, you can make those kinds of decisions, because He will be there to direct you if indeed you are making a mistake.

That is true liberty!

Day 283

Amazed

1 Corinthians 8:2 is a short verse, but one that has come to have real meaning in my life,

And if anyone thinks that he knows anything, he knows nothing yet as he ought to know.

Here is what this verse has come to mean to me: The more I realize of God, the more I realize how little I know of God.

It is almost as if God is represented by this enormous mountain, and it is shrouded in fog. As the fog retreats, I can see how vast this mountain is and how little I have really seen, how little I have explored, how little I have experienced. I am in awe as I look at this enormous mountain.

I once thought, "I'm really mature in God. I've learned so much. Look at these gems I've dug out! And I've experienced this, and I've climbed here, and I've looked from the heights." Then the fog began to roll away, and I realized I hadn't even gotten out of the foothills yet.

God just really amazes me.

Think about God. He merely spoke and created the universe. I read an article not too long ago where scientists now think that perhaps there is not just a "universe" but there is really a "multiverse," or multiple universes.

Whether it is one that spans millions of light years, or multiple universes spanning even greater distances, God made it all just by saying something.

And that is what I mean. The more I learn of God, the more I am amazed at just how little I really know of Him. I hope you too will be amazed, and let that wonder and amazement bring you into the worship of our great and awesome God!

Day 284

God's Priority

In Matthew 28:18-20, we have the top priority on God's list,

> *And Jesus came and spoke to them, saying, "All authority has been given to Me in heaven and on earth. Go therefore and make disciples of all the nations, baptizing them in the name of the Father and of the Son and of the Holy Spirit, teaching them to observe all things that I have commanded you; and lo, I am with you always, even to the end of the age." Amen.*

Just imagine after the Resurrection that an angel comes up to Jesus and says, "Jesus, this is wonderful! You have paid the price for mankind's sin. What are You going to do to let the whole world know that they can be saved and they won't have to perish and spend an eternity without God? What is Your plan? How are You going to do it?"

And Jesus replies by saying, "Well, My few disciples are going to tell people, who in turn will tell other people, who are going to tell other people, who are going to tell other people."

Puzzled, the angel then asks, "Well, do You have a backup plan?" And Jesus says, "No." Still confused, the angel asks, "Well, no offense, Lord, but what if they fail?" Jesus replies by saying, "I have confidence in them."

My friend, there is no Plan B. God has no backup plan. You and I are it! We are Plan A! The problem is too many Christians today do not have God's priority as their priority.

Over the next few devotionals, I am going to share with you what I call the five "P"s of evangelism. I pray they will encourage you to actively share the Good News of our risen Savior!

Day 285

The Prerequisite of Prayer

In yesterday's devotional, I shared that God's priority is to see people come to know Him. Today, I want to give you the first of the five "P"s of evangelism, which I hope will encourage you as you seek to share your faith.

The Scripture is 1 Timothy 2:1-6,

> *Therefore I exhort first of all that supplications, prayers, intercessions, and giving of thanks be made for all men, for kings and all who are in authority, that we may lead a quiet and peaceable life in all godliness and reverence. For this is good and acceptable in the sight of God our Savior, who desires all men to be saved and to come to the knowledge of the truth. For there is one God and one Mediator between God and men, the Man Christ Jesus, who gave Himself a ransom for all, to be testified in due time.*

I want you to notice verse 4 in particular: God *desires all men to be saved and to come to the knowledge of the truth*. He wants them saved and discipled.

As Jesus said, "Go into all the world, preach the gospel to every creature, and make disciples of all nations." Those are our two main jobs. Proclaim the gospel to see people get saved, and then disciple them. God desires all men to be saved and come to the knowledge of the truth.

But did you notice that verse 1 preceded verse 4? Verse 1 says, *Supplications, prayers, intercessions, and giving of thanks be made for all men*. Verse 4 will not and cannot happen until verse 1 happens. First there is *prayer*, then comes sharing the plan of salvation.

We must first talk to God about men before we talk to men about God. We cannot be successful unless we talk to God about men first.

Day 286

Turning Desire into Prayer

I want to follow up yesterday's devotional by turning your attention to something I believe is very profound. It is Romans 10:1, where Paul states,

> *Brethren, my heart's desire and prayer to God for Israel is that they may be saved.*

It is important to pray that people be saved. In fact, I want you to notice how Paul turned his desire into a prayer.

I think if I were to ask any believer, "Do you desire your family to be saved?" they would say yes. Or, "Do you desire your friends to be saved?" they would answer yes. Or, "Do you desire your coworkers to be saved?" they would reply yes.

Well, that is great. That is to be commended, but it is not enough. Your desire must be turned into a prayer. It is not enough just to have a desire that they be saved. That desire has to translate into prayer. Prayer that they may be saved.

It's all right to pray generally, but it is better to pray specifically. I encourage you to make a list of every unsaved person in your life. Start with the network of relationships that already exist in your life. Make a list of family members, friends, and associates who are not saved, and then do your best to pray for the people on that list every day.

Most Christians genuinely desire for folks to be saved, but not all Christians pray for the salvation of people that they love. And even fewer pray for the salvation of folks that they work with.

Turn your desire for the unsaved people in your life to be saved into prayer for their salvation. And start today.

Day 287

How to Pray for the Unsaved

In the last two devotionals, I have stressed the importance of praying for the unsaved people in our lives to be saved. Today, I want to give you four ways you can pray for them:

1. Pray for openness and understanding. Acts 16:14 says the Lord opened the heart of Lydia to heed the things spoken by Paul. Paul was speaking the gospel. And if the Lord can open Lydia's heart, He can open your Aunt Mildred's heart.
2. Pray that God would send laborers to them. In Luke 10:2 Jesus said, "*The harvest truly is great, but the laborers are few; therefore pray the Lord of the harvest to send out laborers into His harvest.*" I am confident that God will answer any prayer He has commanded us to pray, and this prayer is not a suggestion. Jesus commanded us to pray that God would send out laborers into the harvest.
3. Pray that God will visit them and reveal Himself to them. I do not know of a specific promise in the Bible where it says God is going to visit someone in a dream or give them a vision. But I do see in Scripture where God reveals Himself to people in such ways, like Saul of Tarsus, who, on the Damascus Road, had a vision of the Lord Jesus Christ and was saved.
4. Pray for personal direction and for personal opportunities to share. Jesus, in Luke 10:2 said, "*The harvest is great, laborers are few. Pray the Lord of the harvest to send forth laborers into His harvest.*" In the next verse Jesus said, "*Behold, I send you.*" You can become the answer to your own prayer!

So pray for the unsaved people in your life, and do not stop praying until they get saved.

Day 288

The Power of Your Presence

Jesus said in Matthew 5:16,

> *"Let your light so shine before men, that they may see your good works and glorify your Father in heaven."*

The way you let your light shine is just being yourself around people. Witness everywhere you go through your life, and use words, if necessary.

You can sow seeds just by showing people that you are real. Some people call it friendship evangelism: being a genuine friend, touchable, genuinely caring for people, just letting your light shine.

Jesus also said you are a city set on a hill. A city set on a hill cannot be hidden. Nobody lights a lamp and puts it under a basket. You and I are to live a life that brightly shines the gospel to the unsaved.

I read a story years ago about a guy who had his doorbell hooked up to a big buzzer in the back room. The buzzer was really loud. He wanted to change it and put a light there instead that would illuminate when somebody pushed the doorbell. So he rigged it up to do just that.

The problem was the light would barely illuminate. He could not figure out what was wrong, so he called an electrician friend. His friend looked at it and told him, "Oh, you don't understand. It takes more power to shine than it does to make noise."

That is very true. Jesus said, "Let your light shine." Without having to necessarily confront people, they will just notice something different about you. If you are walking with God, it is reflected in your attitude, your work ethic, and your countenance. It is a discernable difference that will lead some people to ask about your faith. You will be able to sow seeds just with your *presence*.

Day 289

The Power of Proclamation

In our last few devotionals, we have seen we are to pray for the unsaved and live lives that shine the gospel.

But there does come a time to speak up. Look at Romans 10:13-14,

> *For "whoever calls on the name of the LORD shall be saved." How then shall they call on Him in whom they have not believed? And how shall they believe in Him of whom they have not heard? And how shall they hear without a preacher?*

When the time does come to speak up, a lot of Christians are like arctic rivers: frozen at the mouth. But someone must tell the story!

Pray for the unsaved, let your light shine, and when the time comes, tell them the gospel story. Paul said in Romans 1:16, *I am not ashamed of the gospel of Christ, for it is the power of God to salvation for everyone who believes.*

Through just a simple *proclamation* of the message, many people, when they hear it, will believe and be saved. The reason for that is found in Romans 10:17,

> *So then faith comes by hearing, and hearing by the word of God.*

A proclamation of the message causes faith to arise in people's hearts. Just simply tell them the gospel story: Mankind was separated from God, Jesus paid the price for their sins, He was raised from the dead, and if you put your trust in Him, you can be saved.

As well as opening your mouth to share the Good News, you might consider writing letters to your friends to simply and clearly share the gospel. Incorporate your own story if you feel it would be helpful.

It is easy to share the gospel if you just remember three things: our rebellion, our ransom, and our response. With those three things, you can share the gospel with anyone.

Day 290

Persuasion

Acts 28:23-24 provides us a great example of the next "P" of evangelism,

> *So when they had appointed him a day, many came to him at his lodging, to whom he explained and solemnly testified of the kingdom of God, persuading them concerning Jesus from both the Law of Moses and the Prophets, from morning till evening. And some were persuaded by the things which were spoken, and some disbelieved.*

Some people are going to need to be *persuaded*, they are going to need more than proclamation, because they are honestly grappling with questions that need to be dealt with. Those questions are like roadblocks in front of them that will need to be removed so they can advance and embrace the gospel.

They may have questions like, "Well, why can't other religions save? Why does Jesus have to be the only way?" Or, "What's this deal about the Jews? Why did the Savior have to come from the Jews?" Or it may be, "What about people who don't hear? How could it be fair that they would perish?"

When people have questions like these, they are genuinely seeking answers, so give them biblical reasons. If you don't have an answer, tell them you don't know. Say, "You know what? That's a good question, and I don't know the answer. But I'm going to find one for you." Then go study your Bible and find the answer.

Or go to the Bible bookstore and find a book that deals with that subject. Or ask a Christian friend who knows more than you do and find an answer. Then go back to the person and give them an answer.

You will find that when you give people legitimate Scriptural answers, they will respond and often be saved.

Day 291

Power

In Acts 9:32-35, we are given the fifth and final "P" of evangelism, and that is *power*,

> *Now it came to pass, as Peter went through all parts of the country, that he also came down to the saints who dwelt in Lydda. There he found a certain man named Aeneas, who had been bedridden eight years and was paralyzed. And Peter said to him, "Aeneas, Jesus the Christ heals you. Arise and make your bed." Then he arose immediately. So all who dwelt at Lydda and Sharon saw him and turned to the Lord.*

Two entire cities turned to Christ because of one display of God's power! One man who had been paralyzed was healed by the Lord Jesus Christ, and two cities came to God.

We have the same gospel. It is the same Holy Spirit; we serve the same blessed Savior, Jesus Christ, who is the same yesterday, today, and forever. We have to pray that God will, if necessary, do the miraculous to save people.

Paul, writing in the book of Romans, says he fully preached the gospel with miracles, signs, and wonders. People will respond today just like they did then. But we need to be bold, step out, and pray for things to happen.

When I was living in Oregon, there was an Indian girl who was very sick and actually at the point of death. The doctors told her she was going to die. She came to a small meeting one night and the evangelist prayed for her. She was healed and then gave her life to Christ. As a result, her dad, a famous rodeo rider, got saved, and her mom was saved also. Then a large group of people from her tribe came to Christ as well.

Evangelism through power. We need to trust God for the supernatural.

Day 292

The Snare of Fear

Proverbs 29:25 tells us,

> *The fear of man brings a snare, but whoever trusts in the LORD shall be safe.*

A snare is a noose used for catching an animal. Fear will cause you to be snared or trapped, just like an animal.

I have a friend in the church who has a very large nut tree in his yard, which the squirrels regularly raid. He put this big net over the tree, but it did not seem to deter the squirrels at all. So he finally got a trap and set it up on the roof right next to the nut tree. To date, he has caught about 120 squirrels.

When the squirrel is in the trap, it is totally at his mercy. It can't go anywhere. He happens to be a fairly merciful gentleman, so he takes them over to a local park and lets them go.

When fear gets a hold of your life, you become like one of those trapped squirrels—you are not going anywhere. You are at its mercy. You will not progress spiritually. It keeps you bound. The fear of man can keep you from obeying God; it will keep you from pleasing God. It will keep you from the joy you would experience when you trust God.

In fact, there is a contrast in our verse today. The man or woman who is bound by the fear of man, will not be trusting God in some area of his life. Look at the two parts of the verse together: *The fear of man brings a snare, but...* in contrast *...whoever trusts in the Lord shall be safe.*

Do not allow the fear of man to control your life. Instead, trust in the Lord.

Day 293

Don't Lose Out

In 1 Samuel 15:18-19, 24-26, Samuel, the prophet, comes to King Saul, and this is what he says,

> *"Now the LORD sent you on a mission, and said, 'Go, and utterly destroy the sinners, the Amalekites, and fight against them until they are consumed.' Why then did you not obey the voice of the LORD? Why did you swoop down on the spoil, and do evil in the sight of the LORD?"...Then Saul said to Samuel, "I have sinned, for I have transgressed the commandment of the LORD and your words, because I feared the people and obeyed their voice. Now therefore, please pardon my sin, and return with me, that I may worship the LORD." But Samuel said to Saul, "I will not return with you, for you have rejected the word of the LORD, and the LORD has rejected you from being king over Israel."*

Saul disobeyed God and then lied about it, tried to cover it, and tried to shift the blame to the people. Did you notice that part? Why? Because he feared the people.

Because of the fear of man, Samuel said to him, "You have lost your place." Later on he says, "God has found a man better than you, a man after His own heart." And He chose David to replace Saul as the king of Israel.

I want you to think about this: God had promised Saul that his seed would sit on the throne, but it was a conditional promise God gave to him.

Saul lost out because of his disobedience caused by the fear of man, and so did his offspring! And David, a better man than Saul, ended up on the throne of Israel, through whom our Savior came.

If the fear of man can rob us of our destiny and affect our offspring, just think what faith in God can do!

Day 294

Not Ashamed

I have a question to ask you today. Has there ever been a time when you were afraid to confess the name of Jesus? In John 9:20-23, we have the example of the parents whose son had been born blind but was healed by Jesus.

Look at their response when asked who healed their son,

His parents answered them and said, "We know that this is our son, and that he was born blind; but by what means he now sees we do not know, or who opened his eyes we do not know. He is of age; ask him. He will speak for himself." His parents said these things because they feared the Jews, for the Jews had agreed already that if anyone confessed that He was Christ, he would be put out of the synagogue. Therefore his parents said, "He is of age; ask him."

How many Christians have held their tongue when they should have been giving praise to the name of Jesus? Praise for answered prayer, for the miracles He has done, but they were intimidated by unbelievers?

I was coming back from Africa when a Muslim man on the plane put a blanket on the floor, got down on his face and began to pray. This man was not ashamed at all about kneeling down on the plane in front of everyone.

I thought, "Oh, Jesus! How many times have Your people kept silent because they were afraid of what someone might think of them?"

Throw off the shackles of fear and timidity, and boldly take your stand for Christ!

Proverbs 28:1 says, *The wicked flee when no one pursues, but the righteous are bold as a lion.*

Day 295

No Worries

I trust that these words from Isaiah will encourage you today. Read carefully what God has to say,

> *"I, even I, am He who comforts you. Who are you that you should be afraid of a man who will die, and of the son of a man who will be made like grass? And you forget the LORD your Maker, who stretched out the heavens and laid the foundations of the earth; you have feared continually every day because of the fury of the oppressor, when he has prepared to destroy. And where is the fury of the oppressor?... But I am the LORD your God, who divided the sea whose waves roared—the LORD of hosts is His name"* (Isaiah 51:12-13 and 15).

God spans the heavens with the palm of His hand. The nations are as a drop in the bucket before Him. There is nothing too hard for Him, and nothing He cannot do.

A number of years ago, I had the chance to go elk hunting with a friend in Montana. We were lying outside under the stars, and I was unprepared for the glory I saw. I have never seen so many stars in my life! It took my breath away!

As we lay there, I said, "You know what? God spans the heavens with His hand, and you and I are worried about paying the rent!" It was just one of those moments. We both just cracked up at how ridiculous it was to worry when God was so big.

What are you worrying about today? Whatever it is, place it into God's hands. After all, His hand spans the entire universe!

Day 296

Your New Nature

As human beings, we are constantly confronted with opportunities to fear. People have fears concerning their health, their finances, terrorism, relationships, their jobs...the list is almost endless.

I want to challenge you with a thought today, and it is simply this: Realize who you are. If you are born again, you are a new creature in Christ Jesus, and it is not in your nature to be afraid.

Consider what the Bible says in 2 Timothy 1:7,

> *For God has not given us a spirit of fear, but of power and of love and of a sound mind.*

Which points to our problem with fear. We listen to our heads, and we listen to our flesh, rather than listening to our spirit. As a result, our lives can be overwhelmed with fear.

I want to challenge you today to listen to your spirit instead of your head. The real you on the inside is made after the image of God. Once you realize who you are and what you are made of, it will help deliver you from fear. Consider these verses that talk about the real you:

- Ephesians 4:24, *And that you put on the new man which was created according to God, in true righteousness and holiness.*
- 2 Corinthians 5:17, *Therefore, if anyone is in Christ, he is a new creation; old things have passed away; behold, all things have become new.*

When you understand your true nature, that you are made after the image of God, you will know freedom from fear.

Day 297

He Has Said, So We May Say

In our last few devotionals, we have been talking about fear, and how to be free from it. Today, I want to give you a final thought to consider on fear. It is based on Hebrews 13:5-6,

> *Let your conduct be without covetousness; be content with such things as you have. For He Himself has said, "I will never leave you nor forsake you." So we may boldly say: "The LORD is my helper; I will not fear. What can man do to me?"*

I want you to notice what the Bible says, *He Himself has said... So we may boldly say.* God says something, so you can say something.

What does God say? He says He will never leave you. He says He will never forsake you. As a result you can say, "The Lord is my helper; I will not fear. What can man do to me?"

When you understand that God will never leave you or forsake you, you can live without fear. And that freedom from fear will be reflected in both your actions and in your speech.

What are you facing today? Would you be afraid if God was standing beside you saying, "It's alright. I am here"? Well He is with you! He said He would **never** leave you or abandon you! You may not see or feel Him, but He is with you—now and always.

It is time to start acting and speaking like you believe it.

Boldly say, "The Lord is helping me! I will not fear!"

Day 298

Life's Proper Focus

Read Luke 12:16-21,

> *Then He spoke a parable to them, saying: "The ground of a certain rich man yielded plentifully. And he thought within himself, saying, 'What shall I do, since I have no room to store my crops?' So he said, 'I will do this: I will pull down my barns and build greater, and there I will store all my crops and my goods. And I will say to my soul, "Soul, you have many goods laid up for many years; take your ease; eat, drink, and be merry."' But God said to him, 'Fool! This night your soul will be required of you; then whose will those things be which you have provided?' So is he who lays up treasure for himself, and is not rich toward God."*

This parable really helps us bring life into the right perspective. The rich man in this story failed to do three things.

- He failed to realize that he was only a steward and not the owner of his goods.
- He failed to have an eternal perspective.
- He failed to consider how brief this earthly life can be.

How did he fail in these three areas? By not understanding just how short life is and where to place his focus.

He talked about building barns but instead he had a burial.

He said he had many years but God said "this night."

He thought he was wise, but God said he was a fool.

Let's learn from his mistakes and bring our life into proper focus.

Day 299

Who Made the Sun Shine?

Look again at Luke 12:16-21,

> *Then He spoke a parable to them, saying: "The ground of a certain rich man yielded plentifully. And he thought within himself, saying, 'What shall I do, since I have no room to store my crops?' So he said, 'I will do this: I will pull down my barns and build greater, and there I will store all my crops and my goods. And I will say to my soul, "Soul, you have many goods laid up for many years; take your ease; eat, drink, and be merry."' But God said to him, 'Fool! This night your soul will be required of you; then whose will those things be which you have provided?' So is he who lays up treasure for himself, and is not rich toward God."*

Take a look at the few words that this man spoke. In his short declaration, he uses the word *I* six times and the word *my* five times!

His perspective was a very selfish one.

Here are a few questions to ponder:

- Who gave the rain that made his crops grow?
- Who made the soil out of which his crops grew?
- Who made the seed he planted?
- Who caused the sun to shine?
- Who gave him the physical strength to work the field?
- Who gave him his soul?

The answer to all of those is God. Yet he makes no acknowledgement of God in his speech, planning, or giving. He should have been thanking God for all His blessings and asking the Lord what He wanted done with His things.

Be faithful to acknowledge God and to ask Him what to do with His resources over which you are a steward.

Day 300

It's All Mapped Out

One of the great truths revealed in Scripture is that the end is determined from the beginning. What I mean by that is God sees the end from the beginning. He already has a plan for you. He has already got the whole thing worked out.

Consider what God told Jeremiah in Jeremiah 1:5,

> *"Before I formed you in the womb I knew you; before you were born I sanctified you; I ordained you a prophet to the nations."*

Before Jeremiah was ever born, God had his destiny, a plan for his life, all worked out. That truth applies to you and me, and that helps me rest at night. It is great to know I do not have to figure this whole thing out. Sometimes we see through a glass darkly. But you know what? God sees everything perfectly.

This same truth is echoed in Ephesians 1:4,

> *Just as He chose us in Him before the foundation of the world, that we should be holy and without blame before Him in love.*

Did you know you were chosen before God laid the foundation for this world? That was a long time ago. God knew you before you ever existed. He knew you before the world was here. You were chosen in Him. You were not an accident. God knew you.

Again, this truth is affirmed in Ephesians 2:10,

> *For we are His workmanship, created in Christ Jesus for good works, which God prepared beforehand that we should walk in them.*

The *beforehand* is before the foundation of the world. Just like God knew you, He prepared specific good works for you that you should walk in them long before you ever came into existence.

He has your life mapped out. What a great comfort!

Day 301

Let God Do His Job

Philippians 2:8-11 shows us how humility precedes honor,

> *And being found in appearance as a man, He humbled Himself and became obedient to the point of death, even the death of the cross. Therefore God also has highly exalted Him and given Him the name which is above every name, that at the name of Jesus every knee should bow, of those in heaven, and of those on earth, and of those under the earth, and that every tongue should confess that Jesus Christ is Lord, to the glory of God the Father.*

If God's good pleasure and His plan are to be worked out in our lives, we must walk in humility. It is a prerequisite for us to pass the test of humility. As we see here, because Jesus humbled Himself, God highly exalted Him. And at that point, no demon in hell could do a thing to prevent it.

When God promotes you, no person, no demon, no ungodly system can hold you back. God's exalting power is irresistible. It is undeniable, and it is undefeatable.

But a humble heart must come first. It has been said that no man stands taller than when he is on his knees before God. Let us humble ourselves and be obedient to God in every area of our lives. If we will lower ourselves, God will lift us. God's job is to exalt us, and our job is to humble ourselves. If we try to do God's job for Him, He will have to do our job for us.

Day 302

Humpty Dumpty?

Proverbs 27:2 gives us very wise words of advice,

Let another man praise you, and not your own mouth.

There are so many people, including Christians, who think God cannot get along without them. They think they are the reason they experience so much success.

It has been said that a man wrapped up in himself makes a mighty small package.

When God grants you success and blesses you, you have to remain humble if you are going to retain your usefulness to God. The Scripture says pride goes before destruction and a haughty spirit before a fall.

There are plenty of men and women who at one time or another were on top, but today are on the bottom. I know examples inside and outside ministry. One story in particular comes to mind when I think of this principle.

There was a minister who once said, while making a plea for money, "No one is doing what we're doing throughout the world, and God needs us to carry on this work. The world cannot be reached without our ministry."

Granted, he was doing an incredible work in a lot of different countries. But the moment he said, "God can't get along without me," I thought of Humpty Dumpty. I just thought, "Oh, no! Oh, no! Oh, no!" I knew he was headed for a fall!

And you know what? That man is no longer in the position of prominence that he once was. And God seems to have gotten along fine without him.

Do not sing your own praises. Let others congratulate you if they will, but at the end of the day offer those praises to the One who really deserves it—the Lord.

Day 303

Faithfulness and Open Doors

In 1 Timothy 1:12 Paul writes,

And I thank Christ Jesus our Lord who has enabled me, because He counted me faithful, putting me into the ministry.

According to Paul, Jesus did three things. First, He enabled him, which means Jesus is the One who puts the gifting in you. He is the One who gives you talent. He is the One who gives you the ability.

Second, Paul says that Jesus counted him faithful. Apparently, Jesus is watching and He expects you and me to be faithful.

Third, Paul says that Jesus put him into the ministry. In other words, Jesus opens doors when we are faithful, doors that no man can shut. When the way seems blocked, Jesus can make a way where there is no way.

Here is the point. It is not enough just to be enabled. Some of the greatest, most gifted, and talented people in the world are living far, far below their potential. While the enablement is there, Jesus has not found them faithful yet, and so certain doors of opportunity remain shut.

Having the gifting is not enough. You need to have both the gifting and be faithful. When both are there, Jesus opens doors.

Recognize and develop the gifting God has given you, but focus on being faithful so that God can open doors in your life.

Here are a few other verses that also make it clear that faithfulness is the road between enablement and open doors,

A faithful man will abound with blessings, but he who hastens to be rich will not go unpunished (Proverbs 28:20).

"His lord said to him, 'Well done, good and faithful servant; you were faithful over a few things, I will make you ruler over many things. Enter into the joy of your lord'" (Matthew 25:21).

Day 304

Not in the Abundance of Things

Then one from the crowd said to Him, "Teacher, tell my brother to divide the inheritance with me." But He said to him, "Man, who made Me a judge or an arbitrator over you?" And He said to them, "Take heed and beware of covetousness, for one's life does not consist in the abundance of the things he possesses" (Luke 12:13-15).

Life is not about things and how much "stuff" you can accumulate. Your identity and value as a person should not be based on the abundance of your possessions.

If, however, your sense of value as a person is wrapped up in your things, what happens if you lose those things?

A relative of mine from a few generations back had all of his property confiscated by the government after the Civil War. He died a broken and bitter man. That is the end of someone whose identity and sense of worth are tied up in their things.

This man that came to Jesus to sort out his inheritance had the real treasure in front of him all the time, but he couldn't see it because "things" were in the way. The real treasure was his brother!

He was at odds with his brother. There was friction and tension between them over their inheritance. Apparently this man was willing to destroy his relationship with his brother for things!

Life does not consist in the abundance of things we possess, but in the riches of the relationships we have!

In tomorrow's devotional I want to share three relationships that make a person rich.

Day 305

Three Relationships that Make Us Rich

Then one from the crowd said to Him, "Teacher, tell my brother to divide the inheritance with me." But He said to him, "Man, who made Me a judge or an arbitrator over you?" And He said to them, "Take heed and beware of covetousness, for one's life does not consist in the abundance of the things he possesses" (Luke 12:13-15).

This man came to Jesus to get him to "sort his brother out" over the inheritance, not realizing that his brother was the real treasure in his life—not the things he might inherit.

Here are three relationships that make us rich:

1. Our relationship with God. To know God makes you rich, no matter what material resources you may or may not have. Some of those that the world would call rich are actually bankrupt when it comes to the most important treasure of all.
2. Our relationship with others. People, not things, are the real treasures in life. I can honestly say that I am a rich man. I have family and friends that I love and that love me. Things lose their meaning, and serve as a very poor substitute for relationships with people.
3. Our relationship with our own heart. *Commune with your own heart...* declares the psalmist in Psalm 4:4 (KJV). That means hold some serious communication with your heart—get acquainted with your heart. Don't let you and your own heart be strangers!

Day 306

Faithful to Another

Jesus, in Luke 16:12, makes a very interesting statement...one that provides a perspective on faithfulness you would not expect,

> *"And if you have not been faithful in what is another man's, who will give you what is your own?"*

Jesus makes it clear. You have to be faithful in something that is someone else's before He will fulfill your dream or open doors for you.

God gives each of us opportunities to help others. And He looks for us to faithfully help others before He blesses us. For example, Joseph had to help Pharaoh with his dream before God allowed Joseph's dream to come to pass.

Maybe you have a dream to be super rich for the purpose of spreading the gospel. You would like to see the gospel go around the world. Or you would like to pay off the debt on your church's building. Or you would like to fund a certain missions organization.

I think the Kingdom could use a multitude of very wealthy people who have a heart for the lost and a desire to see God's work succeed and expand.

But first you need to be faithful working for that person who has hired you. You have to be faithful in that which is another man's. God is not going to open a door for you to fulfill the dream you have if you do not show up for work on time, or if you do not put in a full day's work. Why would God open the door for you to lead your own successful business if you have not been faithful working for someone else?

You must serve that other person with all of your heart, or that other company you are working for first, before God will prosper you. It is a Kingdom principle.

Day 307

The Way Up May Be Down

It is not unusual for God's promotion to look like a demotion at first, to feel like you are going backward rather than forward.

There are a couple of great examples of this in the Bible. For instance, do you remember how Joseph in Genesis 37 dreamt he would one day rule over his brothers? That God was going to promote him to a place of prominence?

So what happened? His brothers threw him into a pit, he was sold to Midianite traders as a slave, and then he was put on the auction block and sold again in Egypt. On top of that, he ended up in prison on false charges and spent several years there, seemingly forgotten.

But without those experiences, Joseph would have never been ready to rule. Preparation comes before promotion. The way up may go down for awhile at first.

David is another example of how God will "demote" in order to promote. Do you remember in 1 Samuel 16:12-13 how David was anointed king while still just a shepherd?

> *Now he [David] was ruddy, with bright eyes, and good-looking. And the LORD said, "Arise, anoint him; for this is the one!" Then Samuel took the horn of oil and anointed him in the midst of his brothers; and the Spirit of the LORD came upon David from that day forward. So Samuel arose and went to Ramah.*

This is a pretty big promotion for a shepherd boy, don't you think? But for years, David lived a fugitive's life—moving from place to place, living in caves, being hunted. He was separated from everyone and all the things that he loved.

His promotion ended up looking more like a demotion, which is often the way God works. In the process of your promotion, He will take you through difficult times to prepare you for that promotion.

Just remember, the way up is often down.

Day 308

Preparation for Promotion

It is easy for us to be impatient with God's timeline of blessing, or to wonder why God is not prospering us as we think we should be.

In 1 Samuel 22:1-2, we are given a snapshot of how God prepared David, a little shepherd boy, to be king,

> *David therefore departed from there and escaped to the cave of Adullam. So when his brothers and all his father's house heard it, they went down there to him. And everyone who was in distress, everyone who was in debt, and everyone who was discontented gathered to him. So he became captain over them. And there were about four hundred men with him.*

Just think how David must have felt. God tells Him, "David, you're going to be Israel's next king!" but Saul is chasing him across the countryside and the people who are following him are all the outcasts, the people with problems, the people who are unhappy, the people who don't have any money.

On top of that, the next few verses of this passage talk about how David had to move his family to a foreign country just to keep them safe. Some promotion!

But you know what? Through it all David was learning how to trust God and how to manage people. His character was being tested. He was being fitted by God to wear the garments of a king: the garment of mercy, fairness, and wisdom, the shoes of decisiveness, the belt of strength, covered with a robe of gentleness.

The fullness of his promotion came in due season, and so will yours. David was not ready to be king when he walked out of the field as a young shepherd boy, so do not be surprised if you also need to be prepared for your promotion!

Day 309

At Just the Right Time

It is easy for us to get anxious when it seems like God is moving more slowly than we would like. But Scripture is clear, God's purposes have their appointed times. They are fulfilled in their season.

Ecclesiastes 3:1 says,

> *To everything there is a season, a time for every purpose under heaven.*

And there is 1 Peter 5:6-7, which says,

> *Therefore humble yourselves under the mighty hand of God, that He may exalt you in due time, casting all your care upon Him, for He cares for you.*

Humility and God's exalting of you are two things that are tied together. Perhaps you are feeling pretty frazzled, wondering, "God, when's it going to happen?" Just continue to cast your cares on Him. He will promote you in due time. Do not worry about it.

In fact, the phrase that says, *that He may exalt you in due time*, literally means "at the set time" or "at the time prearranged by God."

When your character has been shaped and molded enough, and when other events are ready and in their proper place, then God will promote and exalt you.

Think about Moses who had it in his heart to be a deliverer and a judge, but when he first acted on it he failed miserably. He was 40 years early! (See Acts 7:23-34). The Israelites were not ready to be delivered yet. God had to work at the other end of the line.

Remember, God may have put some things in your heart, but the timing may not be quite right. There may be some work He needs to do in your life, or there may be some other factors God is working on. Until those things come together, God will not push you into that position.

So, focus on being faithful and let God worry about just the right time.

Day 310

Attractive...or Unattractive?

Titus 2:9-10 says this,

• *Exhort bondservants to be obedient to their own masters, to be well pleasing in all things, not answering back, not pilfering, but showing all good fidelity, that they may adorn the doctrine of God our Savior in all things.*

Let's focus on that phrase at the end, *that they may adorn the doctrine of God our Savior in all things.* We adorn the gospel. We dress it up in clothes, as it were.

The New International Version says this, *And not to steal from them, but to show that they can be fully trusted, so that in every way they will make the teaching about God our Savior attractive.* We make the gospel attractive or unattractive.

I was returning from Europe one time when, just before they closed the door of the plane, a woman rushed in and sat next to me. She was wearing a baggy wool cap pulled down low, a pair of glasses sticking out from underneath the cap, a big baggy woolen sweater, and a bright orange sweat suit.

When we took off, I closed my eyes and took a little snooze. When I opened my eyes and looked at her, I was startled because there was this beautiful woman sitting next to me. I was really shocked.

She turned out to be an actress who, I guess, was traveling incognito. There was this amazing lady hidden under all this frumpy stuff. Sometimes we take this amazing gospel that we have, and we adorn it in such a way that it is unattractive.

We must be careful to make the gospel attractive. But in order to do that, I believe it is important to see how we make the gospel *unattractive* first.

Our next few devotionals will deal with that subject.

Day 311

Double Standard

I would like for you to read again the Scripture we read yesterday, Titus 2:9-10,

> *Exhort bondservants to be obedient to their own masters, to be well pleasing in all things, not answering back, not pilfering, but showing all good fidelity, that they may adorn the doctrine of God our Savior in all things.*

We make the gospel unattractive when we live contrary to our beliefs. The gospel becomes unsavory and unattractive to those outside the Church when our lives do not match up to what we say we believe.

Take the verses we read here. Paul says, in effect, that we make the gospel unsavory when we pilfer (which means stealing items of small value) or talk back to our boss.

You do not adorn the gospel when you show lack of respect for your boss, rip the company off, use the phones and computers at your job for personal business, take extra long lunch breaks, steal paper, take staplers, steal pens, or whatever you can get your hands on.

You should not dress the gospel in rags and then pass out tracts to all your coworkers or invite your boss to church.

This truth does not just apply to work. Do not live contrary to your beliefs anywhere. Do not live a double standard at home. If you do, it will turn your kids away from wanting to serve Christ. If you are into sports and you curse a lot, cheat, or have a bad temper, you dress the gospel in rags.

In 2 Corinthians 3:2 Paul states that, *You are our epistle written in our hearts, known and read by all men.*

The truth is, we are the only Bible some people will ever read. They are looking at our lives.

Day 312

Sour, Angry, and Negative

We are looking at how we make the gospel unattractive. I believe one of the main ways this occurs is when Christians are sour, angry and negative.

Some people live right but they always look like they have spent the night in a bottle of lemon juice.

If you struggle in this area, you need to listen carefully. Your salvation should be the source of great joy, and that joy and happiness should be expressed in your life in a dynamic way.

For example, Jesus said this in John 15:11,

> *"These things I have spoken to you, that My joy may remain in you, and that your joy may be full."*

And in John 16:22, He said,

> *"Your joy no one will take from you."*

In Romans 14:17, Paul said,

> *For the kingdom of God is not eating and drinking, but righteousness and peace and joy in the Holy Spirit.*

Finally, James 1:2 says,

> *Count it all joy when you fall into various trials.*

Joy is one of the hallmarks of the Kingdom of God. Even when we are going through a rough patch, the Bible says we are to be full of joy.

Joy makes the gospel attractive. If you put on a sour face all the time and you have a negative disposition, you will scare people away from church. You make the gospel seem like something people would never want.

Day 313

Remember

Titus 3:1-7 says,

> *Remind them to be subject to rulers and authorities, to obey, to be ready for every good work, to speak evil of no one, to be peaceable, gentle, showing all humility to all men. For we ourselves were also once foolish, disobedient, deceived, serving various lusts and pleasures, living in malice and envy, hateful and hating one another. But when the kindness and the love of God our Savior toward man appeared, not by works of righteousness which we have done, but according to His mercy He saved us, through the washing of regeneration and renewing of the Holy Spirit, whom He poured out on us abundantly through Jesus Christ our Savior, that having been justified by His grace we should become heirs according to the hope of eternal life.*

Paul tells us to remember where we have come from. Notice he said to show humility to all men and speak evil of no one. Why? Because we also used to be foolish and deceived and disobedient.

I thank God I am a new creation in Christ, but I still blush when I think about some of the stuff I got involved in before I was saved! Disobedient? Been there. Serving various lusts and pleasures? Up to my eyeballs! Plus all the other things Paul mentions in this passage and a few more!

It is amazing how people in the church forget what they were like before the grace of God came into their life. When that happens they tend to get very haughty and judgmental towards those still lost in their sin. A harsh, judgmental church that lacks humility while verbally lashing out at sinners is one of the ugliest garments you can dress the beautiful gospel in.

Day 314

What's Your Motive?

The Bible says in James 4:3,

> *You ask and do not receive, because you ask amiss, that you may spend it on your pleasures.*

James says that you ask, but you do not receive, because you ask amiss. The word *amiss* here comes from the Greek root word that means to harm or to injure. His point is: God will not grant you anything that is going to harm or injure your spiritual life, whether in the short term or in the long term.

When you pray, God is looking out for your best interests.

But then he also said, *You ask amiss that you may spend it on your pleasures*. The word *pleasures* has the idea of sensuality, which means, if I am asking for something just to stroke my fleshly ego, then I short-circuit the prayer by my wrong motivation.

For example, it is great to pray for a car. I live in Southern California where we need a car to get around. And I think God will give you a car that you like. After all, the Bible says He gives us richly all things to enjoy. Jesus said, "*Ask, that your joy might be full.*" So I think God wants us to be happy, and He generally has no problems granting your request for a car you would like.

Yet some people go a step beyond that, and their real motivation is, "Man, I want that car because I would look good in that car! If I came to work in that car, I would really show up so-and-so. People would think I'm pretty fine if I had that car. If I had that car, the chicks would dig me."

Be careful when you pray to not slip over into a motivation that is not really pure. Because you will short-circuit your faith and you will not receive an answer—except "no."

Day 315

Overcoming Barrenness

I Samuel 1:10-11 says,

> *And she was in bitterness of soul, and prayed to the LORD and wept in anguish. Then she made a vow and said, "O LORD of hosts, if You will indeed look on the affliction of Your maidservant and remember me, and not forget Your maidservant, but will give Your maidservant a male child, then I will give him to the LORD all the days of his life, and no razor shall come upon his head."*

These words are written about Hannah, who was barren. But God answered her prayer by giving her a son, and he became one of the most prominent figures in biblical history—Samuel.

Perhaps there is a "barrenness" in some area of your life, and like Hannah, who was tormented by her adversary—so it is with you. Prayer can change things. It did in Hannah's life, and it can in yours. But there are several things about Hannah's prayer that we need to consider:

1. Hannah's prayer was not casual. It was heartfelt and deep. Too much of our praying is "skin deep." Only prayers that originate from deep within us get God's attention. James 5:16 declares that *the effective, **fervent** prayer of a righteous man avails much.*
2. Hannah's prayer was specific. She asked for a male child. Too much of our praying is too general. Don't be afraid to be specific in your requests.
3. Hannah wanted the answer to her prayer to glorify God. Her boy would be dedicated to God's service. When our prayers take on the purpose of glorifying God, we have moved into a higher realm.

If you are experiencing a barrenness in any arena of life, pray. And let your prayers be heartfelt, specific, and for the glory of God.

Day 316

Power in Numbers

By Janet Conley

I believe the Bible teaches us that when we join together the impact is multiplied far beyond just the addition of those who join together. One plus one equals far more than two. Let me show you what I mean.

In Deuteronomy 32:30, it says,

> *How could one chase a thousand, and two put ten thousand to flight, unless their Rock had sold them, and the LORD had surrendered them?*

While this verse deals with Israel's disobedience to God and subsequent retreat from their enemies, think of what might be possible when God's people obey Him! It says that one could chase a thousand, but two could put ten thousand to flight.

While one person can impact a thousand, two people can impact ten thousand. That is a ten-fold multiplied effect!

Leviticus 26:7-8, when God was giving promises to His people if they would walk in His ways, states this,

> *You will chase your enemies, and they shall fall by the sword before you. Five of you shall chase a hundred, and a hundred of you shall put ten thousand to flight; your enemies shall fall by the sword before you.*

Notice God says five will chase a hundred, and a hundred will chase ten thousand. By increasing the number of people times 20, their effectiveness would increase times 100. Again, that is a multiplied effect.

You have probably heard of the Clydesdale horses, those big, strong workhorses that can pull a lot of weight. One horse by itself can pull two tons, but if you yoke two together they can pull 23 tons! That is incredible!

When we join our forces in prayer and connect with heaven, that is what happens. There is a multiplied effect.

Day 317

Unburdened

Philippians 4:6-7 promises,

> *Be anxious for nothing, but in everything by prayer and supplication, with thanksgiving, let your requests be made known to God; and the peace of God, which surpasses all understanding, will guard your hearts and minds through Christ Jesus.*

God is telling us not to freak out about anything. **Anything!** Can you think of anything that does not fit in "anything"? Instead of worrying—pray—about everything!

It is interesting that these verses do not promise God will answer your requests (though it is implied). Rather, what God does promise in these verses is this: If, when you are confronted with difficult things, you will pray rather than worry, God will give you peace. The stress will lift. The pressure will be broken.

In America, people spend millions of dollars visiting their therapists. They talk over all their problems with their therapists to try and relieve the stress and worries of life. I have a confession to make...I have a therapist. I talk to Him every single day. My therapist is my Father in heaven. I bring all my problems to Him. And I talk over everything with Him.

One of the keys in unburdening your heart when you pray is being completely honest. God knows what you are thinking, anyway. You may as well tell Him the truth about what is weighing you down.

It is no accident you are reading this today. Perhaps you are so filled with anxiety and stress that you are working on an ulcer right now. You don't sleep like you should. Your anxieties have robbed you of the quality of life God wants you to have.

God wants you free from your burdens. Take them to God today, and every day, and see how those burdens are lifted.

Day 318

Good...All the Time

John 10:10-11 gives us a great truth,

> *"The thief does not come except to steal, and to kill, and to destroy. I have come that they may have life, and that they may have it more abundantly. I am the good shepherd. The good shepherd gives His life for the sheep."*

Is your concept of God that He is good sometimes, but not all the time? That sometimes He is blessing you; but other times, He is the source of your troubles? If so, I want to put that notion out of your heart and mind today.

Jesus came to give us abundant life, while the devil, the thief, wants to steal, kill, and destroy. God is always a good God, and the devil is always a bad devil.

I remember, as a young Christian, I ran into another new convert in the park one day. He looked troubled, so I asked him what was up. He told me he was sick and had just received some bad news as well. Then he went on to tell me that he was at a Bible study the day before and they told him that God was doing all of these things to him.

It had shaken him to think that God was the source of his troubles, and that He was responsible for all the troubles in his life.

A lot of people tend to think that way, but it is just wrong. God is good all the time. The Bible says in James 1:17,

> *Every good gift and every perfect gift is from above, and comes down from the Father of lights, with whom there is no variation or shadow of turning.*

There is not the slightest degree of variation in this. God is good. And the gifts He gives are good and perfect gifts. I am glad they don't just stay in heaven. God sees to it that they make their way down to you and me.

God is good...all the time.

Day 319

Real Goodness

Romans 2:4 declares,

> *The goodness of God leads you to repentance.*

Ephesians 2:4-6 says,

> *But God, who is rich in mercy, because of His great love with which He loved us, even when we were dead in trespasses, made us alive together with Christ (by grace you have been saved), and raised us up together, and made us sit together in the heavenly places in Christ Jesus.*

God is not holding your sins against you. He sent His Son to pay a debt that had to be paid in order to liberate you from sin. God extends His mercy and forgiveness to you and me even when we do not deserve it.

It was His goodness that arrested my attention and that brought me to the foot of the cross, even when I was in my darkest sin, doing terrible things, abusing my body with drugs and alcohol, and doing things that should have put me in an early grave. In fact, a number of times I nearly died. But God loved me right in the middle of all of that.

I want to tell you, wherever you are right now, God loves you. You may be in the depths of the darkest sin you have ever been involved in, you just feel wretched, but God loves you right where you are.

He loves you so much He doesn't want to leave you there. His grace can reach you, change you and lift you out of any sin or situation if you will turn to Him with all of your heart.

There is no reason to fear or hesitate. Entrust yourself to the goodness of God and say yes to Him today.

Day 320

The First Step Toward Freedom

Now there is in Jerusalem by the Sheep Gate a pool, which is called in Hebrew, Bethesda, having five porches. In these lay a great multitude of sick people, blind, lame, paralyzed, waiting for the moving of the water. For an angel went down at a certain time into the pool and stirred up the water; then whoever stepped in first, after the stirring of the water, was made well of whatever disease he had. Now a certain man was there who had an infirmity thirty-eight years. When Jesus saw him lying there, and knew that he already had been in that condition a long time, He said to him, "Do you want to be made well?" (John 5:2-6).

Jesus asked this man a seemingly ridiculous question, "Do you want to be made well?" It's obvious, isn't it? He is at the pool, isn't he? The only reason people went there was to be healed. What kind of a question is that to be asking? Of course, he wanted to be healed.

But Jesus was not convinced. This man had been stuck in his condition for a long time. He was not only lying down on the outside, he was lying down on the inside.

Sometimes people get used to living in their problems. While they may outwardly be going through the motions to get free (generally because they know that is what is expected of them), inwardly they have given up.

The first step toward getting free from your problems and that which binds and restricts your life is wanting it—really wanting it.

You have to stand up on the inside before you can ever stand up on the outside.

Let me be very bold and ask you: Do you want to be made well? Do you really want things to change? Or have you grown accustomed to living under the devil's heel?

If you are tired of defeat, mediocrity and bondage, then stand up on the inside and say, "Enough is enough!"

It is the first step toward freedom.

Day 321

Stop Blaming and Rise Up

When Jesus saw him lying there, and knew that he already had been in that condition a long time, He said to him, "Do you want to be made well?" The sick man answered Him, "Sir, I have no man to put me into the pool when the water is stirred up; but while I am coming, another steps down before me" (John 5:6-7).

This guy was basically saying, "It's not my fault. I'm in this condition because of what someone else won't do *for* me, and because of what someone else has done *to* me."

Think about it, "I have no man to put me in." Paraphrased that says, "I'm stuck because of what someone won't do for me." Or, "While I'm coming, another steps down before me," which paraphrased says, "I'm stuck because of what someone else has done to me." Either way, "It is not my fault."

After making up our minds that we want to be free, the next step is to stop shifting the blame to others.

A friend of mine migrated from Mexico to the U.S. many years ago. He didn't understand the culture or the language and seemed to be hopelessly locked into a dead end job.

His employer took advantage of him and it seemed like he had no way out. But instead of blaming others for his situation (which would have been easy for him to do), he decided to get unstuck and do something with his life.

It took several years, but today he has several businesses and is quite wealthy.

Do not get caught in the trap of blaming others. Instead, make the decision to *rise up* (something we will be talking about in our next devotional.)

Day 322

Obey and Get Unstuck

Jesus said to him, "Rise, take up your bed and walk" (John 5:8).

These words were spoken to a man who had been sick for 38 years! His bed had been carrying him, and now Jesus was telling him to carry his bed!

We have discussed several keys to getting unstuck from our problems in our last devotions. First, we must genuinely want to be free, and second, we must stop shifting the blame for our problems to others.

The final key I want to share with you is found in the above verse. It is to obey what the Lord tells you. Whether it makes sense or not—obey!

To a man who had been carried by his bed for 38 years, rising up and carrying his bed must have seemed crazy! But the moment he began to obey, new life and strength began to flow into his previously paralyzed limbs.

Listen for the Lord's instructions in your heart. Search for them in His Word. There is no faith without action. There will be something that God will require you to do in order to release or express your faith.

It may make sense to you—or it may not. But to quote Mary, the mother of Jesus, "*Whatever He says to you, do it*" (John 2:5).

After pastoring the same church for several decades, I have observed that many people remain stuck in their problems. Not because the Lord hasn't spoken to them, but because He has and they haven't obeyed.

If there is any unfilled obedience in your life, get busy and do what the Lord has told you to do. It is the only way to get unstuck.

Day 323

Confounding the Wise

In 1 Corinthians 1:20, 27-29, the apostle Paul provides a very powerful word,

> *Where is the wise? Where is the scribe? Where is the disputer of this age? Has not God made foolish the wisdom of this world? But God has chosen the foolish things of the world to put to shame the wise, and God has chosen the weak things of the world to put to shame the things which are mighty; and the base things of the world and the things which are despised God has chosen, and the things which are not, to bring to nothing the things that are, that no flesh should glory in His presence.*

We are often enamored with what the world considers wise and mighty, but God isn't. In fact, He chooses things that are foolish and weak, things the world considers insignificant, and things the world even despises, to put to shame the things that people consider wise.

I really like the King James Version when it states that God does these things *to confound the wise.*

We need to understand that sometimes God turns human conventional wisdom on its head. And I believe Scripture shows us three ways in which He does that.

First, there are times that God turns conventional wisdom on its head with the people He chooses for His purposes. Second, He will confound human wisdom with the plans He unfolds. Whether they are for your deliverance, or plans to further His kingdom and expand His work.

And then, third, God will truly confound the wise of this world with the pardon that He provides.

Through people, plans, and pardon, God does confound the wise!

Day 324

God's Choice of People

1 Corinthians 1:26 says,

> *For you see your calling, brethren, that not many wise according to the flesh, not many mighty, not many noble, are called.*

God does not call a lot of people who our world would consider wise, noble or mighty. He calls a few, but not many. The fact of the matter is, God will use *anyone* who will yield himself or herself to Him.

The idea Paul wants us to understand is that the vast majority of people God chooses are a surprise to everyone else. God's choices are generally not on our "A" list of people.

Think about the apostle Paul himself, who wrote these very words in 1 Corinthians, chapter 15, *I am the least of the apostles, who am not worthy to be called an apostle, because I persecuted the church of God.* And the next words out of his mouth are profound, *But by the grace of God I am what I am.*

Paul was a persecutor of Christians. In fact, he was so filled with hatred he even went to foreign cities to have believers arrested, families split apart, Christians jailed, beaten, and at times even executed. And yet, God chose Paul as His mouthpiece.

It was so astonishing to many in the church that they didn't want to receive Paul when he was first saved. They thought it was a trick. It took them a while to understand that God actually had saved him *and* was using him.

Paul would not have been one of their primary choices as a vessel for God. I love that about the Lord. He uses the unexpected and those we might pass over to carry out some of His most important work.

Day 325

A Seedbed of Faith

In Judges 6:11-15, we read this about Gideon,

> *Now the Angel of the LORD came and sat under the terebinth tree which was in Ophrah, which belonged to Joash the Abiezrite, while his son Gideon threshed wheat in the winepress, in order to hide it from the Midianites. And the Angel of the LORD appeared to him, and said to him, "The LORD is with you, you mighty man of valor!" Gideon said to Him, "O my lord, if the LORD is with us, why then has all this happened to us? And where are all His miracles which our fathers told us about, saying, 'Did not the LORD bring us up from Egypt?' But now the LORD has forsaken us and delivered us into the hands of the Midianites." Then the LORD turned to him and said, "Go in this might of yours, and you shall save Israel from the hand of the Midianites. Have I not sent you?" So he said to Him, "O my Lord, how can I save Israel? Indeed my clan is the weakest in Manasseh, and I am the least in my father's house."*

We often think of Gideon as a great champion for Israel, and he was. But when he was chosen, we found him cowering in the winepress. He was hiding, he was fearful, he was negative, he was doubtful, and he was questioning.

While we might be critical of Gideon, I have found that the only people who never question are those who have been indoctrinated. Sometimes you need to doubt. Sometimes you need to question. In fact, a lot of times uncertainty is the seedbed from which faith grows.

If you are struggling with doubt today, if you have genuine questions, don't panic. If you are sincerely looking for answers, God will meet you, and faith will spring from the answers you find.

Day 326

The Most Important Quality

In 1 Samuel 16:6-7, when Samuel came to Jesse's house to anoint the next king of Israel, we see the criteria God uses to choose people for service to Him,

> *So it was, when they came, that he looked at Eliab and said, "Surely the LORD'S anointed is before Him." But the LORD said to Samuel, "Do not look at his appearance or at his physical stature, because I have refused him. For the LORD does not see as man sees; for man looks at the outward appearance, but the LORD looks at the heart."*

This is a fascinating story with a very strong lesson I want you to understand. Right after these verses, Jesse parades each of his sons before Samuel...except for David. Jesse knows why Samuel is there, but he doesn't even bother to get David.

David's own father had written him off. His own father didn't see enough potential in him to call him before Samuel.

But David was anointed king that day. Not based on what Jesse thought was important, but on what God thought was important... David's heart.

Maybe your own father has written you off. Maybe your parents said you would never amount to anything. Maybe your teacher said, "Look, you're not going to amount to much. You just better get yourself a minimum wage job."

Only God can see things in your heart that your father can't see, that your mother can't see, that your teachers didn't see, that your family doesn't see, that the people around you don't see.

It is not that God overlooks ability or talent or training. All of those things are important. But God looks first at the most important quality for service, and that is the heart.

Don't let someone else write your history before it happens.

Day 327

When God's Plan Doesn't Make Sense

In Joshua 6:1-5 we find one of the most bizarre battle plans, but one with an important lesson for you and me,

> *Now Jericho was securely shut up because of the children of Israel; none went out, and none came in. And the LORD said to Joshua: "See! I have given Jericho into your hand, its king, and the mighty men of valor. You shall march around the city, all you men of war; you shall go all around the city once. This you shall do six days. And seven priests shall bear seven trumpets of rams' horns before the ark. But the seventh day you shall march around the city seven times, and the priests shall blow the trumpets. It shall come to pass, when they make a long blast with the ram's horn, and when you hear the sound of the trumpet, that all the people shall shout with a great shout; then the wall of the city will fall down flat. And the people shall go up every man straight before him."*

When you and I read that today it is easy for us to think, "Oh, that must have been pretty normal and natural to Joshua." But it wasn't. It did not make any more sense to him than it would have to you and me.

Imagine God taking Joshua aside and telling him that all they need to do is march around the city one time for six days. Then on the seventh day march around seven times and shout. It made no sense. Naturally speaking, it was ridiculous!

All of us will face our Jerichos, and sometimes God's plans won't seem to make sense. Our part is to listen and obey—even when God's instructions don't make sense to our natural minds. He has had a lot more experience winning battles than we have!

Day 328

Pursue Peace

In 1 Peter 3:10-11, Peter provides an important command in our relationships with other people,

For "He who would love life and see good days, let him refrain his tongue from evil, and his lips from speaking deceit. Let him turn away from evil and do good; let him seek peace and pursue it."

I want to focus your attention on the last part of verse 11, "*Seek peace and pursue it.*" This means we are to pursue peace with people.

This command is reinforced by the writer of Hebrews in Hebrews 12:14,

Pursue peace with all people, and holiness, without which no one will see the Lord.

I want you to take note of the first part of that verse, *Pursue peace with....* How many people are we to pursue peace with? *All people.* Does that include your neighbor? How about your mom? How about your dad? How about your kids? Your boss? Your relatives? How about that individual who seems to have a gift for getting on your nerves? What about those who are rude and obnoxious?

We are told that we are to pursue peace with *all* people. That is not a suggestion. That is a command. And that command is clarified further in Romans 14:19, which says,

Therefore let us pursue the things which make for peace and the things by which one may edify another.

Things that edify (or build up) create peace. Things that tear down shatter peace. Keep that in mind next time you are having a heated discussion with your husband or wife. Ask yourself, "Are the things that I am sharing at this moment building up my partner? Or, are they tearing them down?"

Pursue peace with *all* people by choosing words and deeds that will build them up.

Day 329

Winning an Offended Brother

Proverbs 18:19 tells us,

> *A brother offended is harder to win than a strong city, and contentions are like the bars of a castle.*

When this verse refers to a "strong city," it means a fortified or a guarded city. You cannot just waltz up to the gate of a fortified city and say "give up." It takes strategic planning to take such a city. You have to think things through and have a plan.

It also means there is going to be strenuous effort involved. And, more than likely, you will be in a vulnerable position. In fact, you don't take a strong city without taking risks, without becoming vulnerable.

The same things come into play when a brother is offended. It takes thoughtful planning, it takes effort, and sometimes you have to become vulnerable when you do not want to be.

Perhaps you are struggling with a damaged relationship today, and you haven't pursued healing this relationship because you don't know how to do it. It always starts with prayer. You talk to God about them and about yourself, and then you need to go and talk to them.

When you do, I want you to listen carefully, it should not be with a view to prove that you are right. Being right is not the goal. Peace is. Most of the time it is more important to be kind than it is to be right.

If you try to work something out, but only with the intention of having them understand your point of view so that you can prove you are right, you may win the argument, but you will never make peace.

So when you are endeavoring to win an offended brother, listen carefully to them, and endeavor to understand where they are coming from. Seek to hear and not just be heard. Though it may be difficult, you can win peace and see a broken relationship restored.

Day 330

Listen...to Understand

In Proverbs 18:2, we are given an important word of warning,

> *A fool has no delight in understanding, but in expressing his own heart.*

It is so easy to play the role of such a fool when we are dealing with a strained or broken relationship. Rather than seeking to understand the other person, we will often feel the need to make the other person understand our hurt.

Like me, you have probably said, "You need to hear me. You need to understand why I'm hurt. You need to understand why I reacted the way I reacted. You need to see that I'm right. I need to convince you that I'm justified in the things I've said and the things I've done."

When we say those things, we are not interested in understanding the other person's point of view to reach a mutual peace. We just want to express our opinions, our hurt, and our reasons.

The Bible says that is the way a fool behaves. I am going to stand at the front of the line and say, "I've been that fool more than once." But we must learn to listen and understand.

Once you have listened and understood, here is an important phrase to learn, "I see what you're saying, and I'm sorry." That does not mean, "I see what you're saying, and I'm sorry you're such an idiot." That means, "I've listened to you, I've heard you, and I'm sorry." Period. "Forgive me."

It is amazing how some people choke on those words. In fact, it is shocking to realize how few people know how to give a proper apology. They offer the rose of an apology by handing it thorn-end first.

Don't play the fool. Listen...to understand.

Day 331

The Power of a Gift

Proverbs 19:7 says,

> *All the brothers of the poor hate him; how much more do his friends go far from him! He may pursue them with words, yet they abandon him.*

Sometimes just pursuing reconciliation with a person through communication is not enough. Sometimes you need to take it to another level. Look at Proverbs 18:16,

> *A man's gift makes room for him, and brings him before great men.*

Sometimes it wouldn't hurt you to offer a gift to someone with whom you are seeking to reconcile. The New International Version says, *A gift opens the way.*

When a brother is offended and the contentions are like bars of iron with the gate shut tight, the thing that opens the way is a gift. The Living Bible says, *A gift does wonders.* The Scripture says in Proverbs 21:14, *A gift in secret pacifies anger.*

It is important to understand that both Proverbs 18:16 and 21:14 are actually shared in a negative sense. They are talking about the power of a bribe. Proverbs is great that way because it gives us both the positive and negative perspectives. It's a truth (that I'm not saying is a good thing) that a bribe can open doors which may not be opened otherwise.

In a positive way, it is true that a gift can do wonders. Not that you are trying to buy someone's favor, but a sincere gift can be a powerful form of communication. The important thing is your motivation behind it.

A gift can say, "You're valuable enough to me that I took some of my hard-earned money and bought this for you." A gift has the power to take things to another level as you seek to make things right.

Day 332

When Peace Isn't Possible

Romans 12:18 says,

> *If it is possible, as much as depends on you, live peaceably with all men.*

By implication, this verse is telling us that it is not possible to live peaceably with some people because they refuse to make peace. They take the posture of being an enemy, being an antagonist, and they refuse to shift from that position no matter what you do.

But as much as it depends on you, you must pursue the things that make for peace. You need to pray, you need to communicate, and if God leads you, you need to give a gift. And certainly with your actions, you need to express the fact that you want peace.

Sometimes somebody may not yield. They may not yield to the influence of God's Spirit; they may not yield to your endeavors. But once you have done all you can do, all you can do has been done.

Does that give you a license to be rude to them or to treat them unpleasantly? No. The next few verses address that. Look at Romans 12:19-21,

> *Beloved, do not avenge yourselves, but rather give place to wrath; for it is written, "Vengeance is Mine, I will repay," says the Lord. Therefore "If your enemy is hungry, feed him; if he is thirsty, give him a drink; for in so doing you will heap coals of fire on his head." Do not be overcome by evil, but overcome evil with good.*

Continue to extend the olive branch. If they never respond, at least you will have a clean conscience. God will deal with the things that you cannot deal with. Do not take matters into your own hands. "*Vengeance is Mine*," says the Lord.

Day 333

Seeing God Through Nature

Hosea 6:3 gives us something we should pursue every day of our lives,

> *Let us pursue the knowledge of the LORD. His going forth is established as the morning; He will come to us like the rain, like the latter and former rain to the earth.*

What a great pursuit! When you pursue the knowledge of God, He will come to you. He will refresh you like the rain, like the early and the latter rain.

These rains would cause the crops to ripen and bear fruit. Scripture is seeking to tell us that when you seek the knowledge of God, a personal knowledge of God, it will cause your life to become abundantly fruitful. It will cause your life to prosper. It will bring refreshment into your life because God will come to you.

The question is: How do you pursue the knowledge of God?

One way is through nature. Psalm 19:1 says, *The heavens declare the glory of God, and the firmament shows His handiwork.* Creation screams, "There must be a Creator! I'm too perfect, I'm too intricate, I'm too glorious to have just happened. There must be a Master Sculptor. There must be a Master Painter. There must be a Creator behind it all."

The stars in the heavens and the moon literally declare God's glory. When you look at the sunset over the Pacific ocean, or look at the mountains, or you look at the grass in your backyard, they scream that there is a Creator.

Take some time to pursue the knowledge of God this week by just observing nature. When you do, you will come to a deeper knowledge of God as you see and understand the beauty and majesty of Him in a fresh, new way.

Day 334

Suppressing the Truth

> *For the wrath of God is revealed from heaven against all ungodliness and unrighteousness of men, who suppress the truth in unrighteousness* (Romans 1:18).

A truth that is suppressed is a truth that has addressed itself to someone, but they do not want to be confronted by it. They do not want it to force them to change, so they keep it down and refuse to look at or deal with it.

What kind of a truth is it that men suppress? Romans 1:19 tells us,

> *Because what may be known of God is manifest in them, for God has shown it to them.*

People are suppressing a knowledge or truth about God. Where did they learn that truth about God that they are suppressing? Verse 20 tells us,

> *For since the creation of the world His invisible attributes are clearly seen, being understood by the things that are made, even His eternal power and Godhead, so that they are without excuse.*

Creation speaks of a Creator. God is understood, it says, by the things that are made. There comes a point in every human's life as they observe nature, where a voice whispers to them, "This didn't just happen. There has to be a hand behind this."

At that point, each person has a choice: Whether or not to suppress that truth. If they do not suppress the truth, I believe God will move heaven and earth to get the knowledge of the gospel to that person.

This is so profound because even on Judgment Day no one is going to be able to stand and say, "Well, I never heard. I didn't have a chance." They will be without excuse, because God is going to take them right back to that experience where He spoke to them through nature.

Day 335

Pursue Hospitality

Romans 12:9-14 says,

> *Let love be without hypocrisy. Abhor what is evil. Cling to what is good. Be kindly affectionate to one another with brotherly love, in honor giving preference to one another; not lagging in diligence, fervent in spirit, serving the Lord; rejoicing in hope, patient in tribulation, continuing steadfastly in prayer; distributing to the needs of the saints, given to hospitality. Bless those who persecute you; bless and do not curse.*

At the end of verse 13, Paul says we are to be "given to hospitality." The word *given* is the Greek word translated "pursue" everywhere else in the New Testament. This could be translated "pursuing hospitality."

Hospitality is actually a compound word in the Greek language. The first part of the word means to be fond of. The second part means guests. So hospitality means to be friendly to strangers, to open your heart and open your home to others.

The Scripture is very strong when it says we are to pursue hospitality. It is one of the greatest ways in all the world to demonstrate the love of God to people who are in need.

I remember like it was yesterday a time I was preaching at a church. It was over 20 years ago, when I was a newlywed. After the service was done, Janet and I were standing around not knowing what to do. No one was speaking to us and the church had made no provision for our lodging or meals.

Just then an elderly couple came up to us and invited us to their home for lunch, which we gratefully accepted.

And you know what? I don't remember what I preached that day, but to this day I remember eating roast in that couple's home. I remember their graciousness, their hospitable spirit, and how much they made us feel welcome.

Pursue hospitality!

Day 336

In the Balance

1 Thessalonians 5:15 is a powerful verse that speaks to everyone,

> *See that no one renders evil for evil to anyone, but always pursue what is good both for yourselves and for all.*

Notice the apostle Paul makes sure no one is excluded. That means you can't get out of this. You are either a "no one," or an "anyone" in this verse!

Paul's point about pursuing *what is good for both yourselves and for all* can be looked at two ways. First, he could be talking about the worshiping community as a whole. His point: Pursue what is good for the church, but also for all those outside the church. You need to think of the welfare of the church ***and*** the community in which you exist.

On a more personal level, Paul could be speaking to the need for you and I to weigh how our words, our actions, and our pursuit of that which is good for us affects others. I have to weigh that in the balance.

While a certain thing may be good for me, I need to think of how it is going to affect others. It is not just about pursuing what is good for me, even if it is something I deserve. I need to ask, "How is it going to affect others...my spouse, my kids, my friends, my church, my neighbor?" I have to factor that in.

Many times people pursue something and they defend their position by saying, "Well, it's time for me to start thinking about myself. I deserve this. This is good for me."

Well, this verse allows for that. In fact, it admonishes you to pursue what is good for you, but it adds the proviso "*and* for all."

Eagerly pursue the things that are beneficial for you, but also that which is good for others.

Day 337

A More Excellent Way

In 1 Corinthians 14:1, we are given a foundational truth,

> *Pursue love, and desire spiritual gifts, but especially that you may prophesy.*

Notice that this verse leads off with a very direct command. We are to pursue love.

It is interesting that this command is given in the context of Paul's teaching on the gifts of the Holy Spirit. In fact, 1 Corinthians chapters 12-14 deal with the gifts of the Spirit: the word of knowledge, the word of wisdom, the discerning of spirits, the gift of faith, the working of miracles, the gifts of healing, the gift of tongues and interpretation of tongues, and the gift of prophecy.

Chapter 12 gives us the definition of those gifts, chapter 13 teaches us the spirit that should characterize their use, and chapter 14 gives us guidelines for their functioning within the context of the local church.

When it comes to the operation of the gifts of the Spirit, Paul is very clear. He tells us, "Desire the gifts. Seek to have these things operating in your life and operating in the life of the local church, but they need to be practiced in love."

It is with that thought in mind that Paul writes 1 Corinthians 12:31. Here is what he says,

> *But earnestly desire the best gifts. And yet I show you a more excellent way.*

As we read the following verses we are told that the more excellent way is love. Again, Paul is giving us the spirit that should characterize the use of the gifts of the Spirit as they function within the context of the local church.

Desire the gifts. Earnestly covet them. But let them operate through a spirit of love.

Day 338

Pursue Love!

In yesterday's devotional, we talked about how love is "the more excellent way." We are to pursue love, especially in how we practice the gifts of the Spirit.

In 1 Corinthians 13, Paul presses home the point of just how important love really is. Let's start with verse 1,

> *Though I speak with the tongues of men and of angels, but have not love, I have become sounding brass or a clanging cymbal.*

Paul does not say the gift of tongues isn't legitimate or genuine. But if there is not a heart of love behind it, it is just noise. You see, the water picks up the taste of the pipe that it flows through. If the pipe isn't clean, the water can pick up a pretty nasty taste, even though it is still genuinely water.

So also the gift can be genuine, but it is more noise than anything else to the hearts of the people who hear it if it is not accentuated by love.

Let's move to verse 2,

> *And though I have the gift of prophecy, and understand all mysteries and all knowledge, and though I have all faith, so that I could remove mountains, but have not love, I am nothing.*

Notice he did not say the gifts are nothing. The gifts are genuine. He says *you* are nothing. From heaven's point of view, you are defined by your character, not by your accomplishments. The world tends to define people by their accomplishments. In heaven's books, however, you are defined by your character.

> *And though I bestow all my goods to feed the poor, and though I give my body to be burned, but have not love, it profits me nothing* (verse 2).

It does not say the poor won't profit, but *you* won't profit. You lose your reward if your heart is not right.

Pursue love!

Day 339

Releasing God's Love

We have been talking about pursuing love in the last couple of devotionals. Today I want to go to a passage where Scripture gives us a snapshot of what God's love looks like. 1 Corinthians 13:4-8,

> *Love suffers long and is kind* (a lot of people suffer long, but they are not very kind while they do it)*; love does not envy; love does not parade itself, is not puffed up; does not behave rudely, does not seek its own; is not provoked* (it is not touchy or fretful or resentful)*; thinks no evil; does not rejoice in iniquity, but rejoices in the truth; bears all things, believes all things, hopes all things, endures all things. Love never fails.*

What you just read about the love of God is already inside of you if you are a Christian. It is not something outside of you that you need to seek. It is something that is in you that needs to be released.

Romans 5:5 tells us,

> *Now hope does not disappoint, because the love of God has been poured out in our hearts by the Holy Spirit who was given to us.*

God's love has already been poured into your heart! The ability to do everything in 1 Corinthians 13:4-8 is already in you. You have the ability to not be touchy, or fretful, or resentful, or seek your own or insist on your own rights; to suffer long and to be kind; to believe the best of every person.

The Bible is not talking about pursuing love as though it is something that is vacant from your life. Rather, you are to pursue the expression of that love purposely and let it work its way into your words and actions.

Day 340

Choose to Love

"You have heard that it was said, 'You shall love your neighbor and hate your enemy.' But I say to you, love your enemies, bless those who curse you, do good to those who hate you, and pray for those who spitefully use you and persecute you, that you may be sons of your Father in heaven; for He makes His sun rise on the evil and on the good, and sends rain on the just and on the unjust'" (Matthew 5:43-45).

These are not suggestions to be considered, they are commands to be obeyed. "A pretty tall order," you say. Perhaps, but definitely within the realm of possibility.

Jesus would never tell us to do something we could not do. That would be unjust. We can bless, we can do good, we can pray for and forgive those who have wronged us.

When people say, "I can't forgive," that generally means, "I won't forgive." The ability to love, bless and forgive is within us—because God is within us. Learn to let His nature of love dominate you. Choose to love. Let what God has put on the inside come out.

The world needs to see real love—the kind of unconditional love that brought us into God's family. And they need to see it in us. If we really are the children of God, then His nature should be displayed in us and through us. The most outstanding feature of God's nature is love. God is love.

One last thing. When you choose to love and forgive those who have wronged you, you set a prisoner free. The prisoner is you.

Day 341

The Qualities of Love

For the last number of devotionals, we have focused our attention on how love is such a vital quality to the Christian life. We have seen that unless we love, any of the spiritual gifts are meaningless.

We have also seen that God has deposited His love in us already, and as a result, it is our responsibility to choose to express that love. It is not something we can put on God's shoulders. We must take on that obligation.

So what do those qualities of love really look like? I want to share with you 1 Corinthians 13 from the Amplified Bible, but I want to do it with a twist. I want to make it personal and show how, if we choose to love as God has asked us to love, it will look.

1 Corinthians 13:4-8 from the Amplified Bible...personalized (read it out loud),

> *I endure long, and I am patient and kind. I am never envious or boil over with jealousy. I am not boastful or vainglorious. I do not display myself haughtily. I am not conceited, arrogant, or inflated with pride. I am not rude or unmannerly. I do not act unbecomingly. God's love in me does not insist on its own rights or its own way for I am not self-seeking. I am not touchy or fretful or resentful. I take no account of the evil done to me. I do not rejoice at injustice and unrighteousness, but I rejoice when right and truth prevail. I bear up under anything and everything that comes, and I am ever ready to believe the best of every person. My hopes are fadeless under all circumstances, and I endure everything without weakening. God's love in me never fails.*

I challenge you to read this out loud to yourself every day for a month, and see if it does not change your life!

Day 342

Spiritual Metamorphosis

Romans 12:1-2 says this,

> *I beseech you therefore, brethren, by the mercies of God that you present your bodies a living sacrifice, holy, acceptable to God, which is your reasonable service. And do not be conformed to this world, but be transformed by the renewing of your mind, that you may prove what is that good and acceptable and perfect will of God.*

First, notice that it is your responsibility to present your body to God. God will not do it for you. You have to do it. But Scripture doesn't leave us there. We are shown how we are to do that in verse 2 above.

First, when it says, *Do not be conformed*, that word *conform* means to be pressed into a mold by outward pressures. Instead of being conformed we are told to be *transformed*. That is actually the Greek word from which we get our English word *metamorphosis*. It means to let what is on the inside come to the outside.

One day many years ago, my kids came home from school with some silk worms. We were supposed to put them in a box and feed them mulberry leaves. I couldn't believe how many leaves these worms ate! They ate leaves until they turned a translucent green!

Then they wove cocoons and went through a metamorphosis. They went from being these ugly ol' fat green transparent worms, to the most beautiful fuzzy huge white moths. It was amazing to see!

My friend, you renew your mind by feeding on God's Word, the same way that those silk worms fed on the mulberry leaves. As you are filled with His truth, it causes a metamorphosis to take place. It brings what is on the inside—God's nature—to the outside.

So feed on God's Word and watch your life be transformed.

Day 343

The Love of Money

In 1 Timothy 6:9-11, Paul gives us a critical insight,

> *But those who desire to be rich fall into temptation and a snare, and into many foolish and harmful lusts which drown men in destruction and perdition. For the love of money is a root of all kinds of evil, for which some have strayed from the faith in their greediness, and pierced themselves through with many sorrows. But you, O man of God, flee these things and pursue righteousness, godliness, faith, love, patience, gentleness.*

I want you to notice: Before Paul tells us to pursue righteousness, godliness, faith, love, patience, and gentleness, he says we must first flee the love of money. You have to be willing to flee the wrong things before you can pursue the right things, because you cannot go in two directions at once.

If you are pursuing riches, and the gaining of wealth and the achievement of success have become your number one priorities, pushing everything else, including God, to the side, then you are pursuing the wrong thing.

You may be thinking, "Well, that's great for some people, but that doesn't apply to me." You need to understand that you can be eaten up with the love of money and not have a dime in your pocket. All of us are subject to such a temptation and such a trap.

It's fascinating that Paul uses the word "drown" here. I live by the Pacific Ocean, and generally people who drown do so because, (a) they overestimate their own abilities as a swimmer; or (b) they underestimate the power of the ocean.

If you overestimate your ability to be free from this type of a temptation, or you underestimate the power of this type of a temptation, you are setting yourself up for disaster.

Flee the wrong and pursue the right. Stay on course with God.

Day 344

The Main Pursuit

Ezekiel 33:30-32 provides some pretty direct and challenging words from God,

> *"As for you, son of man, the children of your people are talking about you beside the walls and in the doors of the houses; and they speak to one another, everyone saying to his brother, 'Please come and hear what the word is that comes from the LORD.' So they come to you as people do, they sit before you as My people, and they hear your words, but they do not do them; for with their mouth they show much love, but their hearts pursue their own gain. Indeed you are to them as a very lovely song of one who has a pleasant voice and can play well on an instrument; for they hear your words, but they do not do them."*

I think, for some people, church is almost like going to a concert, especially if the preacher is flashy and the music is great. They are not listening with a view to imbibe God's truth and then put it into practice in their lives.

What is the reason for this disconnect? People are pursuing something else in their hearts. Sure, they are showing up at church, they are listening, they are even saying "amen" at the right time, but they are not applying God's truth to their lives. Why? Because they are pursuing something else in their heart.

This is the same thing that Paul talked to Timothy about in yesterday's devotional. Remember? Like Ezekiel, he said, *Their hearts pursue their own gain.*

It is very simple: If your focus is on the pursuit of things, your focus will never be on the One who has created all things. It really boils down to this one question: What is the main pursuit of your life?

If it is not God, then your life is going in the wrong direction!

Day 345

Sowing Righteousness

The Bible says in Galatians 6:7,

Whatever a man sows, that he will also reap.

And in Proverbs 11:18 it says,

The wicked man does deceptive work, but he who sows righteousness will have a sure reward.

The Bible teaches the law of the harvest, that what you sow, you will also reap. If you treat others fairly and uprightly, it will come back to you.

We live in a world that doesn't put much stock in integrity, fairness, uprightness, and righteousness. We must be careful to not give in to that influence. We need to be different.

How? By not cutting corners. By putting in an honest day's work. By giving people what they pay for and more. If you will pursue righteousness, it will come back to you.

You may remember a story back in the eighties about an armored car that crashed in Columbus, Ohio. Two million dollars in cash spilled out on the highway, and the motorists helped the armored car company gather all of its money.

But, when it was all said and done, only $400,000 of the $2 million made its way back to the armored car company. $1.6 million ended up in the pockets of the people who stopped along the highway to "help."

I'm sure they had every excuse under the sun. Some probably even said, "Well, I've been praying for God to meet my needs, and it was a miracle!" No, it was not a miracle. They were thieves!

You cannot make an excuse for that kind of thing. And yet that is the way the world thinks. There should be a difference between us and the world. We need to pursue uprightness, integrity, honesty, and godly character. They need to be hallmarks of our lives.

Day 346

The Reward of Godliness

In today's devotional, I want to draw your attention to the importance of the pursuit of godliness. Let's look at 1 Timothy 6:6,

Now godliness with contentment is great gain.

What an incredible truth. Godliness coupled with contentment is great gain. Not just gain, GREAT gain!

Over and over in Scripture, God highlights the importance and reward of godliness. For instance, it says in Psalm 4:3, *That the Lord has set apart for Himself him who is godly.* 2 Peter says the Lord knows how to deliver the godly out of temptations. Those are great rewards!

But there is more. Look at 1 Timothy 4:7-8,

But reject profane and old wives' fables, and exercise yourself toward godliness. For bodily exercise profits a little, but godliness is profitable for all things, having promise of the life that now is and of that which is to come.

It could not be more clear! There is profit in godliness, and that profit is not only in this life, but in the life that is to come. Godliness is going to pay off in both this life and into eternity!

So it makes sense to make this pursuit of godliness a priority! Even if people want to kick you every time you do something that is right, you need to stay with it.

Determine today to make godliness an everyday pursuit. If you do, you will reap the rewards of godliness, great gain and profit, not just in this life, but for eternity.

Day 347

Strengthening Your Faith

Romans 10:17 is the verse I would like for you to read today. It says,

> *So then faith comes by hearing, and hearing by the word of God.*

To fully understand this verse, you need to know that if you are saved, faith has already been deposited in your heart. It is part of your spiritual DNA. Romans 12:3 says that, *God has dealt to each one a measure of faith.* Faith is something He has already given.

It is up to you to develop that faith. It is up to you to do something with it. How do you develop it? You develop it first by hearing the Word of God.

The Bible—God's Word—is the food. As you feed upon it, your faith will be strengthened.

You know those body builders, men and women who are constantly pumping weights? Well, if you talk to any serious body builder, one of the first things they will refer to is diet. You have to eat the right kind of diet if you are going to build muscle mass. Usually, their diet is protein-rich.

They faithfully drink their protein shakes and eat their tuna fish sandwiches, which, when they are consumed and digested, become the raw materials that build muscle mass.

As you feed upon and digest God's Word, that truth becomes the raw material that will build faith. It is faith food.

Most people who struggle with their faith are feeding on the wrong things. Faith comes unconsciously when you feed upon God's Word.

So today, if you feel like you are struggling in your faith, then change your diet. Start feeding more on God's Word!

Day 348

Exercising the Muscle of Faith

Yesterday we looked at the importance of God's Word to strengthen our faith. Yet there is something more we need to do to see our faith grow. We must use it.

In 1 Timothy 6:12, Paul says this about faith,

Fight the good fight of faith.

Faith is made for conflict. It does not grow without conflict. It does not grow without pressure. You need to use it.

Remember our illustration of the body builders and how a proper diet is essential to building muscle mass? Well, they will also tell you that it is not enough to drink protein shakes and eat tuna fish, you have to work those muscles if they are going to grow. They work those weights every day in order to build their muscles.

The same thing is true when it comes to faith. Faith is a muscle that you have to use. It is not enough just to listen to your Bible teaching CDs all day long. Hearing alone is not enough to develop faith. You must use your faith muscle.

That is what the fight of faith is all about. You exercise your faith when you are standing in the midst of your storm, and you are assailed by temptations and every kind of trial that tells you you're not going to make it, that you are going down with the ship.

As you stand in the midst of your storm, and the wind is howling around you, and the lightning is flashing, and the waves are breaking over the bow of your little ship, stand up and say, "I believe God, that it is going to be just as it was told me." That is where the fight of faith comes in.

No matter what you may be going through today, exercise that muscle of faith. Trust God to do just as He has promised.

Day 349

Understanding Faith

In the last two devotionals, we have been talking about faith and the importance of both the proper diet of God's Word, and exercising our faith if we are to see it grow.

The natural question is, "What is faith?" Most Christians probably know the technical definition for faith from Hebrews 11:1,

> *Faith is the substance of things hoped for, the evidence of things not seen.*

The New International Version says, *Faith is being sure of what we hope for and certain of what we do not see.* That is pretty clear. But it becomes even more clear when you plug that definition into 1 Timothy 6:12,

> *Fight the good fight of* [the substance of things hoped for, the evidence of things not seen. Fight the good fight of being sure of what you hope for and being convinced of what you do not see.]

When the answer to your prayers is not on the horizon, when you don't feel differently, you need to fight the good fight and say, "You know what? God's Word says it and that's all the evidence I need. It is the evidence of things not seen, and I'm going to stand on that truth. I don't care what the world says, I don't care what circumstances say, I am going to fight the good fight of the substance of things hoped for, the evidence of what I do not see."

And you stay with it until, as they say, "Faith turns to sight."

What are you struggling with today? What challenge is testing your faith? Stand firm on the truth of God's Word. Trust Him, no matter what others may say.

Real faith is standing firm in the midst of the storm. So stand firm!

Day 350

Your Professional Trainer

As we continue to look at faith, I want you to read Hebrews 12:1-2,

> *Therefore we also, since we are surrounded by so great a cloud of witnesses, let us lay aside every weight, and the sin which so easily ensnares us, and let us run with endurance the race that is set before us, looking unto Jesus, the author and finisher of our faith, who for the joy that was set before Him endured the cross, despising the shame, and has sat down at the right hand of the throne of God.*

What this passage teaches about faith is vital for you to understand if you are to progress in your faith. That truth is simply this: Jesus is the Author and Finisher of our faith. He not only authors it, He is the One who is the developer of our faith.

Remember the analogy of the body builder from the last few devotionals? Well, if your faith is like a body builder, Jesus is your weight trainer. Many of the people who are seriously into body building have a professional trainer who will work with them to be more effective in building muscle mass and sculpting their body.

Just like the professional weight trainer for a body builder, Jesus is your professional faith trainer. No one knows more about faith than Jesus. If you want to learn about faith, you need to listen to Jesus. You need to follow His guidance on how to build your faith.

Over the next few devotionals, I will show you three levels of faith Jesus talks about. Through that process, I pray you will discover where you are and see where you need to go and what you need to pursue in order for your faith to grow.

Day 351

God Does Care

In yesterday's devotional, I told you about the three levels of faith Jesus talks about. The first of these levels is found in Mark 4:37-40,

> *And a great windstorm arose, and the waves beat into the boat, so that it was already filling. But He was in the stern, asleep on a pillow. And they awoke Him and said to Him, "Teacher, do You not care that we are perishing?" Then He arose and rebuked the wind, and said to the sea, "Peace, be still!" And the wind ceased and there was a great calm. But He said to them, "Why are you so fearful? How is it that you have no faith?"*

The first level of faith that Jesus speaks about is *no faith*. No faith believes God does not care. It is typified by the disciples who woke Jesus in the midst of the storm and said, "Lord, don't You care that we're perishing?"

Perhaps you are in a storm today; and, to you, it seems like God is asleep and that He doesn't even care. That He is aloof, disinterested, and disconnected from you. That you are going through hell and He doesn't care.

Do not believe that lie. If you buy into the lie that God does not care, it robs you of faith. And you cannot get any lower than that.

Do not believe the lie that God is detached and unconcerned. Don't think, "If God cares about me, why would this have happened? Why am I going through this storm? Why is this happening in my life? God doesn't care about me. He doesn't even know my name."

My friend, God does care. He is not going to let you perish. He is interested in even the smallest details of your life.

1 Peter 5:7 says, *He cares for you*!

Day 352

Little Faith

In our last devotional, we looked at the first level of faith: no faith. We learned that no faith is based on the belief that God does not care, and that such a belief is completely false. God does indeed care for you!

Today we are going to look at the second level of faith. It is found in what Jesus says in Matthew 6:30-34,

> *"Now if God so clothes the grass of the field, which today is, and tomorrow is thrown into the oven, will He not much more clothe you, O you of little faith? Therefore do not worry, saying, 'What shall we eat?' or 'What shall we drink?' or 'What shall we wear?' For after all these things the Gentiles seek. For your heavenly Father knows that you need all these things. But seek first the kingdom of God and His righteousness, and all these things shall be added to you. Therefore do not worry about tomorrow, for tomorrow will worry about its own things. Sufficient for the day is its own trouble."*

This second level of faith is *little faith*. As we see in this passage, little faith is a worried faith, worried about tomorrow and occupied with lack instead of being occupied with God.

While people with little faith believe God cares, their focus is wrong. They are concentrating on, "What am I going to eat? What am I going to wear? How am I going to get by?"

Now, those are all legitimate things; and your Father knows you have need of those things. So rather than focusing on your lack and being worried about tomorrow, pulling tomorrow's clouds over today's sunshine, let your focus be on God and His sufficiency, His care, and His abundant love.

Do not live a life of little faith.

Day 353

Great Faith

In today's devotional, I want to look at the third level of faith. It is found in Matthew 8:5-10,

> *Now when Jesus had entered Capernaum, a centurion came to Him, pleading with Him, saying, "Lord, my servant is lying at home paralyzed, dreadfully tormented." And Jesus said to him, "I will come and heal him." The centurion answered and said, "Lord, I am not worthy that You should come under my roof. But only speak a word, and my servant will be healed. For I also am a man under authority, having soldiers under me. And I say to this one, 'Go,' and he goes; and to another, 'Come,' and he comes; and to my servant, 'Do this,' and he does it." When Jesus heard it, He marveled, and said to those who followed, "Assuredly, I say to you, I have not found such great faith, not even in Israel!"*

We saw in previous devotionals that the first level of faith is no faith, the second is little faith, and now the third is *great faith*.

Great faith says, "Lord, Your word is enough." The centurion said, "*Only speak a word.*" He understood the authority of Jesus' words. He said, "Jesus, all You have to do is say it. You don't even have to come into my house. I don't have to see anything. Your word is all the evidence I need."

That is what great faith says, "Lord, Your Word is all the evidence I need. Things don't have to look differently and I don't have to feel differently. Your Word is it. I don't need any other kind of confirmation. It doesn't matter what the circumstances say. Lord, Your Word settles the issue for me."

That is great faith, and that is what we should be pursuing.

Day 354

Your Purpose

Today I want to speak to you about your destiny and purpose. First, read Ephesians 2:10,

> *For we are His workmanship, created in Christ Jesus for good works, which God prepared beforehand that we should walk in them.*

The word *beforehand* refers to before the foundation of the world. What the apostle Paul is saying in this verse is that before we were ever born, God prepared good works for us to walk in them. God decided that we would be doing certain things.

Listen to that same verse from the Knox Translation, *We are His design. God has created us in Christ Jesus, pledged to such good actions as He has prepared beforehand to be the employment of our lives.* I like that.

Paraphrased, "You were designed with a unique purpose, and that is what you should be doing with your life."

In Philippians 3:12, Paul also states,

> *Not that I have already attained, or am already perfected; but I press on, that I may lay hold of that for which Christ Jesus has also laid hold of me.*

The phrase "I press on" literally means "I pursue." What is it that Paul states he is pursuing? He is pursuing his purpose.

On that Damascus road, Jesus laid hold of Saul of Tarsus, and He did it for a reason. There was a purpose involved. From the day that Jesus Christ laid hold of him, Paul's life became a progressive search to lay hold of the answer to the question, "God, why have You laid hold of me? What is my purpose?"

My point? You have a God-designed purpose in life! There is something that you are wired up to do as the employment of your life.

Day 355

The Place of Blessing

In Genesis 12:1-3 we read,

> *Now the LORD had said to Abram: "Get out of your country, from your family and from your father's house, to a land that I will show you. I will make you a great nation; I will bless you and make your name great; and you shall be a blessing. I will bless those who bless you, and I will curse him who curses you; and in you all the families of the earth shall be blessed."*

Notice how God says to Abram, "Abram, I'm going to bless you, and you will be a blessing." But here is what I want you to see: Abram's being a blessing was tied to being in God's purpose. He could only become a great blessing if he followed God's calling.

You will never be the blessing God intends for you to be if you are not flowing in your purpose.

Was there risk involved for Abram? You bet! He had to leave everything that was familiar to him, all of his security, everything that was comfortable and familiar.

He left Ur of the Chaldeans, which history tells us was one of the most highly developed cities of the ancient world. They had cobblestone streets, an underground sewage system, and it was a place of world trade.

Abram left all of that and went out on an adventure by faith, pursuing the purpose that God had for his life. And in pursuing that purpose, God blessed him, and he became a blessing.

But think about this. What if he had stayed back? What if he had said, "I'm secure here; I have it made; I have a nice house and everything I need. I think I will stay put." We would not even know his name.

Pursue your purpose. That is the place of God's blessing.

Day 356

The Signpost of a Provoked Heart

Without a doubt, God has plans for you. Your life is no accident. You have a purpose. In today's devotional, we will discover an important key to help you understand your calling.

Let's look first at Acts 17:16-17,

> *Now while Paul waited for them at Athens, his spirit was provoked within him when he saw that the city was given over to idols. Therefore he reasoned in the synagogue with the Jews and with the Gentile worshipers, and in the marketplace daily with those who happened to be there.*

The word *provoked* literally means that his spirit was deeply troubled, his spirit was grieved within him.

That gives us the first step in understanding your purpose. What grieves your heart? Paul was grieved about this city wholly given over to idols. And the next verse begins with the word *therefore*. He did something about it.

Generally, the things that grieve you in your heart are things that God has gifted you to change. They point you to your purpose.

For instance, in Job 30:25, Job said, "*Has not my soul grieved for the poor?*" If you read Job's story, a big part of his ministry had to do with helping the poor. It was tied to what caused his heart to grieve.

Then there was David who was grieved and provoked as Goliath was taunting the Israelites. Why? David was called to be a leader and a warrior in Israel. It was a signpost pointing to his calling.

What is it that provokes you in your heart? Whatever it is, do something about it.

Day 357

Intimacy with God

Paul, in Philippians 3:10-12, gives us the other principle for discovering your purpose,

> *That I may know Him and the power of His resurrection, and the fellowship of His sufferings, being conformed to His death, if, by any means, I may attain to the resurrection from the dead. Not that I have already attained, or am already perfected; but I press on, that I may lay hold of that for which Christ Jesus has also laid hold of me.*

Paul said, "I am pursuing my purpose," but it was a purpose based on knowing God. Look at what he said in verse 10, *That I may know Him.*

The understanding of his purpose came out of that primary desire and pursuit of knowing God Himself and living in intimacy with Him.

Perhaps the most important thing you could do in your life right now is to just lock yourself away, grab your Bible, and go sit at the beach. Find that place of communion with God. As you get to know Him, you will also discover your own heart and the dreams and desires that God put within you.

They are there. They may be covered with debris, they may be covered with dust, but they are there. You can find out what they are if you will develop that intimate relationship with God.

It is in closeness with God that His breath blows the dust off of undiscerned and unrecognized purposes and dreams.

Day 358

Weeping

In 1 Samuel 30:1-4 we read,

> *Now it happened, when David and his men came to Ziklag, on the third day, that the Amalekites had invaded the South and Ziklag, attacked Ziklag and burned it with fire, and had taken captive the women and those who were there, from small to great; they did not kill anyone, but carried them away and went their way. So David and his men came to the city, and there it was, burned with fire; and their wives, their sons, and their daughters had been taken captive. Then David and the people who were with him lifted up their voices and wept, until they had no more power to weep.*

David experienced the sudden loss of his family and it tore his heart out. Notice that David and his men lifted up their voices and wept until they had no more power to weep.

Feeling sorrow and anguish and expressing it is not wrong. In fact, it is normal, especially when you have experienced a sudden and personal loss.

Perhaps, like David, you have lost family members. Or maybe you have wayward children. They were brought up in the way of the Lord, but they are living a lifestyle that is diametrically opposed to the ways of God right now, and your heart is broken when you think about it.

Maybe you have experienced some other loss in your life, something of value, something that is important to you, something that has meaning to you. If so, it is okay to grieve!

God has wired us to be emotional beings. We are not robots. It is right for loss to affect us on a personal, emotional level. As the Bible says in Ecclesiastes 3:4, there is *a time to weep*.

> *Weeping may endure for a night, but joy comes in the morning* (Psalm 30:5).

Sorrow has its place and its time, but there is also a time for it to end and to be replaced with something else.

Day 359

Someone Else's Fault

In the devotional yesterday, we saw how it is okay when we experience loss to weep and to grieve. I want to point you to verse 6 of that same passage to learn another important lesson related to experiencing loss. 1 Samuel 30:6 says,

> *Now David was greatly distressed, for the people spoke of stoning him, because the soul of all the people was grieved, every man for his sons and his daughters. But David strengthened himself in the LORD his God.*

David was greatly distressed because the people spoke of stoning him. David was not only grieving for the loss of his own family, but he was now being blamed for the whole thing. In fact, they were blaming him to the point that they wanted to take his life.

When you experience troubles, do not be someone who always wants to blame others. I know that it is human nature to want to point the finger and to lash out at somebody else when we are in trouble or when we have experienced loss.

In fact, I think blaming others is just part of our fallen fleshly DNA. Just take a look at what Adam and Eve did in the garden when they messed up. When God turned up and asked what happened, Adam said, "Well, it's the woman that You gave me. She gave me from the tree, and I ate."

And when God asked Eve what happened, she replied, "Well, it was the serpent. It was the snake."

So Adam blamed his wife, and blamed God who gave him his wife, and Eve blamed the snake. Neither Adam nor Eve took personal responsibility. It was somebody else's fault.

If the problems you are experiencing today are your fault, take responsibility, and do not blame others.

Day 360

Strengthen Yourself

For today's devotional, I would like you to read 1 Samuel 30:6 again as it contains another truth I want you to see,

> *Now David was greatly distressed, for the people spoke of stoning him, because the soul of all the people was grieved, every man for his sons and his daughters. But David strengthened himself in the LORD his God.*

Notice that this verse begins by saying, *David was greatly distressed,* but it ends this way, *But David strengthened himself in the Lord.*

It is all right to weep, but when you are done, you need to strengthen yourself. It is all right to grieve, it is all right to express those emotions, but when you are done, you need to strengthen yourself in the Lord.

You need to connect with God in whatever way you find is best for you. If it is lifting your hands and worshiping Him, then that is what you should do.

If it is getting into His Word (which I would suggest for everyone) and spending time feeding your spirit, then do that. If it is reminding yourself about how God has helped you in the past, you need to do that.

Personally I believe that is what David was doing when the Bible says he "strengthened himself in the Lord." I think David was reminding himself about:

- How God delivered him from the lion and the bear;
- How God delivered Goliath into his hands; and
- How God delivered him when Saul tried to kill him.

I am confident David was thinking, "You know, God hasn't delivered me so miraculously in my past to get to this point and to let go of my hand and abandon me. I know He is going to help me now."

David was strengthening himself in the Lord, and you need to learn to do the same thing.

Day 361

Inquire of the Lord

1 Samuel 30:8 tells us what David did next as He sought to deal with the troubles that besieged him. After grieving and strengthening himself in the Lord, here is what he did,

> *So David inquired of the LORD, saying, "Shall I pursue this troop? Shall I overtake them?" And He answered him, "Pursue, for you shall surely overtake them and without fail recover all."*

David inquired of the Lord.

There is a story in the book of Joshua that shows the importance of inquiring of God, of seeking His guidance, no matter how things may seem.

The nation of Israel had entered the Promised Land and they were gaining great victories. One day a group of Gibeonites showed up. They had bags full of old moldy bread, their sandals were worn out, their water skins were cracked and old, and their clothing was old and worn.

They told Joshua and the leaders that they had come from a country far, far away. They went on to tell them they had heard about the great things God was doing through Israel, and they wanted to make sure they would not be attacked. So they had traveled from afar to make a covenant so that when Israel eventually reached them in the future, they wouldn't attack the Gibeonites.

The Bible says specifically that Joshua and the men did not inquire of the Lord. Rather, they looked at the people's provisions…the moldy bread, the old sandals, the old water skins…and they made a covenant with them.

It turns out they were the next door neighbors and Israel had been deceived. And it caused huge problems in Israel's future.

I am telling you, things are not always as they appear. It pays to inquire of the Lord when you are going through difficult times. He will lead you.

Day 362

Global Harvest

In Mark 16:15 Jesus said,

"Go into all the world and preach the gospel to every creature."

In Matthew 13:38 He said,

"The field is the world..."

We need to lift up our eyes upon the harvest field "of the world."

It may sound crazy, but God is expecting us to do something about the salvation of the whole world!

In James chapter five, we are told that God is like a farmer waiting patiently for the precious fruit "of the earth." The implication there is that the Lord is coming, but there is a great global harvest coming first.

Here are some things you can do to be a part of reaching the world for Christ:

- Pray – Matthew 9:37-38 says, *Then He said to His disciples, "The harvest truly is plentiful, but the laborers are few. Therefore pray the Lord of the harvest to send out laborers into His harvest."*
- Give – Generously support ministries that are reaching the lost. Make the mission outreaches of your own church a priority.
- Go – Jesus' command to go is to all believers. At the very least, take a short term missions trip to share the Good News with others.

Remember, the only things we will take to heaven with us are the precious souls we have brought to Christ.

Day 363

Two Voices that Cry Out

Your gold and silver are corroded, and their corrosion will be a witness against you and will eat your flesh like fire. You have heaped up treasure in the last days. Indeed the wages of the laborers who mowed your fields, which you kept back by fraud, cry out; and the cries of the reapers have reached the ears of the Lord of Sabaoth (James 5:3-4).

These words are written to believers, to Christians who are hoarding up wealth rather than giving to support the spread of the gospel.

The reapers in verse 4 are those preaching and working out in the harvest fields of the world. Notice it says that the Lord has heard their cry. But if you read carefully, you will find that another cry has entered the Lord's ears as well.

"The wages" of the laborers cry out to God as well! The tithes and offerings that have been withheld cry out. Monies that should have been sown into the cause of Christ are raising their voices in a mighty chorus to heaven!

Large amounts of undesignated and unused funds that sit in bank vaults cry out. Funds God has graciously given to His people that have been withheld from their purpose—to bring a living Jesus to a dying world—cry out and cry out and cry out!

Are you sitting on a talking wallet today? Is your purse crying out to God? If you could hear their voice, what would they cry? "China! Europe! Africa! The Middle East!"??

Are you generously supporting the work of your own local church? Do not let your money testify against you! Give where, when, and how much God directs—consistently—into the work of His Kingdom.

If the precious fruit of the earth is going to be reaped, we have to support those who labor in the field.

Day 364

A Chain Reaction

Again, the next day, John stood with two of his disciples. And looking at Jesus as He walked, he said, "Behold the Lamb of God!" The two disciples heard him speak, and they followed Jesus (John 1:35-37).

When John opened his mouth about Jesus, two people who heard him speak followed the Lord. We must open our mouths about the Lamb of God if we want people to follow Him.

Look what happens next in John 1:40-42,

One of the two who heard John speak, and followed Him, was Andrew, Simon Peter's brother. He first found his own brother Simon, and said to him, "We have found the Messiah" (which is translated, the Christ). And he brought him to Jesus.

We have a chain reaction happening here. John says, "*Behold the Lamb of God*," and two men follow Jesus. One of the men, Andrew, goes straight to his brother and brings him to Jesus. It is interesting to note that it says he "first" found his own brother—indicating that Simon was not the only one that Andrew found and brought to the Lord.

The remainder of this chapter in John tells us how Philip told Nathaniel about Jesus and was able to persuade him to meet the Lord with the words "come and see."

These stories from the first chapter of John reveal to us what we should be doing once we meet Jesus. We need to bring our friends and loved ones to the Lord. We should be inviting them to "come and see."

Take a moment right now and ask God to show you someone who you should talk to about Jesus. Then get busy and do it. You just may see a chain reaction of salvations.

Day 365

Through Kindness and Love

In Romans 12:20 we read a startling truth,

> *"If your enemy is hungry, feed him; if he is thirsty, give him a drink; for in so doing you will heap coals of fire on his head."*

Our natural inclination is to hate our enemies, isn't it? But the Bible gives us a very different perspective and direction. We are to care for and love our enemies. In fact, some of the greatest antagonists to the gospel have been won through love.

We once had a neighbor next to our church building who was very set against us and very vocal against the church. He would voice his opinion in meetings at the city hall and, on occasion, he would even accost people as they were walking to church. He would shout things at them and harass them a bit from his front yard.

Well, we had one of our pastors go out of his way to show this guy love. He would compliment this man on how well he took care of his lawn, and he began to build a relationship with him. Then one day he actually led the man to Christ!

That same man who would yell at the church members as they walked by his house came into our auditorium and repented before me with tears in his eyes and apologized. He said he had lashed out because he was afraid. But now he had come to Christ, and he had been saved.

It is a glorious thing. He was won to the Lord through kindness and through love.

Think about God. I am so glad that He did not judge us and let the hammer fall on us because of our sins. Instead He extended kindness and mercy to us.

Win your enemy to Christ by showing him kindness and loving him today!